W9-BFQ-568

DATE DUE

BROCKTON PUBLIC LIBRARY

3 3738 00059 2655

DISCARD

BROCKTON
PUBLIC LIBRARY

SETTLED 1700 · A TOWN · 1821
INDUSTRY
EDUCATION · PROGRESS
SACHEM'S ROCK
1649
CITY OF BROCKTON 1881.

Added Sept. 14, 1972

Book No. BK352d

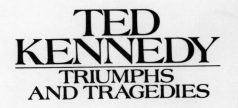

TED KENNEDY
TRIUMPHS AND TRAGEDIES

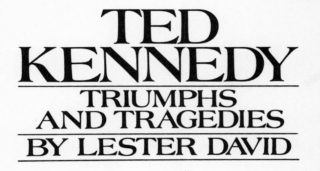

TED KENNEDY

TRIUMPHS AND TRAGEDIES

BY LESTER DAVID

GROSSET & DUNLAP
A National General Company

Publishers   New York

Copyright © 1971,1972 by Lester David
All rights reserved

Library of Congress Catalog Card Number: 70-183019
ISBN: 0-448-01767-9

Published simultaneously in Canada

Printed in the United States of America

B
K352
d

For Margery and Susan,
with love

SEP 14 1972

5·30 Eastern

Acknowledgments
and Sources

I want to express my special thanks to Senator Edward M. Kennedy for taking valuable time from work and vacation in Washington and Hyannis Port to answer my endless questions, and to Mrs. Joan Kennedy for sharing her thoughts and memories. I am indebted, too, more than I can say to Senator Kennedy's staff in Washington and Boston for opening doors and providing free access to material I requested, particularly to Richard Drayne and Loretta Cubberley.

I acknowledge herewith the gracious cooperation and assistance of the following: Richard Clasby, William Frate, George Anderson and Edward Carey, Kennedy's Harvard roommates, and also George McCauley, Harvard '54; former Professor Arthur N. Holcombe of Harvard, Arthur Hall, former dean of Milton Academy, and the staffs of the University of Virginia Law School and Manhattanville College, all of whom had a role in the education of Edward Kennedy. Most helpful and informative were Dave Powers, David Burke, Gerard F. Doherty, Senator John V. Tunney of California, Representative Thomas P. O'Neill of Massachusetts, former Massachusetts Governor Foster Furcolo, Joseph Ward, once a candidate for the Massachusetts State House; former Massachusetts Attorney General Edward J. McCormack; nurses Luella Hennessey and Rita Dallas; a long-time family friend, Mrs. Vincent Greene, and by no means least, Candace McMurrey, sister of

Mrs. Joan Kennedy. For their invaluable recollections, my grateful thanks go to journalists Robert Healy, Liz Smith and Joe McCarthy, and to young James A. Spada, editor of EMK, a journal devoted to the activities of Senator Kennedy. It is impossible to list the many others who helped satisfy my curiosity about Edward Kennedy but to them all my deepest gratitude.

Numerous publications were consulted, particularly the Boston *Globe, American* and *Post,* the Washington *Post* and *Star, The New York Times, Post,* and *Herald Tribune,* Los Angeles *Times,* Springfield, Mass., *Union,* and, in London, The *Times, Observer, Daily Express, Daily Mail* and *Daily Telegraph.* Books that proved particularly helpful included: *Divided They Stand,* by David English and the staff of the London *Daily Express; Robert Kennedy, A Memoir,* by John Newfield; *Robert Kennedy at 40,* by Nick Thimmesch & William Johnson; *The Remarkable Kennedys,* by Joe McCarthy; *On His Own, RFK 1964–68,* by William vanden Heuvel & Milton Gwirtzman; *The Unfinished Odyssey of Robert Kennedy,* by David Halberstam; *The Next Kennedy,* by Margaret Laing; *The Kennedy Legacy* and *Kennedy,* by Theodore C. Sorensen; *Decision for a Decade,* by Edward M. Kennedy; *The Founding Father: The Story of Joseph P. Kennedy,* by Richard J. Whalen; *The Bridge at Chappaquiddick,* by Jack Olsen; *Kennedy Campaigning,* by Murray B. Levin; *Honey Fitz* by John Henry Cutler; *Rose,* by Gail Cameron; *The Lost Prince,* by Hank Searls; *U.S. Senators and Their World,* by Donald R. Matthews; *Halls of the Mighty: My 47 Years at the Senate,* by Richard L. Riedel.

I owe a deep debt of gratitude to John Mack Carter, editor of the *Ladies' Home Journal,* and Richard Kaplan, managing editor, for their help, encouragement and undimmed enthusiasm. To Hy Cohen, my editor at Grosset & Dunlap, my thanks for his wise guidance, superb editorial skill and unfailing good humor. Can there be anywhere a more cooperative and thoroughly able manuscript typist than Corinne Boni? And finally, to my wife Irene, who suffered through the labor pains with me and, despite the pressure of running a home and teaching fourth graders, provided valuable help as well as support and understanding, no thank-you words can be sufficient.

Woodmere, N.Y.
January, 1972

Contents

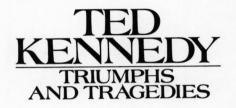

TED
KENNEDY
TRIUMPHS
AND TRAGEDIES

They say best men are moulded out of faults . . .

— Measure for Measure
SHAKESPEARE

I

One Long Day

1. Morning in McLean

He awoke in the 25-foot pink, green and white bedroom of his home in McLean, Virginia, and quickly showered and shaved. Edward Kennedy and his wife Joan have "his" and "hers" bathrooms; hers, alongside, is pink, frilly and feminine, with a bank of sunlamps set into the ceiling above the sunken tub. From one of the closets lining the hall outside the bedroom — the sleeping area itself has none — he selected a blue summer-weight suit, light blue shirt with fashionably long-pointed collar and a striped blue and yellow necktie which he wrapped into a wide knot.

From his bedroom windows, he could see the fast-flowing Potomac 150 feet down the slope. An hour before, the river had been steaming like a witch's cauldron but now the sun's rays, slanting eastward from Washington, had burned away the mist. He could see the heat shimmering through the glass. It would be a day like the one just gone, sunny and miserably hot.

By 7:20, he was in the breakfast room with Joan, his daughter Kara, age eleven and growing tall, and his son Ted Jr., ten. Joan, in a pale blue dressing gown, wore no makeup; her thick, lemon-yellow hair framed her sun-tanned face. Kara, freckled and bearing a strong resemblance to Caroline Kennedy when

1

the President's daughter was younger, was in the fifth grade at the National Elementary School in Washington. Ted was a fourth-grader at St. Albans School for Boys at Massachusetts and Wisconsin Avenues, nearby. The baby, orange-haired Patrick, though not quite four, was enrolled at a Montessori School; he was still asleep. Both boys, but especially Patrick, look startlingly like their father did as a child. Neighboring mothers formed car pools to deliver the children to school and Joan takes her turn regularly.

Kennedy prizes these moments with his family and wishes there were more of them during his long days. He joked with the children, asked them about school and their friends, talked about their plans for the weekend. Andrée Imbert, the Kennedy's French cook who once worked for his father and, before that, for the Duke and Duchess of Windsor, slipped a plate of lightly scrambled eggs before him as he talked. He ate rapidly, kissed the children, told them to have a good day, kissed Joan and went to his study, a small room where he works at home.

On a chair rested a worn green leather briefcase with EMK stamped in gold in front, wide open and crammed with papers. A transcript of a hearing he had been reading before going to bed had been stuffed into it, not neatly. It's his "traveling office"; into it, his staff places the papers he must see, letters that need answering. He generally uses the morning minutes before going to work to scrawl notes atop the letters or along the margins. His secretary, tall, brunet Angelique Voutselas, later deciphers them at the office and shapes them into full, formal replies.

In his inside coat pocket, Kennedy always carries a sheaf of $3'' \times 5''$ index cards stapled together, his hour-by-hour routine for the day planned by himself, his appointments secretary and several key aides. The schedule is typed up the previous after-noon, the items often followed by terse, candid comments of staff members. One function or meeting might be stressed as "important," another, though, as a "stop-by," meaning skip if pressed. Interviews with newsmen often must be squeezed in between stops; on this day, the cards noted that John Lindsay, who was preparing an article on him for *Newsweek* magazine, would jump into a car with him for a half-hour conversation en route to Capitol Hill. On this day, too, the cards noted that Lester David would be dogging his footsteps.

Usually, Kennedy drove himself to work in his year-old Plymouth Fury, leaving about 8:30 and arriving at the Old Senate Office Building about twenty or thirty minutes later, depending on traffic. But the correspondence had backed up alarmingly the past several days, so he had arranged to have a staff aide pick him up. He would use the traveling time to catch up.

Promptly at 8, Philip Heller rolled into the driveway. A moment later, Heller's dark green LeMans, with its EMK 4 license plate, was heading up Route 123 toward the George Washington Parkway and Washington. At 8:45, Ted Kennedy walked into the Hotel Sonesta on Thomas Circle near the downtown section for the first engagement of his day.

McLean, where the Kennedys make their permanent home, is a sprawling, gasoline-alley kind of community, proud of its rise from a crossroads hamlet in the 1950s into a bustling area of some 15,000 inhabitants and five drive-in shopping centers. The Kennedys live in the "estate section" north of the town center, an area of attractive to palatial residences bordering Chain Bridge Road. Hickory Hill, where Robert Kennedy's widow, Ethel, lives with her eleven children, is about one mile from Ted's home. Stewart Udall, former Secretary of the Interior, is another neighbor.

The Ted Kennedys live at 636 Chain Bridge Road. The atmosphere of subdued wealth is apparent the moment one comes upon the long, low, double level structure of grey shingles, brick and glass, with its peaked roofs and jutting wings. It was designed by John Carl Warnecke, the celebrated San Francisco architect who created the John F. Kennedy Memorial at Arlington National Cemetery and, in 1969, Hawaii's $26.6 million state capitol. From the outside, hidden by tall trees, there is little hint of its magnificence. The house, on five and one-half acres of heavily wooded land, rests in a hollow scooped into the top of a bluff that overlooks the rushing Potomac.

The site was chosen after a long search, the rooms and the decor carefully planned to achieve an atmosphere of warm informality. The materials, such as the open ceiling beams and matching-grain oak floors and the eighteenth century Mass-achusetts paneling, were sought for months and gathered from all over. The Kennedys paid $125,000 for the land alone while the overall cost from start to move-in finish has been estimated somewhere between $500,000 to $750,000. The Kennedys have never pinpointed the exact figure but admit this range is accurate.

Visitors enter a circular driveway, then walk through a pair of wooden gates into an enclosed court surrounded on three sides by the house itself and on the fourth by a garden wall. Off the huge entrance foyer are three arched doorways leading to the major rooms of the house — a drawing room, dining room and a den.

The 32- by 21-foot drawing room, in yellows and coral pinks, has a vast vaulted cathedral-like ceiling with arched oaken beams and oak floors secured by wooden pegs instead of nails. A piano stands in a corner; there are five sofas upholstered in yellow-white English Radziwill chintz and standing on an eighteenth century Oushak rug. There is a breakfront filled with fine antique glassware collected by Joan, a fireplace faced with white marble with an eighteenth century English mantel of hand-carved wood. The dining room, with white damask walls and two huge built-in cupboards, has a square table designed to Ted Kennedy's specifications; it seats six—eight with a leaf inserted. The 20- by 16-foot library is paneled in the wood sought by Joan and discovered in a Massachusetts barn, and has a huge fireplace of grey stone. Each of these rooms has one wall entirely of glass, twenty-five feet high, which can be slid open; and each commands a breathtaking view of the Potomac and the tree-bordered banks beyond.

These three rooms form the core of the house. There are separate wings for the master bedroom suite and the culinary area, the latter large enough to serve a middle-sized hotel. A square, sunny yellow kitchen has two sinks, two stoves, a breakfast bar with stools, and large tables for food preparation. Next to it is the breakfast room and, completing the suite, a serving pantry lined with cupboards for china, silverware and utensils. Another wing contains the children's rooms and one for the governess. On a lower level — from the outside one would never guess the house had a lower level — are guest bedrooms and a large paneled playroom. On the grounds are a cork tennis court, a gracefully curved forty-four-foot swimming pool and a much-trampled lawn where the children and their friends play hard at outdoor games.

The Kennedys run the house with a full-time staff of four: Andrée, the cook; Theresa Fitzpatrick, the children's governess; Florence Evans, the maid; and a man who doubles as a butler and gardener. There is also petite, attractive Rosalie Helm, Mrs. Kennedy's social secretary. Like all Kennedy homes, family photographs are everywhere, on the walls, tables, mantels, the piano. It is a Kennedy photo gallery showing them all as babies, as students, at sports, on the campaign trails, as public officials.

All the rooms are wired for stereo and connected by an intercom system. The moment an intruder or uninvited guest comes upon the property, his presence is immediately detected by an elaborate security system installed all over the house and grounds.

2. Morning in Washington

In the Normandy Suite at the Sonesta, waitresses weaved through the narrow aisles between the tables with trays of scrambled eggs and sausages for the 150 officials of the powerful American Federation of State, County and Municipal Employees Union gathered for a breakfast meeting. There had been three days of leadership conferences during which the union, considerably respected by politicians, had been addressed by five of the leading candidates for the Democratic Presidential nomination the following year: Senators Hubert H. Humphrey of Minnesota, Birch E. Bayh of Indiana, Henry M. Jackson of Washington, Edmund S. Muskie of Maine and Harold Hughes of Iowa.

At a rear table, a delegate watched a technician test the lights for a television camera set up in the middle of the room. "Damned interesting," he mused as he poured himself another cup of coffee. "We had all those other guys and the television never showed up. But when Teddy comes, we get the TV."

At 8:50, five minutes late, Kennedy strode into the room to a standing reception, walked to the head table and shook hands with New York State president of the State, County and Municipal Employees Union, Jerry Wurf, who is also a vice president of the AFL-CIO. Wurf, who had been discussing union affairs, interrupted his talk to introduce Kennedy as "the only senator who has introduced a comprehensive health measure into the

Senate." Kennedy was a co-sponsor of the hotly controversial Health Security Act, backed by the AFL-CIO, which would create a system of national health insurance. All persons living in the country would be eligible for benefits under the program, which would not involve a test of means, as in Medicare, and which would cover all health services for the prevention and early detection of disease, care and treatment of illness and medical rehabilitation. As chairman of the subcommittee of health of the Senate Labor and Public Welfare Committee, Kennedy had been conducting hearings on the measure across the country during March and April. The plan had been sharply attacked by President Nixon, the American Medical Association and the private medical insurance companies as too costly and unwieldy. Kennedy, citing the existence of a pervasive health crisis cutting across all political, social, economic and geographic lines, had been fighting hard for this measure for months, and on this morning he was to make a new plea for support.

Rising, he warmed up the audience like a trained actor. "It must really be a relief to listen to someone who's not running for anything," he said. A small ripple of laughter. "You know," he went on, "you may have a strong union but the place where I work these days is even stronger." Appreciative chuckles.

And talking of unions and working men . . .

"One day," he said, "during a political campaign, my opponent got really wound up and finally he pointed to me and said: 'And furthermore, this man never worked a day in his life.' Well, I was all ready to come out and get at this guy, but the moderator got up and said thanks very much and that ended the evening.

"Next morning I was outside a plant gate just outside Boston about five in the morning and some burly worker came up to me and grabbed my hand and he said: 'Kennedy, I heard what that guy said about you last night, that you never worked a day in your life. Well, let me tell you something. You haven't missed a thing!' "

The delegates howled. It was a joke Kennedy uses often, and it always goes over big. Then Kennedy spoke for ten minutes, rapidly, intensely:

"We have a health crisis in the nation, a crisis in very human terms. Our committee had eight weeks of hearings here in

Washington, and then we went out into the field, to Maryland, up to New York, into West Virginia, Ohio, Illinois, Iowa, through the Rocky Mountain states and out to the West Coast. We found that every day across America, real tragedies are happening because in the richest nation of the world, health care is a forgotten right.

"There's a union brewer in New York City whose life depends on a kidney dialysis machine which costs $10,000 a year to maintain. With the cutbacks in city and state funds, he's afraid that machine is going to be unplugged and he's going to die, because he hasn't got the money to pay for it himself.

"There's a paint sprayer in Nashville who lost his job after working for one company for fifteen years. His wife went into a hospital and he had a $700 medical bill to pay. Well, you talk about catastrophic illnesses. To a worker, a $700 bill is as catastrophic if he hasn't got it as a $50,000 medical bill would be to a middle-income person. That paint sprayer had to go into personal bankruptcy. They took everything — his car, his icebox, his stove. They ruined his credit so that he was unable to charge anything to provide basic necessities for his family.

"There's a college professor who died at forty-six of a brain tumor, after spending tens of thousands of dollars. Now the lives of his wife and children are mortgaged for years in the future.

"There's a black father in Chicago whose son died outside the emergency room door while the hospital was making a credit check on the father to see if he could pay the bill.

"These are not isolated cases. In every city we have visited, from New York to California, from Nashville to Des Moines, we have heard such stories from people in all walks of life, victimized by a health-care system that is a disgrace to modern life."

He had delivered the same speech many times before, but he spoke it with conviction, at times with fire, and at the end the audience rose and applauded for three minutes. Jerry Wurf said a few minutes would be allotted to questions. At once a man rose and asked Kennedy:

"If you were drafted for the Presidency, would you run?"

"Hey," Wurf began, "none of that now. . . ."

Kennedy, grinning, leaned into the microphone and said

quietly: "I indicated previously that I would not. I haven't changed my mind." The man sat down.

At 9:15, after three more questions, Kennedy quickly left the room and climbed into the car for the drive to Capitol Hill. Lindsay, the *Newsweek* correspondent, squeezed in beside him for a fifteen-minute interview.

Lindsay, fortyish, wearing a rumpled grey suit, wanted to talk to him about the subject apparently on many other minds, the possibility that Ted would seek the Presidency in 1972. Later, his dispatch would say: "Edward Moore Kennedy introduces himself to audiences as 'the only senator who isn't running for President.' Everybody laughs, and nobody quite believes him." In the car, he asks him and Kennedy says he will remove his name from every primary. How about the vice presidency? Would Kennedy accept the number two position with Humphrey as number one? "No, no, no, no," Ted answered. He couldn't imagine himself as a vice presidential candidate under any circumstances . . .

At 9:35, Heller drew up at the Delaware Avenue entrance to the Old Senate Office Building. Kennedy bade Lindsay goodbye at the door of his suite and walked inside. Lindsay remained in the anteroom to chat with thirty-four-year-old Richard C. Drayne, Kennedy's crisply efficient, thoroughly professional press secretary who had been loaned to Bobby in 1968 to work on the nomination campaign. Drayne, who had replaced Frank Mankiewicz as road man while Frank worked on policy and operations in California, was only a few feet away when Bobby was shot down in the serving pantry of the Hotel Ambassador in Los Angeles on June 5.

Ted Kennedy works in No. 431 of the Old Senate Office Building, a five-room suite staffed by twenty-seven aides and secretaries and filled with Kennedy memorabilia. The walls of all the offices are almost entirely covered with huge posters and photographs of the Kennedy brothers, alone, with each other and with world notables, and their families. In the reception room hangs an impressionistic painting of the French Riviera, done by Ted from memory while he was recovering from a broken back suffered in the 1964 plane crash that almost took his life. Below it is a framed letter from the illustrator Norman Rockwell, admiring the effort and telling the senator if he ever wanted to get out of politics, he had a "real future in landscape painting." Kennedy admitted that he was pleased, though he felt Rockwell was stretching a point.

In one of the offices, a secretary had hung a hand-lettered quotation from Albert Camus, the late French existentialist author: "To be born, to create, to live, to win at games, is to be born to live in time of peace. But war teaches us to lose everything and become what we were not. It all becomes a question of style." Several bumper-stickers, "Hays Stowe for President," have been stuck on the walls and desk sides; Hays Stowe was a Kennedy-style United States senator portrayed on television by Hal Holbrook as part of a series called "The Bold Ones" in 1971.

Kennedy's private office is large, 30 by 20 feet, and is similarly embellished with such poignant reminders as notes, paintings and assorted handicraft samples by his children.

On his desk is a paperweight engraved with the George Bernard Shaw quotation that Bobby used over and over during his 1968 campaign for the presidential nomination: "Some men see things as they are and say, *why?* I dream of things that never were and say, *why not?*" There is a humidor bearing a small copper plaque that lists all the United States senators from Massachusetts since the Republic was founded, from Tristram Dalton to Edward Kennedy. To the left of the desk, an entire wall is covered with photographs of the families in happier times. In a frame are John Kennedy's Navy dog tags on a chain. On either side of the mantel on the opposite wall are the flags that stood in the Oval Room of the White House when his brother was President, presented to Ted by Jackie.

Teddy junior is well represented. His painting of the senator's twenty-eight-foot sailboat, the *Victura* — the water a bold blue, the sails sharp white — has a place of honor. It is signed "To daddy, love from Teddy, Merry Christmas, 1969." Atop the mantel is young Teddy's laboriously constructed replica of the aircraft carrier *John F. Kennedy*, made of wood, bottle tops and ten-cent-store airplanes. On a wall is Teddy's description of his father done as a homework assignment: "My father is medium. He weights 230 pounds. My father is a majority leader of the Senate. He is nice and he plays football with me. His hobbies are eteing candys." And near it is young Teddy's manifesto, proclaiming a fifth freedom: the right of a child to perform his homework without parental supervision. On the morning of April 16, 1969, Teddy senior found the following crayoned message Scotch-taped to his bedroom door: "You are not ascing me qestungs about the 5 pages. You are not creting [correcting— ed.] my home work. It is a free wrold." *

In the summer of 1971, Kennedy employed an administrative assistant, two "LAs" (legislative assistants), a press secretary, an executive assistant and a special assistant — all young men. The others are secretaries and clerical workers. A special aide had to be hired to take care of the voluminous mail; some days as many as 2,000 letters can be dumped on the floor in a sack. Official letters are placed on his desk at once, while all the others are read and eventually answered. "There are quite a few hate letters," an aide told Frances Spatz Leighton, the Washington journalist. "I hate all Kennedys and no one with that name will ever be President again, if my vote means anything," one letter said. "I don't think you're fit to be Senator, President, or dog ketcher," said another. Threatening letters are turned over to the Federal Bureau of Investigation.

The door to the suite is always open and visitors drop by constantly hoping to catch a glimpse of the senator. They are all given folders explaining how the Senate operates, and Kennedy buttons from a glass jar on the blond receptionist's desk. The jar has to be refilled at least once a week.

The staff is never fazed by the odd requests and pleas that come to the office by mail or phone, not even when one young woman telephoned long-distance from Boston, challenging Ted to swim the Charles River with her. "Then he would see, smell and taste at firsthand the terrible pollution of the river and *do* something about it," she said. Dick Drayne politely explained that the senator did not have to swim the Charles to realize what was in it, and he sent her a position paper he had prepared on the subject.

*Kennedys are fired by independence early in life. That same summer, Bobby Kennedy Jr. registered some solid Kennedy-type indignation at what he felt was unwarranted and excessive police power.

There had been a party at the home of one of Bobby's friends, a young GI shipping out to Vietnam. Neighbors had complained of the noise and the police, answering the call, had raided the premises.

Bobby had not been present at the party but was incensed by the police action. The next morning he drew up a proclamation on the sanctity of individual rights and the dangers inherent in the abuse of police power. When he finished, he told his mother Ethel that he and his friends were planning to make hundreds of copies and post the document on trees and fences all over the neighborhood.

Eventually, the idea of posting the proclamation was dropped after the politically astute Stephen Smith, Jean Kennedy's husband, counseled it might be unwise.

At 9:45, Mark Schneider, Kennedy's bearded young LA, was on the phone from the Senate cloakroom. "You'll be called in ten minutes," he told Kennedy. "I'll be right down," the senator replied and quickly left for the Senate floor.

The bill to extend the draft another two years, which included the hotly controversial McGovern-Hatfield proposal requiring all U.S. troops to be withdrawn from Indochina by year's end, had been under consideration by the Senate since early May. Sen. John C. Stennis, the Mississippi Democrat who was chairman of the Armed Services Committee and floor manager of the draft bill, had submitted an amendment setting a top limit of 150,000 men that could be called up in each of the following two years. However, Stennis had written an escape clause: the President could exceed the ceiling if, in his judgment, "urgent national security reasons" demanded more men.

Kennedy wanted this escape clause removed. He had written an amendment to the Stennis provisions which would call upon Congress, and not the President, to raise the quota if the upper limit proved inadequate. Schneider was telling Kennedy his amendment would be brought up within minutes.

Kennedy entered the floor and went to his desk, No. 91 in the rear row on the west side of the aisle, between Ernest Hollings of South Carolina and Philip Hart of Michigan. James L. Buckley, the Conservative from New York, was in the vice president's chair as presiding officer. The summer tourists in the half-filled galleries stirred and pointed as they recognized Kennedy. Senators' desks, which conform rigidly to the style used in 1819, are small; each has an inkwell, a penholder, and a glass shaker filled with blotting sand. Atop the narrow mahogany surface, a portable lectern had been placed on which Kennedy spread open a black looseleaf notebook containing his prepared remarks on behalf of his amendment.

The chair recognized Kennedy, who rose and faced the platform where Buckley sat before a panel of Hauteville cream marble flanked by red Levanto marble columns and pilasters. On either side of the rostrum, tucked in recesses, were two old snuffboxes, relics of another age which are faithfully kept filled by Senate employees. Three pages, two of them girls, dressed in identical uniforms of white shirts and blue slacks, sat on the rostrum steps below the four official Senate clerks.

Kennedy thrust his hands into his jacket pockets and began

his speech, which would go largely unreported by the press and mostly unheard by the Senate: only eight members were in their seats throughout most of his address. But it contained a ringing affirmation of the historical constitutional prerogatives of Congress to raise and support armies, and a plea to return to the tradition of close congressional checks over the executive branch's military manpower decisions.

"Mr. President," he began, "simply stated, my amendment presents the Senate with a single issue and that is: Who decides how many men is enough for the armed services, Congress or the President? For that reason I have not tampered with the number of 150,000 inductees authorized by the Committee on Armed Services. . . . My amendment simply would assert that Congress has the right and responsibility to establish no-lift ceilings on the number of men the President may induct each year and that the Congress, not the President, shall determine whether that ceiling will be lifted. . . ."

He argued against the "unfettered power" of the President "to impose endless and unrestricted inductions at his pleasure and for foreign policies of his design." He reminded the Senate sharply that, for the past seven years, "the tragedies of Vietnam have occurred apace with the diminution of congressional influence over the nation's foreign policies." Congress has stood by, he said, as year after year, under Democratic and Republican administrations, the number of draftees soared — from 107,000 in 1964 to 364,700 in 1966, and then above the 200,000 mark for the next three years.

He had taken his hands from his pockets and was gripping the lectern. A lock of hair fell over his right eye and he pushed it back; it fell again and he left it. Muskie of Maine had come onto the floor and sat at desk No. 93, one removed from where Kennedy was standing. Mike Mansfield, the majority leader, had gone to his seat, No. 9, in the front row, and was listening, a forefinger at his temple. Stennis stood at the rear of the chamber. Slowly, as Kennedy spoke, the chamber began filling up.

Kennedy's voice rose. "Vietnam," he said, "has harshly exposed the consequences of giving the President a blank check for manpower. The steady stream of men into Indochina could only take place because the Congress did not have to debate annual requests by the President to lift the ceiling on the draft. If we are to prevent a recurrence of the tragic story of Vietnam, one sure way is to place strict limits on the number of men the President may draft."

At five minutes before eleven, he concluded his arguments and sat down. Senator Stennis walked by and conferred with him at his desk, then both went into the cloakroom. Five minutes later, they emerged and the reason for the huddle became clear.

Stennis announced a concession. He agreed that, since the time the bill was drawn, the need for troops had lessened considerably and therefore the escape clause could safely be eliminated. "I do not think it [the clause] is anything near as important as it was when we wrote the bill. . . . If anything extraordinary should arise, such as trouble in the Middle East, or anything that could not be reasonably met otherwise with the manpower, the President naturally would want to come to Congress anyway."

Stennis proposed, therefore, that the Kennedy amendment, which specified that "not more than 150,000 persons may be inducted" be changed to "not more than 130,000 for 1972," and "not more than 140,000 for the year following."

Kennedy accepted the change and Stennis's amendment to the Kennedy amendment was put to a vote. It won, 67 yeas to 11 nays. The Senate then voted on the Kennedy amendment, accepting it overwhelmingly, 78 to 4.

Following the victory for his amendment, Kennedy went around the floor and into the cloakroom, rounding up the members of his health subcommittee. An executive session had been scheduled for Room 4232 of the Senate Office Building, but with the draft bill debate heating up, he thought it would be a good idea to stay close by. He got the senators together and found an empty room in the Senate wing of the Capitol for the meeting.

While he was away, dark, slender Sen. Robert Dole of Kansas, chairman of the Republican National Committee, rose to deliver a bitter attack on Ted Kennedy. Two days before, Kennedy had made a strong anti-Nixon speech before the National Convocation of Lawyers to End the War. "At last," he had said, "the ultimate and cynical reality of our policy is beginning to dawn on the American people. The only possible excuse for continuing the discredited policy of Vietnamizing the war, now and in the months ahead, seems to be the President's intention to play his last great card for peace at a time closer to November, 1972, when the chances will be greater that the action will benefit the coming presidential election campaign."

Now Dole counterattacked. "Some members of the other party," Dole was saying, "are willing to exceed the bounds of partisanship, reason and common decency in their efforts to downgrade the president and advance their own personal interests." He called Kennedy's charge "the meanest and most offensive sort of political distortions . . . as inexcusable as it is outrageous." He accused Ted and others who had attacked Nixon of "irresponsibility and blind personal ambition."

Senators rarely pass up a chance to make political hay, and Hubert Humphrey didn't let this opportunity go by. Looking gaunt from strenuous dieting, he also rose to express sharp disagreement with Kennedy's views and to support Nixon's conduct of the war.

He began jocularly. "I have been given, out of historical precedent," he said, "the dubious honor of being the titular leader of the Democratic party. I say dubious because I have never found out what that title meant, except that the one who had it lost." But at once he grew serious.

"Insofar as this senator is concerned, and this Democrat is concerned," he said, "I do not believe the President is playing politics with Vietnam. . . . I do not think it is a matter of the President being cynical or of the President trying to prolong the struggle. I think the President wants peace and that he wants it as badly as anyone in the Congress or in the country."

At this point in history, nobody was sure what Kennedy might do about 1972. Liberal commentators saw in Humphrey's remarks a growing worry that eventually Kennedy might make a declaration. The following day James A. Wechsler observed in the *New York Post:* "It [the incident] underlines Humphrey's apparent resolve to seek to identify Kennedy as the thunderer on the left. By laying down so blunt a challenge at so early a stage, he has confessed his belief that Kennedy, not Ed Muskie, George McGovern or anyone else, is the real threat to his dream of another chance."

Kennedy, told of the attacks by Schneider in the Senate corridor, listened quietly, nodded, and during the afternoon session asked for the floor to respond. He said he stood squarely behind the remarks he had made and hoped that every senator would read the address in full which had been reprinted in the Congressional Record.

"I would add one further comment," he said. "It is my understanding that, as a matter of long-standing procedure in the Senate, a member traditionally has the courtesy to inform his colleagues when criticism of the sort made by the senator from Kansas is to be delivered on the floor of the Senate. I received no such notice, and was actually engaged in a meeting of the Senate Health Subcommittee at the time the senator from Kansas delivered his remarks."

Later in the afternoon, Senator Dole's office delivered a copy of the statement to Kennedy's office. "Damned nice of him!" muttered Drayne.

3. Afternoon

Kennedy glanced at his index cards:

12:30 p.m.–STOP BY. Rm. S-120; Senate Demo Campaign Comm. Lunch for Jim Wilmot (N.Y. pres. of Page Airways) who's running June 29 dinner.

12:30 p.m.–Amb. Orlando Letelier, Rm. 431, lunch; from Chile.

He walked quickly back to his office. There was no time to drop in at the Wilmot lunch; he was already late for his appointment with the Chilean ambassador. Angelique had ordered lunch from the Senate dining room which had already arrived: tomato juice, chef's salad, fresh strawberries and iced tea. (In Washington, Kennedy usually has a quick lunch on a tray in his office, a twenty-minute affair during which he discusses business with a staff aide. Angelique generally orders jellied consommé, a medium rare hamburger and iced tea, varying the fare on occasion with a grilled cheese sandwich or a bacon, lettuce and tomato on toast.) Ambassador Letelier arrived promptly and the two closed the door for a private conversation which lasted an hour.

After the ambassador left, Kennedy took six telephone calls, conferred with Dick Drayne over questions asked by columnist Stewart Alsop and Walter R. Mears of the Associated Press, and got quick briefings from staff aides on forthcoming committee meetings. Kennedy is a member of four Senate committees: Judiciary, Labor and Public Welfare, the Special Committee on Aging, and the Select Committee on Nutrition and Human Needs. He also serves on eighteen subcommittees of these major groups. Thus, the details that must be absorbed, the issues that must be decided, are overwhelming in number and complexity. He relies a great deal on his staff to brief him on the facts and holds many short conferences with aides throughout the day, sometimes at lunch, sometimes during walks to the Senate or to his next appointment.

1:30 p.m.–Center for Urban Ethnic Affairs, Rm. 318, Caucus Rm.; Msgr. Geno Baroni (Bob).

Bob Bates, a black LA on Kennedy's staff, stood outside the high oak doors of the Senate caucus room waiting for the boss. Room 318 was the ornate chamber in which the Army-McCarthy hearings had been held seventeen years before and from which Robert Kennedy had announced his candidacy for the Democratic Presidential nomination in 1968. Inside, some 300 educators, social workers and clergymen were having a luncheon conference, discussing issues facing blue-collar workers and urban ethnic communities. Kennedy had arranged to have the Center, which is affiliated with Catholic University, use the Caucus Room for its luncheon meeting as part of a five-day conference.

At 2:10, Kennedy, accompanied by Dick Drayne, came down from his office on the floor above and received a standing ovation as he walked to the front of the room and shook hands with Father Baroni. He talked for ten minutes and left for the Senate floor.

Kennedy, Drayne and I walked across heavily-trafficked Constitution Avenue toward the Capitol just as the light changed. As the cars moved past, he grabbed my arm. "Look out," he called, "we don't want to lose you."

The cars had begun moving around the senator too. "We don't want to lose you, either, Senator," I replied. The comment was banal, almost stupid; only later did I realize it had its source in some deeper labyrinth of the mind. If Kennedy understood or even heard, he made no sign.

In the Senate, the debates continued on amendments to the draft extension bill.

By a unanimous vote, 76 to 0, the Senate approved an amendment by Harold Hughes, Democrat of Iowa, providing for the identification and treatment of drug- and alcohol-dependent persons in the Armed Forces.

By a vote of 72 to 1, it approved an amendment by Sen. Jacob K. Javits, New York Republican, calling on the President to take all possible means through international cooperation to reduce the illegal importation of heroin and other narcotic drugs into the United States.

4. p.m.–Gov. Milton Shapp, Rm. 431.

Kennedy glanced sharply at his watch, saw it was late and hurried off the floor for his appointment with the Pennsylvania governor. In the reception room of his suite, two long-haired youths and a pretty girl in cut-off dungarees were signing the visitors' book. "Hi," he called, smiling and extending his hand. "Awfully glad you stopped by. Where you from?" The young people, ecstatic, mumbled replies. Waiting unobtrusively inside was a man named Robert Kelly, his wife Thomasine, and their two children, Maria, 12, and Susan, 9. Kelly, who was 41, had lost his job as an electrical engineer for a Boston firm. Unemployed for months, he had come to Washington to ask Senator Kennedy to help him get placed. Kennedy talked to Kelly quietly for a few moments, then said he would ask his Boston office to make some calls in his behalf. He turned to the children and signed his name in their autograph books, shook hands with Mrs. Kelly. Kelly left, not completely happy, but more cheerful than when he came.

Governor Shapp, waiting in his office, remained forty minutes. At 5 p.m., Kennedy saw a representative of the Robert F. Kennedy Memorial, of which he is a trustee. The memorial awards "action fellowships" to outstanding young people who contribute their talents to projects closely identified with Bobby Kennedy in all parts of the country. At 5:30, Joseph Kraft, a columnist, came in for an interview.

At 6:15, Phil Heller drove him back to McLean.

Traffic was heavy. Kennedy cannot sit idle, even in a moving automobile. He pulled documents from his briefcase and began to read, scrawling notes in the margins. He got to the letter section and answered two dozen (again with scribbled notes for Angelique to decipher) by the time the Le Mans pulled into the driveway. Kara, Teddy junior and little Pat piled out to greet him. Smiling broadly, calling out "Hi's," he slung Pat on his back, grabbed Ted around the waist and, after hugging Kara, walked inside with the noisy brood.

Most evenings he has dinner at home with Joan and the family. Andrée, the French cook, who can do wonders with gourmet specialties, must restrain her culinary flights and stick to plain dishes such as roast beef, steak, and chicken, the Kennedys' customary fare. She does go to town, though, with vegetables, no special favorite of any of the family except when Andrée prepares them. She also bakes chocolate cake and chocolate chip cookies, which the senator devours, even while protesting that he must watch his weight.

After dinner, Kennedy usually spends time with his children before returning to his den for homework. An associate says: "He doesn't go to most of the things he's invited to — he's not much on the party circuit, doesn't go to many embassy balls, although you might think he would from the way he and Joan keep getting their names in the paper, she with her hot pants or whatever." On this evening, though, he had an engagement, the final item in his stack of index cards:

8 p.m. Sen. Javits dinner for Erik Erikson, informal, Watergate West #1504; 2700 Va. Ave. NW; stag (12 attending).

Javits, a good personal friend and, though a Republican, a valuable ally in liberal causes, had asked him personally to attend the small function for the eminent psychoanalyst, recently retired from Harvard University. Dr. Erikson, who was visiting Washington, had told Senator Javits he was particularly interested in meeting Ted Kennedy. Kennedy changed to another dark suit and arrived at the exclusive apartment house and hotel complex near the Lincoln Memorial a few minutes late. Meanwhile, Joan watched the television news with the two older children, listened to them as they said their prayers and, after they went to bed, talked on the telephone, read, and listened to Mozart on the stereo. When Ted is home, he is always present at go-to-bed prayers. Bedtime is between 8 and 8:30.

Ted Kennedy returned home at midnight. He discussed the day's events with Joan for a quarter of an hour, went to his den to read more documents to prepare for the day ahead and got to bed at 1 a.m. Another long day was over.

II

Baby of the Family

1. Kid Brother

Teddy was the perfect kid brother: Adoring and agreeable, never a pesky, whining, run-to-mommy pain in the ass, always ready to run his fat little legs off for the bigger guys.

The three of them — Joe junior, Jack and Bobby, from seventeen to six years older — never had a minute's trouble with him, though they gave him plenty. In that family during the 1930s, the hand-me-downs were not clothes, because Joseph Kennedy Sr. was already many times a millionaire; they handed down the athletic chores. So for hours Ted would race barefoot across the grounds at Hyannis Port under a hot sun, shagging flies for Jack who batted them down-lawn from the wire screen in front of the tennis court. He scuttled after the tennis balls that bounded loose, hauled out whatever equipment was needed and rose at dawn to rig the sailboats so they would be ready when the big brothers came down to the dock.

He took a lot of teasing from his older brothers in the early years but he never complained or tattled, not even when Joe, in a fit of anger, tossed him into Nantucket Sound a mile from shore. Teddy, then barely six years old, had asked if he could crew for him during a race and Joe, though dubious, had agreed. Five years later Ted, with complete candor, set down what happened in a book privately published by the Kennedys after

Joe's death in World War II. When the book, *As We Remember Joe*, was being planned, Teddy told his brother Jack and sister Eunice he wanted to make a contribution. "Say how wonderful and strong and calm Joe was," Eunice suggested. Teddy replied: "But Joe wasn't calm." A short while later, he handed them his contribution:

"This was the first race I had ever been in," Teddy wrote, when he was twelve. "We were going along very nicely until suddenly he told me to pull in the jib. I had know idea what he was talking about. He repeated the command in a little louder tone, meanwhile we were slowly getting further and further away from the other boats. Joe suddenly leaped up and grabed the jib. I was a little scared but suddenly he zeized me by the pants and through me into the cold water.

"I was scared to death practully. I then heard a splash and I felt his hand grab my shirt and he lifted me into the boat. We continued the race and came in second. On the way home from the pier he told me to be quiet about what happened in that afternoon."

Teddy, obedient, kept his mouth shut. "He was such a good little boy, so cheerful and docile," recalls Mrs. Vincent Greene of Brookline, Massachusetts, one of Rose Kennedy's oldest and closest friends. "He never got into scrapes at home like Joe and Jack and Bobby. Rose had to turn the older ones over her knee now and then and let them have it properly. But Teddy was rarely spanked."

Ted remembers one of those rare times: At Hyannis Port, he walked home from kindergarten instead of waiting for the school car to transport him, a distance of more than a mile. A coat hanger, which Rose employed interchangeably with a hairbrush, was applied to his bottom.

It is not uncommon for the baby of the family to become the parents' favorite, especially if the last child arrives when the others are nearly grown. This was Teddy's privileged position. Often, Rose Kennedy referred to him in precisely those words, "baby of the family." And for babies there must be gentler care, less rigorous discipline.

John Kennedy teased Ted about this in later years; the folks had eased up on the reins by the time Ted joined the family. Rose knew she had, admitting that after almost two decades of intensive child-rearing a certain weariness does set in. "We tried to keep everything more or less equal," she says, "but you wonder if the mother and father aren't quite tired when the ninth comes along." One can conjecture, though, that the steel-willed Rose could have kept up the discipline just a while longer had she chosen to do so. As Mrs. Greene remembers: "Rose and Joe had a special feeling, a special tenderness for Teddy because he was the youngest, because he was so very gentle and lovable."

None of this means, however, that Ted did what he wished and got what he wanted. Indeed, the opposite was true in many ways. His older brothers and sisters had the best rooms, the first choice of boats and the more desirable assignments on them, even the most complete wardrobes. Ted remembers that his sister Kathleen — the lovely "Kick" who died when her light plane crashed in France in 1948 — once hustled him off to the stores because he owned only one pair of pants that wasn't torn.

Nor was he supplied with unlimited pocket money. He received an allowance of ten cents a week when he was six, raised to a quarter two years later when Bobby was getting only fifteen cents more and John, away at Choate, was struggling along on a couple of dollars. Every one of the Kennedy boys had to find supplemental income. Bobby undertook to sell magazine subscriptions and Teddy mowed lawns — mostly for neighbors because "the pay was usually better than at my house." Once Ted, eager to buy an old boat, had to float a five-dollar loan from his father that took three months to repay. Despite his tearful pleas, Joe Kennedy was convinced it was a bad investment, that Teddy's interest would wane and the five dollars would be shot. "In the end," Ted says, "he gave me the money with the understanding that if I did lose interest before the summer was over, I'd have to pay him back out of my allowance. For two weeks I practically lived in the boat, and then I just forgot about it. I spent most of the next winter paying him back."

Joe Kennedy wasn't about to let any of his children get used to the easy way of doing things. When Teddy was eleven, he and a cousin took a sailboat on an overnight trip. They met with foul weather which kept them up all night. Too weary to sail back, they rowed to shore in a dinghy and called home. A handyman came to fetch them in a car.

Joe saw the bedraggled kids going upstairs and asked what had happened. Ted related the story, adding that neither of them had slept all night. Joe wasn't impressed. If you start something, finish it. Don't quit on the job, no matter how pooped you may be. He told them to get right back up there and sail the boat to home port. They did.

The older boys taught Ted how to sail, ski, play baseball and football and he learned well; indeed, he was to be the only one of four to make the regular lineup of the Harvard varsity. Years later, he and John were to form a formidable touch-football combination.

Dave Powers, former Presidential assistant who has known the family since 1946: "Jack loved to throw passes, and Ted, with those big ham hands of his, could catch anything. They planned and perfected a play they called the buttonhook. It was simple but it worked great. When the ball was snapped, Ted would run down the field, then stop in his tracks and double back, his path forming a kind of buttonhook. The rest of us would be running ahead and Ted was generally clear and would be able to catch the President's passes. It was a great play and it worked nearly every time. The President liked it because it helped his average — the Kennedys kept count of passes attempted, failed and completed."

2. Father and Son

If Ted's post position in the family did not win him special privileges or material advantages, it did result in a closeness to his parents, particularly his father, that was to last through the years.

Joe McCarthy, author and family friend: "There is no question that Ted was a great favorite of Joe's. The old man would talk about him at great length and often, saying over and over, 'You'll love that boy, he's a great fellow, a great fellow.' I suspect that part of the reason lay in the fact that this last boy resembled the first one so closely. Joe was crushed when his eldest son was killed. For months afterward, he would sit alone in the darkness, listening to symphonic music; thereafter, he would weep at the mention of his name. Ted was built like Joe junior, large and muscular, and his smile was the same."

For his part, Ted returned the affection and devotion of his father in full measure.

On a sunny afternoon late in December, 1961, Joe Kennedy suddenly sat on the grass at the Palm Beach Golf Club in the midst of a round. He told his favorite niece, Ann Gargan, that he wasn't feeling well. Ann drove him to his winter mansion on North Ocean Boulevard where he warned, "Don't call any doctors" and went to his room to rest. Later, he suffered a stroke — a blood clot formed in an artery in the left central hemisphere — that was to immobilize him, and leave him speechless until his death late in 1969.

Back in 1961, the Kennedys rushed to their father's bed. Ted flew in from Boston in a military jet, accompanied by Dr. William T. Foley, a specialist in vascular diseases. For three days and nights, he remained at his father's bedside in Room 335 of St. Mary's Hospital, where Joe had been given the last rites of the Roman Catholic Church. He sat quietly, hands clasped before him, intently watching his father's face for signs of arousal from a deep coma. President Kennedy came, remained for a while, and left to attend to official business. Robert Kennedy, then the Attorney General, also sat for long periods. But Ted stayed on, sleeping fitfully in his chair, rousing to study his father's face, then drifting off.

On the afternoon of the first day following the stroke, Joe Kennedy opened his eyes and Ted was the first person he saw. Ted grinned at him. In a few moments, he was telephoning the President at the estate owned by C. Michael Paul, a broker and philanthropist. "Dad's awake," he said happily. The President left for the hospital where he remained almost a half-hour. For the next eight years until the elder Kennedy died, Ted would see his father at every opportunity. Rita Dallas, old Joe's nurse in his last years, says: "Mr. Kennedy couldn't speak but you could tell how glad he was to see Ted; you just could tell."

It was Ted who insisted on breaking the news of President Kennedy's assassination to his father. He flew to Hyannis Port and, with Eunice, walked into the old man's bedroom and sat at his side. The evening before, the night of the murder, he had ripped the wires from the television set in the room and pretended it was out of order. But he could delay no longer. "There's been a bad accident," he told his father. He paused and the next words came in a rush. "As a matter of fact he died."

Ted watched in anguish as his father, his face pale, the skin stretched taut over the bones, sobbed for his dead son, his shoulders heaving, the tears flowing down the cheeks, but no sound coming from his paralyzed vocal cords.

During the six immobilized months Ted spent in a hospital after he broke his back in the crash of a private plane in 1964, Ted Kennedy showed his devotion to his father by writing Joe Kennedy's biography.*

Ted wrote to almost a thousand persons — business associates, friends, relatives, classmates, everyone who knew his father and had a story to tell and a memory to share. He read all entries personally, edited them to size and personally followed every stage of the book's creation, even to selecting the dark grey cloth cover and expensive glossy paper. He chose the title, too, *The Fruitful Bough*, from the 49th chapter of Genesis: "Joseph is a fruitful bough, even a fruitful bough by a well; whose branches run over the wall: The archers have sorely grieved him, and shot at him, and hated him: But his bow abode in strength, and the arms of his hands were made strong by the hands of the mighty God of Jacob. . . ."

Ted Kennedy said that he compiled the volume to keep Joe Kennedy's memory alive for his more than two dozen grandchildren. "They knew and loved their grandpa, but they couldn't know the kind of human being he really was throughout his life."

In a cold fury, the senator lashed out at a news magazine for what he felt were cruel and untruthful remarks about his father following his death on November 18, 1969. "I never saw the boss so pissed," says an aide. "Usually he lets press criticism roll off his back. He knows it's all part of the business he's in. But this time he was almost white with anger. Because this hit at the memory of his dad."

His letter, which he wrote in longhand before handing it to a

*Twenty years before, John Kennedy had done the same thing for their brother Joe while recuperating from a spinal operation after his patrol boat, the famous PT-109, was rammed by a Japanese destroyer. *As We Remember Joe* contained anecdotes, observations and reminiscences from many dozens of persons who had known him. Prof. Harold Laski, the great Socialist economist under whom Joe studied for a year (and disagreed with all down the line) contributed; so did Joe's Negro valet at Cambridge; Arthur Krock of the *New York; Times* Joe's landlady at law school; and a great number of Harvard jocks. The book, privately printed, has become a collector's item; the Parke-Bernet Galleries in New York sold two copies by auction for $1,500 each in 1945.

secretary, bristled with indignation. The article about his father, he said, contained "unjustified statements"; it was "unnecessarily cruel, and its presence in our home, so soon after his death, added to my mother's grief and the sorrows the rest of my family had to bear."

He was especially irate at a statement that his father "sired" his children and left them to be raised by Rose while he went off to make his millions. To this he retorted: "My mind fills with examples of his presence, patience and love at every stage of my growing up. This was true with all my brothers and sisters. It was his example and encouragement, above all, that inspired President John F. Kennedy and Sen. Robert F. Kennedy to enter public service and make the contributions they did to their country.

"I wish you could have devoted at least a line," he went on, "to the generosity, humor and heart my father had in such abundance, but nowhere were these qualities indicated. I could not recognize my father from your portrayal of him. . . . We who are in public life must learn to live with petty gossip and baseless slander. My mother, however, is not in public life, nor are her grandchildren — and they will want to know in later years what kind of man their grandfather was. So I must protest for their sake when my father is maligned at the last moment by those who never knew him and made no effort to find out."

A tall, skinny young man with reddish hair, a red face and light blue eyes, Joe Kennedy was the son of stocky, mustachioed Patrick J. (P.J.) Kennedy. Patrick had been a poor Irish lad from County Wexford who clawed his way up to become a powerful ward boss in East Boston and an often reelected Massachusetts State Senator. Joe, however, never considered a career in politics for himself. He wanted money, a lot of it, and fast. P.J. made enough in various enterprises, including saloons, a coal business and a bank, to send Joe to Boston's elite Latin School, even then more than 250 years old, and from there to Harvard. At Cambridge, Joe was candid: he let it be known to his classmates that he intended to become a millionaire by the time he was thirty-five — even though he was forced to drop a course in banking and finance because he couldn't get the hang of it. . . . And he made it, with years to spare.

Two years after graduation, at twenty-five, he was the youngest bank president in the country, head of the Columbia Trust Company which his father helped establish. When World War I ended, he became an investment banker on his own in Wall Street, where the great boom of the twenties was getting underway. He and the Street prospered together. Later, toward the end of the decade, he anticipated disaster and sold his holdings before the crash wiped out almost everyone else.

With his mounting assets, he looked around for investment fields and foresaw the meteoric rise of the motion picture and radio industries. He bought a chain of thirty-one New England movie theaters. He invested $120,000 in a motion picture, *The Miracle Man*, and got back $3,000,000. Before long, he was board chairman of the vast Keith-Albee-Orpheum enterprise, and financial adviser (with a piece of the action) to four other film and radio companies. By 1926, he was a millionaire many times over. Seven years later, convinced the Prohibition amendment would be repealed, he made a deal with Haig and Haig, Ltd., John Dewar and Sons, Ltd., and Gordon's Dry Gin Co. in England for exclusive rights to handle their lines in the States. In addition, he was cagey enough to get medicinal licenses to import and stockpile vast quantities of liquor here. Thus, when the long dry season ended, Joe Kennedy was ready to slake America's thirst, making huge profits in the process.

Many claim that Joe Kennedy came on too strong. He has been portrayed as a hard-charging man, on the make, driven by a burned-in resentment of anti-Catholic prejudice in the Boston of his boyhood where the help-wanted advertisements often would carry the line: "No Irish need apply." He has been described as a razor-sharp and super-aggressive operator who split a few legalistic hairs to accumulate his incredible fortune.

Parts of this stereotype may have some basis in fact. Joe Kennedy did indeed remember all his life the anti-Irish slurs of his boyhood, and fought all the harder to give his family money and prestige. Nor could he have amassed his great wealth without a combination of shrewdness, single-minded determination, a certain amount of business cruelty and the expenditure of enormous amounts of time. He was, in John Gunther's words, a "majestic speculator."

Ted Kennedy is aware of this. But he also knows that his father hardly "abandoned" his family to Rose. Joe Kennedy once said that none of his interests was as great as his interest in

his children. Another time he remarked: "The measure of a
man's success in life is not the money he's made. It's the kind of
family he raised." Richard J. Whalen, in his admirable biography, *The Founding Father*, has written that, to different people
in different places, Kennedy in the prime of his career was known
as a banker, a showman, a speculator and a New Dealer, but,
"within the tight circle of Kennedys . . . he came literally and
figuratively to rest, revealing that the only occupation to which
he ever committed himself was fatherhood. . . . He felt an extraordinary responsibility for, and participation in, the success of
his children."

If Rose Kennedy pervaded her children's lives, watching over
their hour-by-hour activities, Joe, though absent, was a powerfully felt presence.

Even though he was away from home a great deal in the
early years, rarely a day passed without a long telephone call
home and lengthy conversations with Rose and the children.
Because of the diversity of his interests, Joe, unlike ordinary
traveling men, could not leave a single phone number where he
could be reached, so he set up a telephone central at his offices in
Rockefeller Center, New York. If Rose or any of the children
wanted to talk to him, a call would be put through to this message center which would track down Mr. Kennedy and get him
to a phone. Sometimes it would take hours to find him, but the
calls always got through, eventually.

With her much-publicized card file, Rose kept track of their
illnesses, allergies, dental work and shots. She spanked them
when they misbehaved, set their allowances, tirelessly shepherded them on visits to historic places, planted and nurtured their
religious faith, sat with them at meals, read to them, discussed
current events with them, helped with their homework and
badgered them to do better when they brought home poor marks
from school. (Years later, Ted Kennedy got an opportunity to
rib his mother gently on the subject of grades. He came across a
report card from Dorchester High School, dated 1906, when his
mother was fifteen, and wrote her this note: "I thought that
your grades would have compared favorably with those of your
sons. However, I noticed in 1906 you had some trouble with
geometry, which you obviously were careful to conceal from
your children." Rose sent the note right back with her comments
scrawled on the bottom: "Never had any trouble! Your record

must have been incorrect. Always 'A' in everything. Mother."
Ted wasn't wrong, however; the yellowed report card clearly
shows a "C" in geometry, though she did rank among the top
three students in her graduating class of 285.)

But it was Joe Kennedy who made many of the basic decisions
— if Rose brought up the children, Joe directed how it should be
done.

Although Rose, who attended mass faithfully each morning,
would have preferred otherwise, Joe believed that his sons
should be educated in non-parochial schools. He himself had
attended Catholic schools in the earlier grades and discovered
that being steeped too long and too deep in religious training
could restrict a man's thinking. Later he was to say: "Their
mother insisted that the girls go to Catholic schools. I had other
ideas for the boys' schooling. There is nothing wrong with
Catholic schools. They're fine. But I figured the boys could get
all the religion they needed in church, and that it would be
broadening for them to attend Protestant schools." Bobby, the
most devout of the brothers, attended Portsmouth Priory, a
school run by the Benedictine Order in Rhode Island, for
several years, but Joe senior ordered him transferred to Milton
Academy near Boston. John went to the Canterbury School in
New Milford, Connecticut, when he was thirteen, and Rose
had been quite delighted when he wrote home: "We have
chapel every morning and evening and I will be quite pious I
guess when I get home." Still, after a year, John left Canterbury
for the Episcopal prep school, Choate, in Wallingford.

It was Joe who decided that his eldest son, and later John,
would study in London under Laski; a rather remarkable decision in view of that Fabian socialist's strong views against the
type of American capitalism that had made Kennedy rich. And
it was he who decreed Harvard for the boys and to Harvard
they all went. Joseph Kennedy set the course of their lives,
insisting that he had made enough money for them all, that
America had been very good to the Kennedy family and that they
all "darn well better put something back into it" through careers devoted to public service.

Joe knew who was having trouble in what subject, which
Kennedy needed coaching in what sport, who had won a sailing
race and who had lost. When his sons played football, he was in
the stands, roaring for the team. When he moved his family from

Boston to New York in 1926, it was not so much that his business interests had shifted to the larger city, as most biographers have stated, but because of the children. The "proper Bostonians" who turned up their noses at the rising Kennedys angered him. "They wouldn't have asked my daughters to join their debutante clubs," he told Joe McCarthy, the author. "Not that our girls would have joined anyway — they never gave two cents for that stuff. But the point is they wouldn't have been asked in Boston."

And the point about Joe is that he did have the time and the energy to run both a financial empire and his large family. Nature had gifted him with a truly enormous physical capacity which he took care not to abuse. He neither smoked nor drank; he watched his diet carefully, slept a full eight hours, and exercised regularly. Whenever he could, he rose early and rode horseback for a half-hour. A British newsman, watching Kennedy in action during his years as Ambassador to the Court of St. James's, observed: "He finds an immense stimulus in everything that happens to him . . . he is never bored. It is pure gusto, the sheer zest of living, which has kept him young after galloping through three separate careers. . . . He squeezes the orange of life dry."

Joe Kennedy cherished all his children and probably never realized that a special love arose for the one who came last. Others, though, noticed.

Richard Clasby, Ted Kennedy's Harvard classmate, captain of the 1953 football team and an all-American tailback: "At the dinner table at Ted's house in Hyannis Port, Ted was always the fair-haired boy. He could do no wrong in his father's eyes. The others, — well, Joe Kennedy would tell them they ought to do better in things, but he treated Teddy differently."

3. Born Rich

If it were not for Rose Kennedy's allegiance to her obstetrician, Ted would have been the only Kennedy unable to claim Boston area as a birthplace.

After his marriage in 1914 and a two-week honeymoon at White Sulphur Springs, Joe Kennedy took his bride to a square frame house with grey siding at 83 Beals Street. He bought it for $6,000, borrowing $2,000 for the down payment. Rose pronounced it not only beautiful but practical. It was a roomy, comfortable dwelling on a quiet, tree-shaded street, with neatly trimmed hedges in front, a spacious front porch and, most important of all, five bedrooms, three on the second floor and two smaller ones on the third. Obviously, they were intending to raise a large family.

Babies came rapidly, four in the first five years. In 1915, Joseph Patrick Jr. was born in his grandfather's summer home at Hull, a resort community on the tip of a long finger of land across the harbor waters east of Boston. John Fitzgerald arrived in 1917, Rosemary in 1918, and Kathleen in 1920, all at the Beals Street residence which, by that time, seemed a good deal smaller than it did when the newlyweds moved in.

Joe took his family deeper into Brookline, into the more exclusive Naples Road where the children, except Jean, were born. Here Rose settled the problem of sibling squabbling by sectioning off the large front porch with folding doors, thus keeping the babies in compartments. That way, she pointed out sensibly, they wouldn't knock each other down or gouge one another with toys.

By the time Ted came along, Joe Kennedy was a multimillionaire and had purchased a $250,000 mansion on Pondfield Road in Bronxville, a fashionable suburb in Westchester County, New York. But early in 1932, Rose was expecting again, and she wouldn't hear of giving birth anyplace but Boston, or of being attended by anyone but Dr. Frederick L. Good, one of the city's most distinguished gynecologists and obstetricians.

Dr. Good, who died in 1962, was one of only two physicians who lived to see a baby he delivered elected President. (The other was the doctor who brought Theodore Roosevelt into the world in 1858.) After John Kennedy's nomination in 1960, Dr. Good, then in semi-retirement, organized a "Doctors for Kennedy" committee.

When her time drew near, Rose kissed her children goodbye and went to visit her parents on Welles Avenue in Dorchester, a section of Boston lying between the heart of the city to the north and South Boston. By this time Rose's father was rising seventy but waggish as ever and still cock o' the walk. John F. (Honey Fitz) Fitzgerald, three times a congressman and twice Mayor of Boston, greeted his daughter warmly and soon had her squealing with laughter at his stories. He was as ebullient as his wife,

Josie, was shy; as friendly as she was reserved; as outgoing as she was prim and proper.

Josie, a great beauty in her day, hugged her Rose and took good care of her. She took her on long walks because she believed firmly in "exercising the mother and baby," and prayed with her for the successful outcome of the ninth pregnancy. Honey Fitz was casual about it all; he had been through all this six times with Josie.

On February 21, 1932, Rose entered St. Margaret's Hospital in Dorchester and the following day, the 200th anniversary of the birth of George Washington, Dr. Good delivered his ninth and last Kennedy baby.

Rose remained in the hospital almost two weeks, and while there she received a short unsigned note on Choate stationery from her son John:

> Dear Mother,
>   It is the night before exams so I will write you Wednesday. Lots of love.
>   P.S. Can I be Godfather to the baby

A month later, John Kennedy, neat and solemn in a dark blue suit, made the Profession of Faith at the baptism of his baby brother. The boy was christened Edward Moore Kennedy for plump and faithful Eddie Moore, whom his father met in the early 1920s and who remained his lifelong friend and confidential secretary.

Bronxville, then as now, was a big money town. It exuded elegance. You could see it, even feel it, the moment you entered this community. From the railroad bridge in the center of town, the proud old buff-colored Hotel Gramatan on Sunset Hill dominated broad Pondfield Road, the main artery, with its stretch of fine shops and diagonally parked, expensive automobiles. "Every other car a Cadillac," recalls an old resident.

After a half-mile, the stores stopped abruptly. Beyond Terry's tasteful red-brick gasoline station at No. 117, well-known to the community, was the newly-constructed public school complex, a palatial structure with a sweep of well-tended lawn that housed kindergarten to twelfth grade. Both the gas station and the local school were snubbed by the Kennedys.

One day Joe senior drove down to Terry's in his chauffeured

Cadillac and told the proprietor that another station on nearby Palmer Road was offering him a two-cent discount on each gallon of gas bought for his cars. If Terry's would grant the same, he would give the place his business because it was closer to his home. Terry's refused, explaining it had a one-price policy for all customers. Though his fortune was then estimated at $9,000,000 and climbing, Joseph Kennedy took his business to Palmer Road. As for the school, which educators even then considered one of the best in the area, if not the entire east, the Kennedys sent their children there for only a short while, transferring them to private or religious schools soon after.

Past the school grounds, Pondfield Road wound, rose and dipped, bordered by increasingly larger homes and more imposing estates. A half-mile from the center of town, atop a hill near Crampton Road, was a twenty-room Georgian mansion of clean red brick, set down in the midst of five acres of lawns and gardens. It cost $250,000 and was considered one of the areas showplaces, though some neighbors felt the Kennedys disfigured it by enlarging the premises to accommodate all their children. "Imagine!" one horrified neighbor said. "They built a room above that lovely porte cochere."

This was just one of Teddy's childhood homes. There were three other large houses, each with its special kind of opulence.

The Bronxville mansion echoed with the yells of young Kennedys, the thud of racing feet and, on more than one occasion, the wails of upstairs maids when they discovered that young John had forgotten to turn off the water in the bath. Since his bathroom was on the third floor, directly above his parents' bedroom, Rose Kennedy could look up from her bed and watch in dismay as water dripped from the ceiling onto her rugs.*

The lawn and even the garden were turned into athletic fields by the Kennedys for uninhibited games of tag, baseball and, their favorite pastime, touch football. Ted's earliest introduction to these rugged activities — and rugged they were because it was not unusual for a Kennedy or two to be knocked senseless in a game — was from a baby carriage.

---

*As a teenager, the future President was hardly neat. Hank Searls, in his story of Joe junior, *The Lost Prince*, writes: "In later years, when the boys went away to school, it was Jack's vacation time that the maids tried to predict and to match, to be away from the house when he was home."

Even before he could walk, the family took him up to House number 2 — the sprawling, fifteen-room, nine-bath place Joe had bought on a bluff at Hyannis Port, the summer colony at Cape Cod. This Big House, which Rose furnished in Early American and eighteenth century English, was to become the nerve center of the famous Kennedy Compound where President and Mrs. Kennedy, and Bobby and Ethel Kennedy were to maintain smaller houses. Brother-in-law Sargent Shriver, married to Eunice Kennedy, purchased a home nearby and Ted himself would buy a ten-room cottage on Squaw Island a mile and a half away for his family. Here, in the salt air of the Cape, Ted Kennedy learned to love the sea and draw solace from it.

Swaddled in blankets, the infant Ted would be put aboard the *Onemore*, the sailboat his father bought and named for him after he was born. (There was another craft called the *Tenovus*.) He would stare big-eyed at the broad expanse of blue water, stare up at the sky, and fall asleep with the gently rocking motion of the boat.

The third house was for the winter season. The year after Teddy was born, his father paid $100,000 for a neo-Spanish villa on broad, palm-shaded North Ocean Boulevard in Palm Beach, Florida, the cold weather refuge for the socially prominent. Though smaller than most of the other private estates along this "millionaire's row," the stucco house with the tile roof contained sixteen rooms. Of course, there was also a tennis court and a swimming pool on its two acres of perfectly groomed grounds. The house overlooks the Atlantic Ocean, from whose ravages it was protected by a seawall, built after the Palm Beaches suffered severe damage during a hurricane in 1928.

Though undeniably opulent, this house too managed to acquire the typical Kennedy lived-in atmosphere. Rose ordered green and white flowered chintz for the slipcovers and devised a unique decorative touch to keep the place from being wrecked by the rambunctious youngsters: she arranged the furniture in the living room with aisles through which the kids could dash.

In later years, Rose and Joe Kennedy were to spend many months of the year at Palm Beach. Joe would sit at the pool and, in bathing trunks and a pad at his side, conduct his affairs on the telephone. "I used to work hard," he once said. "Now I just sit here by the pool and make more money than I ever did." After his election in 1960, President Kennedy came down for a vacation and used the house for conferences with advisers on setting up the machinery for his coming administration.

House number 4, perhaps the grandest of the lot, where Teddy spent three years, was in London. We will visit there presently.

4. The Old Man and the Boy

Throughout his early childhood, Ted enjoyed a warm and beautiful relationship with his elderly grandfather, Honey Fitz. When he was seventy-five, the old gentleman would take his six-year-old grandson by the hand for day-long hikes all over Boston. "I would meet him at the Bellevue Hotel, next to the State House," Ted has recalled. Honey Fitz and Josie were living in the Bellevue at the time in a cramped suite on the third floor. "We would have lunch in the dining room where all his political friends would stop at his table to say, 'Good to see you, Honey Fitz,' and he would introduce me, very solemnly. In the same way, he would take me to the kitchen to meet the chef and his staff."

Honey Fitz was a feisty little man (he stood barely five feet two inches tall) who played the mountebank to win votes. He told jokes, made outrageous promises, claimed credit for practically everything good that happened in Boston. He knew everyone, and everyone knew him. He would stand on a barroom table, on a street corner or any stage and, in a high Irish tenor, sing the song that came to be known as his theme melody, *Sweet Adeline*. On his visits abroad, he would be invited to sing it at official receptions before heads of state, and he never refused. He was a master back-slapper who was adored by the electorate for his shenanigans and, at the same time, mistrusted by many of the politicians of his era. Honey Fitz, President Kennedy was to say, "exuded enough blarney to charm the shamrocks off a glen in Dunmore."

But despite his flamboyance, Honey Fitz knew and loved Boston, and he communicated his love to his grandson. After their lunch at the Bellevue, the bouncy old man would go hand in hand with the large-eyed, pink-cheeked little boy through the busy city. Honey Fitz, the everpresent boutonniere in his lapel, held Ted enraptured with a stream of talk about the historic shrines they passed.

There — pointing — was the Old State House, probably the oldest public building in the country. Did Ted know about the Declaration of Independence? Well, it was proclaimed from that balcony, the one facing State Street. And the Boston Massacre occurred just outside its windows. Ted's eyes opened wide as Honey Fitz told him the story of the Redcoats who fired into the crowd of colonists protesting against the quartering of British troops in town.

Down Park Street they would roam, past the Old South Meeting House where another great event, the Boston Tea Party, was plotted. And there was the Park Street Church where the song *America* was sung for the first time. It was known as Brimstone Corner, Honey Fitz explained, because brimstone for making gunpowder had been stored here in the cellar. Then on to Boston Common — now a park, but once the place where the British soldiers drilled.

Ted remembers those walks well: they would wander to Spring Lane, where once there was a well from which Boston had drawn its water for a great many years. On Beacon Hill, Honey Fitz showed him Louisburg Square whose cobblestones — or so the story goes — were used as ballast in ships that brought the immigrants to these shores. The pair would see the harbor where the smell of rotting fish hit their noses, and Honey Fitz complained that there weren't enough big vessels moving in and out. Why shouldn't Boston have become the great port of the east, he would ask. After all, wasn't it 200 miles closer to Europe?

These walks with his grandfather in his early, impressionable years gave Ted Kennedy an abiding love for his native city, a pride in its spirit and a reverence for its history. Years afterward, when he was a United States Senator, he would write about Boston in an almost poetic vein.

"Boston is a feeling — a sense of having learned long ago what it is that makes a city appealing. If the finest architects and landscapers and the best experts in modern living were asked to plan an ideal city, they would come up with much that Boston already has.

"Like a river. Every great city should be on a river. It gives a feeling of space and sky, majestic by day, shimmering by night. . . . Sailboats and sculling boats fill the waters. Students study on its banks. I take my children to the Esplanade on the riverbank to hear concerts by the Boston Pops Orchestra. . . .

"Or like a Common in the middle of the city, and a Public Garden. Not a small park tucked away between skyscrapers, or a meager piece of green space in a new development where pathetic little trees are tied to wooden rods for safety — but seventy-two acres of the most valuable real estate in town. The Common gives every man in Boston an estate, a place to relax in the sun before plunging into the life of the city. In the spring it is full of flowers; in summer it is a lazy place where children ride on swan boats in a lagoon; at Christmas, it is a wonderland with lights and caroling and live animals in the manger.

"Or a way of doing business that is graceful and unhurried. Boston is the mercantile center for almost ten million people, but men still work at standup desks and eat at restaurants with sawdust on the floor. . . ."

Once this closeness between Honey Fitz and the boy was responsible for a confrontation between the old pol and his arch-rival, James Michael Curley, also a former mayor of Boston. And Fitz came off second best. Curley and Honey Fitz clashed repeatedly through the years, accusing one another of assorted acts of political chicanery and worse. Honey Fitz proclaimed himself "the last honest mayor of Boston"; Curley, who served after him, replied in a similar vein to the integrity of Honey Fitz.

In the late spring of 1947, Ted came up from Milton Academy and, with his grandfather, was waiting for brother John in front of an old drug store. The boy, who was carrying his books in the green flannel shoulder bag used by Miltonians, asked his grandfather to hold his books while he went in for an ice cream soda. Honey Fitz obligingly shouldered the bag and waited at curbside. At this moment, Jim Curley walked past. Spotting Honey Fitz, and without breaking his stride, he called out: "Still carrying your burglar's tools, eh?" For one of the few times in his life, Honey Fitz was speechless.

Ted remained close to his grandfather throughout his growing up years until the old man died in 1950. One may speculate that, despite Joe senior's personal guidance from afar, the boy needed and wanted physical presence of a grown male, and that Honey Fitz served as a father substitute. Ted plainly worshipped the old charmer. After he was elected senator, Kennedy hung a portrait of His Honor, the Mayor of Boston, in the most prom-

inent position in his Washington office, above the fireplace, and
it has remained there ever since.

Ted's decision to enter the political arena may have resulted
from his parents' suasion and his brothers' examples, but the
seed had been planted by Honey Fitz. And Ted is aware of this.
Once when he was asked why he worked so hard and exposed
himself to the inevitable nastiness, and worse, of political battles
when he could relax with his millions, he shook his head. "I
don't know," he replied. "You get this tradition from your
family. From my grandfather, John F. Fitzgerald. . . ." Honey
Fitz's influence upon his grandson should not be minimized.

And Ted Kennedy adopted, or perhaps inherited, the old
man's style of political campaigning. Once, watching him sing
in a South Boston tavern, joke with voters at a rally and gab
with strangers on a busy corner, an old Irish politician shook his
head and muttered: "It's Fitz all over again."

III

In London Town

1. Life in an Embassy

Two days out of New York Harbor, on March 11th 1938, the S.S. *Washington* of the United States Lines ran headlong into the worst storm she had experienced in her four years of service on the North Atlantic.

Rain whipped the big vessel, lightning flashed around her, 90-mile-an-hour winds screamed across her decks. Fifty-foot whitecaps smashed against the bow and sides, receded, reared upwards and attacked again. A number of passengers suffered broken bones as the great ship rolled, pitched and tossed in the boiling sea. The captain slowed speed to minimize the buffeting, and at one point he cut the engines completely.

In those pre-Dramamine days, most passengers were seasick through the storm which continued unabated for four days. There weren't many who could enjoy the luxuries of this beautiful liner: a day after the storm broke there were fewer than a half-dozen persons in the dining room. The fancy shops eventually shut down and the swimming pool was unused.

Among the passengers were Rose Kennedy and five of her children — Teddy and Bobby, and Jean, Pat and Eunice. For the first time, the exuberant, irrepressible clan lost its zest. The children did not race the decks or play games as they did the first day out. They just lay or sat, miserably seasick, in their cabins.

And they were all delighted when at last the skies cleared and the long voyage was over.

The Kennedys were on their way to London for a new chapter in their lives. For Joe Kennedy was now the American Ambassador to the Court of St. James's.

By the mid-thirties, the elder Kennedy had already moved into the arena of politics and government service. A powerful backer of Franklin D. Roosevelt and his New Deal, as well as a heavy contributor to FDR's 1932 and 1936 campaigns, Kennedy was rewarded with several key appointments. He was the first chairman of the newly-created Securities and Exchange Commission (though he had hoped for a cabinet post as Secretary of the Treasury) and later, in 1935, he served as chairman of the Maritime Commission. In 1936, Joseph Kennedy organized a businessman's committee for Roosevelt's reelection and, with Arthur Krock of the *New York Times*, he wrote a trenchant little book called *I'm for Roosevelt*. He was still trying to reorganize the country's merchant navy when Robert W. Bingham, Ambassador to Great Britain, died. Roosevelt offered Kennedy the job.

The appointment was greeted with modified rapture in Foggy Bottom. In *The Remarkable Kennedys*, one of the first of the family biographies, Joe McCarthy wrote: "An Irish Catholic hardly seemed right for the Court of St. James, especially such a hot-tempered, blunt and outspoken one." Hitler and his National Socialist Party were growling menacingly; it seemed to professionals at the State Department that if ever there was need for a diplomat in such a key post, this was it. But Roosevelt was also aware that America's trade relations with the British could stand improving and he felt that Joe Kennedy, an acknowledged business and financial genius, could be enormously helpful in working out more satisfactory Anglo-American trade pacts and perhaps get some action on the matter of Britain's still-unpaid war debt to the U.S.

So Joe Kennedy went to England. As soon as arrangements could be made he sent for Rose and the family. The size of the brood and its impending arrival were already headline news in London — "Nine Children and Nine Million Dollars," the *Daily Express*, awed by both accomplishments, had said in huge type The new ambassador, greeted on his arrival as "America's nine-child envoy," kept the quips going himself. The week before

Rose and the children sailed, Kennedy, a nine-handicap golfer, had teed off with an iron on the 120-yard second hole at the Stoke Poges Club with Arthur Houghton, a former theater manager from the States. The ball hit the green and rolled unerringly into the cup for a hole in one. Delighted, but ever the family man, Joe told newsmen: "I am much happier being the father of nine children and making a hole in one than I would be as the father of one child making a hole in nine."

On March 15, the great ship steamed around Lands End into the English Channel and up the Sound in Plymouth Harbor. Kennedy, who had journeyed down from London by train to greet them, was taken to the vessel as it rode at anchor in the yacht of Adm. Sir Reginald Plunkett-Ernle-Erle-Drax, commander-in-chief of the Plymouth region. On board, the children mobbed him, barely allowing him near Rose, simultaneously shouting out the news of the big four-day storm, how terrible it had been and how a lot of people were hurt and scared and . . .

Suddenly Joe frowned as he looked at them, then shouted: "Hey, where's Teddy?" Bobby solemnly reassured his father that Teddy hadn't been lost in the storm, but everyone, newsmen included, began scouring the ship for him. He was finally discovered far up the deck, staring entranced at a dredging vessel and a fleet of barges which were deepening the harbor.

En route to the train station, Bobby fell in step with Patrick Murphy, a British reporter, and asked him: "Do you know what schools Ted and I are going to? If they are boarding schools, don't tell me about them. I want to go to day school, so I can be home at night." The incident, long since forgotten by the Kennedys, is recalled because almost thirty years later Bobby's son, Robert junior, also had strong views on day versus boarding school, but diametrically opposite to those of his father. Bobby junior insisted on getting away from what he called "this confusing family" — and he did.

Joe took his family back to London — on a borrowed $120. At the station, he discovered he had only one ticket and no money. Reporters loaned him the price of six first-class rides.

House number four was a 36-room mansion with twenty-three servants and three chauffeurs for its fleet of cars, appreciably the largest and most elegant home in which Ted lived as a child.

Walk up busy Exhibition Road in Kensington Borough. At the corner of Kensington Gore, a much traveled road, is the headquarters of the Royal Geographical Society where a statue of Ernest Henry Shackleton, the British arctic explorer, stares over the traffic. Turn right into quiet Princes Gate, a private little street with a single row of aristocratic four-story houses of a faintly-yellow stone. Each is either a private residence or a foreign embassy. At the end is the largest and most imposing of the group, poised like a mother hen watching over her chicks. This is No. 14, six stories high; and it is here that Teddy came to live.

He didn't enter quietly. Jerome Beatty, an American magazine journalist, went to call on the Kennedys soon after their arrival. He wrote in *Woman's Day* that Teddy's arrival in the mansion would be remembered for a long time by the very proper English staff which had been accustomed to the museum-quiet of a residence inhabited by the childless Binghams:

"Before his busy mother could shush the first real American boy that the magnificent and stunningly caparisoned butlers, footmen and valets ever had seen in the place, Teddy commandeered the elevator with whoops and imperious orders, and while they murmured, 'Rully, Mawstah Edward, what *will* the Ambassador sigh?' ran loads of them between cellar and attic playing what he called 'department store.'"

The ambassador said plenty and said it loud. Henceforth, Teddy will not, does he hear, ride the elevator. But while many in the world of high finance might tremble at Joe Kennedy's anger, Ted did not. He rode the elevators anyway, though not when his father was home. On several occasions, Teddy was manning the lift when Joe arrived home. He would quickly race away, forgetting in his haste to shut the inner and outer doors. The elevator would then remain inoperable until someone came up to close them.

But Teddy was hardly the only Kennedy to import some American-style behavior and attitudes.

Take nine-year-old Jean: On her first day of school at the Convent of the Sacred Heart in Roehampton near London, she was reminded during an arithmetic lesson that five does not go into nine twice, at least not exactly. Jean, obviously trying to con her teacher, earnestly told her: "Well, it does back home in America!"

Take Eunice, who was 17: Playing her first game of field hockey with English girls, she kept up a running fire of instructions and bellowed: "Atta Boy! Shoot it to me! Come on-n-n-n!!" This Hyannis Port-style enthusiasm didn't go on English playing fields, Eunice was told by team-mates when the game was over.

Take the American ambassador himself: He astonished British newsmen by planting his feet on the desk at his first press conference. He announced that he certainly had no intention of wearing the traditional knee-breeches when he presented his credentials to the king at Buckingham Palace, and he didn't. (He was only one of five males at the reception in long pants and the other four were waiters.) He said he liked to read detective stories, eat chocolate cake and listen to Beethoven's Fifth Symphony. His blunt straight-from-the-shoulder talk on matters, from the British war debt to the length of British shirt tails, raised eyebrows. His even blunter language in private shocked his secretaries.* His favorite word was "bellyaching"; he did not like complainers and he bellyached constantly about them.

Or take the big house itself: The latest American phonograph records ("A-tisket A-tasket," "Jeepers Creepers," "I Married an Angel," "I'll Be Seeing You," "Change Partners") were played almost constantly. The exquisite Louis XVI furnishings had to compete with U.S. factory-made lamps which may have marred the uniformity of the decor but gave more light. The immense formal garden at the back was turned into an athletic field for touch football and baseball. A long marble terrace, shared with all the other houses on the street and thus stretching for hundreds of feet, was converted into a private bicycle path. The Kennedy girls preferred U.S. nylons to the British "fully-fashioned" hose, and they were delivered along with the State papers in the diplomatic pouches. Cold bottles of American soft drinks were always available in the vast kitchen. American food was served — steaks, chops, hamburgers. The young Kennedys never took to mutton or cabbage. (Inevitably, the children adopted a number of British words and phrases. Teddy and

---

*Joe Kennedy did not watch his language even with presidents other than his son. Once as head of the Maritime Commission he had ordered a group of mutinous sailors put into irons. President Roosevelt telephoned to suggest he ease the stern edict which had not gone down well with the public. Arthur Krock, who was present when the call came, records that Joe insisted the discipline had to be enforced. He began the conversation with plenty of "Yes, Mr. Presidents" and "Yes sirs" but, as Roosevelt continued to press him, he changed. "Listen, boy," he told F.D.R. at last, "if we do that we'll land in the shit house." The President guffawed.

Bobby began using the word "topping" with increased frequency until Joe, for reasons he did not explain to them, ordered them to stop. They substituted "jolly.")

On the first and second floors of the mansion were the reception halls, the big formal dining room and a vast ballroom. The family occupied the third and fourth floors. Ambassador and Mrs. Kennedy and Rosemary had their rooms on the third floor; Teddy, Bobby, Miss Hennessey and Elizabeth Dunn, the children's governesses, were on the fourth. When they came home from school, Jean, Eunice and Kathleen were also quartered on the fourth, as were Joe and Jack when they were staying in London.

As for school, Bobby got his wish: He and Teddy were sent to day schools, first the Sloane Street School for Boys, later to the more exclusive Gibbs. The boys would rise at seven sharp and by eight, they were driven off, dressed in the traditional fashion of upper-class English schoolboys — gray flannel trousers or shorts, maroon jackets and tiny top-of-the-head caps. Bobby couldn't stand the caps; Teddy was too young to care.

They would come home about five for a father-imposed hour of homework, followed by an exercise period before dinner. Afterward there would be another homework period, mostly for Bobby, and quiet games. Bobby would fiddle with his camera and Teddy with a new stamp collection. Midweek bedtime was about nine.

The other seven Kennedys were widely dispersed. Jean 10, Pat who was 14, and Eunice, 17, all attended the Convent of the Sacred Heart; Kathleen, 18, who had graduated from the Parsons Art Institute in New York, was continuing with studies in interior decorating and serving as assistant Embassy hostess. Joe junior, 23, and John, 21, were still students at Harvard. Rosemary, 19, went to Visitation Convent in London. Four years later, Rosemary — a mental retardate whose condition was gradually deteriorating — was sent to an institution in Jefferson, Wisconsin, where she has remained ever since. The Joseph P. Kennedy Jr. Foundation, created because of Rosemary, supplies considerable sums annually to support mental retardation care and research.

Kensington Gardens, the 275-acre western extension of Hyde Park, lay only a few hundred feet from the mansion. Accompanied by their governess, the youngsters would go through nearby Alexandra Gate into the lovely park to play in the fields adjoining Rotten Row, the famed *Route de Roi* where the gentry and nobility of another day had once strolled, and which had become a bridle path. The ambassador, who never slept later than 6:30 a.m. in his life, would ride here for about an hour most mornings.

In London, Teddy and Bobby drew closer despite the six-year difference in their ages, probably because they were the only small boys in the mansion and they were thrown together more. Luella Hennessey, a former private duty nurse who had been hired by the Kennedys in 1937 to supervise the brood and who had been brought over to England by Rose Kennedy, has vivid recollections of the two at play. Miss Hennessey — "Lulu" to the Kennedys — remained with the family for many years, and helped to raise the young Kennedys and assisted at the births of *their* children. Baby nurse for twenty-seven of Rose and Joe Kennedy's twenty-eight grandchildren, Miss Hennessey, now a community mental health adviser in Walpole, Massachusetts, was most recently summoned to Washington to assist at the birth of Ethel Kennedy's last baby, Rory Elizabeth, born six months after Bobby's assassination.

Miss Hennessey: "Bobby played with Ted a great deal. The three of us would ride our bikes up and down that long marble terrace in the back of the house. Then, when Bobby's friends would come over to play after school, he'd always include Teddy. There never was any of this: 'These are my friends and we don't want you along' as you'll find in many other families. They just *liked* each other.

"And always afterward, there seemed to be something very special between Bobby and Ted. They were so different, Bobby the intense one and Ted so easy-going, and yet they understood each other so well."

If Bobby or the others resented Ted's status as family pet, it was not apparent to Miss Hennessey or anyone else. And pet he frankly was. Hank Searls records Teddy's was "the first room Joe junior would visit when he returned from a trip." Luella herself admits: "Nobody could ever make me think anything wrong about Teddy. The other children all noticed and they told me so. When he was much older and already a senator, Bobby once told me that the whole family knew Teddy was my favorite. Teddy remembers, too, and he kind of blushes and laughs as he talks about it."

Joe Kennedy rented a big house at Ascot, twenty-five miles southwest of London, where the family spent most weekends. Winter vacations were at St. Moritz in Switzerland, and for summers there was a villa above the Grande Corniche near Cannes on the French Riviera, reached by narrow, tortuous roads. Knowing that Joe junior and Jack were fast drivers, Rose worried a great deal that one day they might come to grief on the curves. She hit on the idea of plunking Luella Hennessey into the back seat each time the boys went to spend an evening in town. Her theory was that with Miss Hennessey along, they would take fewer chances with the roads. It worked well, and Miss Hennessey got many leisurely trips to town.

If Ted learned about Boston from Honey Fitz, he absorbed some important lessons about world history and the fate of nations from his brother John. Having, by his own admission, "fiddled around at Choate," John Kennedy had become a serious student of history and politics in his last two and a half years at Harvard. At this point in his life, though he had traveled extensively through Eastern Europe, Russia, the Middle East and the Balkans, he was not considering a political career. Instead, he was debating the merits of law, journalism, the foreign service, or the academic life as a professor of history or political science. He was already awake to the threats of totalitarianism, and he expounded on the theme to his brothers and sisters from time to time.

One stormy afternoon in the Cannes villa, a fire dancing and crackling in the grate, John Kennedy held an audience of younger Kennedys spellbound with stories about Hannibal, Julius Caesar and Napoleon, all military geniuses, each a strong, dictatorial ruler.

Round-eyed they listened as he told them that each of their countries basked in moments of greatness but at terrible cost. Though the nations won great renown, the *people* got nothing from any of the glory. And often they became so frustrated, so angry at the terrible lives they had to lead that they revolted violently against their rulers, throwing them out of power. But then, another strong man would rise up and he too would rule harshly until the inevitable revolution came once again. And this, he said, would continue until at last the once-glorious nation would lose its power and importance, or perhaps would no longer remain alive as a nation.

Miss Hennessey, seated nearby and observing the scene, records: "The United States, Jack said, would soon become the most powerful nation on earth. It was inescapable, and this time it would be largely because the U.S. was a democracy where the people held the real power. Then the great question for Americans would be how to keep that position, how to avoid the mistakes that had led to the fall of other countries, and how at the same time to preserve their freedom."

Luella marveled at Jack's eloquence and even more at young Teddy, who was listening avidly and, at the end, wanted to hear more.

2. Little Celebrity

Even at six, Teddy was a little celebrity in London. Three months after his arrival, wearing a belted camel's hair coat and his choir-boy smile, he officiated at a civic function. Prof. Julian Huxley, the eminent biologist and secretary of the Zoological Society of London, handed him a pair of shears with which he officially cut the tape opening a new Children's Zoo in Regents Park. Professor Huxley gave him and Bobby some books and other souvenirs and showed them the animals, which had been specially chosen to appeal to children.

Bobby and the girls (Joe and John too, when they came over from America) were invited to the best homes by the best people, including the Royal Family. Once Bobby spent a half hour with Lilibet — Princess Elizabeth, now the Queen — talking about skiing. Rose, along with Eunice, Kathleen and Rosemary, were presented at court. The older boys cut a romantic swath wherever they went.

In June of 1939, Teddy put on a new blue suit and lined up with his brothers and sisters to greet King George VI and Queen Elizabeth who came to dinner at Princes Gate. When they reached him, he bowed stiffly from the waist and stuck out his hand, which the monarch and his queen shook gravely. At dinner, the five older children were seated at a special table while the four younger ones went upstairs.

Teddy wasn't pleased with the arrangement and said so. He had never been impressed with the upper class British custom of exiling children to their chambers for dinner with their nannies while the parents dined by themselves; nor, indeed, did the

Kennedys observe this ritual. Usually, Teddy had his dinner with the family.

Few little boys of seven meet kings and queens, fewer still get to sit on a Pope's lap. And none before Teddy had been given his first communion by a reigning Pontiff in his private chapel at the Vatican.

When Eugenio Cardinal Pacelli was papal secretary of state, he had met Joe Kennedy a number of times and once had been a guest at his home in Bronxville. In 1939, when Pacelli was elected Pope, Joe Kennedy was instructed by President Roosevelt to represent the United States at the coronation.

He took his entire family with the exception of Joe, who had gone to Spain to observe the Civil War at first hand and had found his way into Madrid which was then being starved into submission by the encircling Nationalist forces. Joe was able to send a message to his father from the besieged city. The day after the colorful and moving rites, the Kennedy family had a private audience with Pius XII.

The Ambassador went in first. The Pope demonstrated his regard for Kennedy by departing from precedent; instead of remaining seated, he rose to greet his visitor. Later, Rose Kennedy entered accompanied by the children, Luella Hennessey, Mr. and Mrs. Eddie Moore and Franklin C. Gowen of the U.S. consular staff. The Pope told Teddy he remembered him very well, recalling that on his visit to Bronxville, the little boy had sat on his lap and twisted the cross that hung around his neck. The Pope went to a table at the side of the room and handed each member of the group a rosary.

The Pope then said that Teddy should have his first communion from the Pontiff himself in his private chapel. Arrangements were made and the ceremony was held the following day. Vatican authorities could not recall that any other little boy had ever attained this distinction.

Outside, after the audience, Teddy held a press conference. To reporters crowding around him, he said: "I told my sister Patricia I wasn't frightened at all. He patted my hand and told me I was a smart little fellow. He gave me the first rosary beads from the table, before he gave my sister any."

Following the audience, the Kennedys called on Luigi Cardinal Maglione, papal secretary of state, and Teddy was singled out once again. The cardinal remarked that since he himself had been the ninth child in his own family, he especially wanted to meet the ninth Kennedy. He shook hands with Teddy, beamed upon him and wished him good luck in Italian.

3. Home Again

The lowest dip in Joe Kennedy's political fortunes was now approaching.

Hitler was cranking up his German war machine. Almost daily, signs of what Winston Churchill was to call the "gathering storm" were becoming increasingly ominous. In defiance of the Treaty of Versailles signed at the end of World War I, Hitler had enlarged his army far beyond the 100,000-man limit imposed, built more than the allotted six battleships, and was producing masses of military aircraft, forbidden under the pact. He was proclaiming his intention of sweeping all German-speaking Europeans into the new German empire, and he seemingly had the strength to fulfill his design.

Or so Joe Kennedy thought, for his cables and telephone talks with President Roosevelt were filled with warnings that the British could not win if a war came. He exhorted Roosevelt to stay out of any conflict; the President, he said, should not be left "holding the bag in a war in which the allies expect to be beaten."

Throughout the tense months of 1938, Joe Kennedy kept urging the U.S. to avoid a collision. A few minutes past midnight of September 30, Prime Minister Neville Chamberlain signed the Munich Pact giving Hitler the coveted Sudetenland, and returned home proclaiming that "peace in our time" had been assured. Kennedy praised the gaunt prime minister for his "all but superhuman efforts in behalf of peace."

It was a major diplomatic blunder on Kennedy's part, for Britain was now turning against Chamberlain's policy of appeasement. Kennedy, though, continued to talk isolation, right through Hitler's invasion of Czechoslovakia and all the way up to September 1, 1939, when the Wehrmacht rolled into Poland and the war began.

Rose and the children were immediately moved to a house in the country for safety. Three weeks later, they once again boarded the S.S. *Washington* for the trip back home. This time, the luxury liner encountered no gales, but the passage was anything but luxurious. There were so many Americans fleeing the war that every available space, even the swimming pool, was occupied by emergency sleeping arrangements.

On October 19, Kennedy's popularity in England plummeted even further when he delivered a speech at the annual observance of Lord Nelson's victory at Trafalgar over the French and Spanish fleets. Kennedy voiced a sentiment that was to haunt him for the rest of his life:

"It has long been a theory of mine that it is unproductive for both the democratic and dictator countries to widen the division now existing between them by emphasizing their differences, which are now self-apparent. Instead of hammering away at what are regarded as irreconcilables, they could advantageously bend their energies toward solving their common problems by an attempt to reestablish good relations on a world basis.

"It is true that the democratic and dictator countries have important and fundamental divergencies of outlook, which in certain areas go deeper than politics. But there is simply no sense, common or otherwise, in letting these differences grow into unrelenting antagonisms. After all, we have to live together in the same world, whether we like it or not."

If Joe Kennedy's warm relationship with the British people had cooled, a free-swinging interview he gave in November, 1940, positively iced them. On a trip back to Washington for an interim report to the president, he talked with Louis M. Lyons of the Boston *Globe* in his suite at the Ritz-Carlton in New York. Suspenders flopping loose around his pants, spearing at a slab of apple pie topped with cheese, Joe spoke his mind as follows.

About the U.S. involvement in the war: "I'm willing to spend all I've got to keep us out of the war. There's no sense in our getting in. We'd just be holding the bag. What would we get out of it?"

About England: "Democracy is finished in England. . . . It isn't that she's fighting for democracy. That's the bunk. She's fighting for self-preservation, just as we will if it comes to us."

About Charles A. Lindbergh, the aviation hero who was also a non-interventionist: "Lindbergh isn't crazy, either."

About Queen Elizabeth (now the queen mother): "The queen is one of the most intelligent women you ever met. It will be the queen who will save what's left of England and not any of the politicians. . . . She's got more brains than the cabinet. . . ."

About American legislators: "Our Congressmen are dopes who don't understand the war or our relationship to it."

Joe Kennedy hadn't expected his words to be published. He thought he was giving the reporter off-the-record background, but since the ground rules had not been clearly established at the start, Lyons did not feel himself bound by any restrictions.

Ruefully, Joe Kennedy told Joseph Dinneen, a *Globe* man whom he'd known for years: "He didn't miss a thing. He has destroyed me as an ambassador. There is nothing left for me now but to resign."

What angered the British most was Kennedy's remark that "democracy is finished in England," a statement that was splashed across all newspapers. Tall, aristocratic Sir Evelyn Wrench, founder of the English-Speaking Union who was in Boston for a speaking engagement, expressed the views of his countrymen: "I cannot believe that Mr. Kennedy made so ridiculous a statement. If he did, he was wasting his three years in England. He has entirely misunderstood the British attitude."

Kennedy tried to remove the sting by disavowing the interview, claiming his remarks had not been intended for publication and, in any event, the reporter had not quoted them accurately. He demanded the newspaper publish a retraction but the *Globe* stood by its reporter and its story.

Fatal damage had been done. The British, as Arthur Krock records in his memoirs, "rose in indignation that developed into a dislike for the U.S. Ambassador that remains unabated. No one at that time could have foreseen that a son of Kennedy's would become the most popular of all American presidents with the British people."

Joe Kennedy returned to London to close up shop and soon was back in the United States, a private citizen once more, earning more millions.

The war years plodded on in England. Grosvenor Square became "Eisenhowerplatz" to American GIs because the Supreme Commander's headquarters were located at No. 48. A huge barrage balloon, which someone named Romeo, was anchored in the center of the greenery and floated high above the square to snag enemy aircraft. On windy days, Romeo would be blown backward and forward, often leering into the windows of No. 48. Still later, a statue of Franklin Roosevelt would be erected in the Square and a new Embassy built.

As the 1970s got underway, the house at 14 Princes Gate was unoccupied. (The American ambassador's residence was located inside Regents Park.) A policeman directing traffic on Kensington Gore doesn't remember that the Kennedy family lived nearby. Mothers watching their children in Kensington Gardens inside Alexandra Gate are astonished to hear that Teddy and Bobby had played there too.

But Ted Kennedy remembers his London years clearly. He talks about them fondly with Luella Hennessey, recalling the things they did, the fun they had. And we can easily understand why he looks back upon those times with a special joy: they were the golden years, the years before the great tragedies would strike so suddenly and with such terrible regularity that he would be moved to say in anguish: "I sometimes wonder whether some awful curse did actually hang over all the Kennedys."

PUBLIC LIBRARY BROCKTON, MASS.

IV

Harvard Man

1. Preppie

Even though Bobby once described Ted as "a better natural politician than any of us," the youngest Kennedy was hardly a ball of fire in the first hurrah of his life.

Back in Bronxville, he was enrolled at the Lawrence Park Country Day School on Palmer Road three miles from his home. In the fall of 1940, as the national election drives grew hotter, headmaster George Collen turned the school into a political arena for a few days to give the students a first-hand lesson in current events. A brief but enthusiastic campaign-in-miniature was conducted, climaxed by a rally in the school gym.

A key spokesman for the Democratic Party and its standard-bearer, Franklin D. Roosevelt, then seeking his third term, was eight-year-old Ted Kennedy. His opponent, stumping for the Republican challenger, the industrialist Wendell L. Willkie of Indiana, was Westbrook Pegler II, whose uncle was the Roosevelt-hating columnist for the Hearst syndicate. Amid cheers from his side and derisive comments for the G.O.P. supporters, Ted mounted the podium and spoke his rehearsed piece.

"Today we are facing a crisis. (Applause.) Across the seas, nation after nation whose belief in democracy has been as strong as ours, have gone down before the Nazi war machine. (Hisses.)

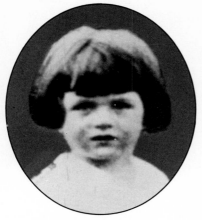

Teddy in 1934.
United Press International

1938. The Kennedys in their home in Bronxville, New York. Seated from the left are Eunice, Jean, Teddy on Joseph Kennedy's lap, Patricia and Kathleen. Standing: Rosemary, Robert, John, Rose Kennedy, and Joseph Jr.

Wide World

Wide World

1938. Teddy mugging for the camera aboard the liner Washington, *en route to join his father, the new U.S. Ambassador to England. Flanking him, left to right: Kathleen, Robert, Rose Kennedy, Patricia and Jean.*

1942. John F. "Honey Fitz" Fitzgerald.

Wide World

United Press International

1955 Harvard-Yale game. Ted (left) grimaces in despair as the ball sails past, too high, in the Yale end zone. Yale won, 21-7.

Ted strikes the kind of pose that footballers dream about.

Wide World

Wide World

1956. Harvard commencement when Ted Kennedy graduated, and Senator John Kennedy received an honorary degree.

United Press International

1958. Francis Cardinal Spellman celebrates the nuptial high mass as Ted weds Joan Bennett at St. Joseph's Roman Catholic Church in Bronxville, New York.

Below are the newlyweds leaving the church.

Wide World

MASSES
SUNDAYS 8-30 8 9 10 15 11 12
HOLYDAYS 630 7 730 8 9 10
FIRST FRIDAYS 630 7 & 8
WEEKDAYS 7 & 8

MIRACULOUS MEDAL NOVENA
MONDAY EVENING AT 81

CONFESSIONS 4 TO 5.45 & 730 TO 9

APPOINTMENT

DOWNSTA RS

Y 4 30

VE

7 1660

1958. The triple threat image that would soon loom large across the landscape of national politics.

1959. Ted visits brothers John and Bobby, who was then counsel to the Senate Rackets Investigating Subcommittee, during one of the committee hearings.

United Press International

"MINE CAN LICK YOURS!"

Ben Roth Agency

*1962. The race for the Massachusetts seat in the Senate is repre-
sented here as a dynastic battle involving the Kennedys versus
the McCormacks versus the Lodges.*

United Press International

1960. Robert and Ethel Kennedy team up against Ted in a game of touch football on the beach in Acapulco, Mexico.

At a time like this, we must get things done whether it is good for private business or not. (Applause, boos.)

"For this task, we must step on the toes of some people and institutions which Mr. Willkie favors." (Loud applause, foot-stomping, cheers.)

In rebuttal, the youthful Pegler, expressing the thesis thundered by his famous uncle, argued that Roosevelt was leaving the nation dangerously exposed by arming it with "toy guns" and disregarding warnings of military experts to shore up the country's defenses.

The Republican heritage of the young private school students showed clearly in the voting: Roosevelt, and the Kennedy who backed him, were buried under a Willkie landslide. Fortunately for the Democratic Party, as Lawrence Park Country Day School went, the rest of the nation did not: in the real election, Roosevelt defeated Willkie 449 electoral votes to 82.

Reminded of the incident years afterward, Kennedy remarked with a laugh: "It was my first and only mistake." Well, almost the only one. In any case, young Pegler retired from politics soon after that, and Ted went on to become, by 1971, a twice-elected United States senator and one of his party's best campaigners.

Because Joe Kennedy moved his family around a great deal, Ted rarely spent more than a year at any one school up to the time he entered Milton. His elementary education was acquired at nine separate institutions, including two in London, several in Massachusetts, several more in New York and one in Palm Beach. Bobby racked up an even higher total — twelve in all.

At Milton, Ted's easy-going nature and athletic talents won him a host of friends though his academic achievements were somewhat less than spectacular. Arthur Hall, retired dean of students at the academy, remembers Ted well. Hall came to Milton as a teacher and head football coach in 1932 and remained until 1969, serving as dean of students for the last seventeen years.

Dean Hall: "Ted was a very good-humored, fun sort of kid but he was not a good student. In fact, he was the favorite customer of the school's tutor, Kernel Holloway, who was known as "the colonel" because he came from Kentucky. He was an extraordinarily good tutor and he got Teddy through.

"Teddy had a regular schedule of tutoring. Each evening, he would be working with the colonel who, by the way, was not somebody who would be used as a prop. He would take you back to the point where you were comfortable and go on from there, building up. The long-range effect of Kernel Holloway on Teddy was that he could finally pass and graduate and go on to Harvard College.

"He graduated as a straight C student — with help.

"Bobby was a more able student, though he was not as well liked. He used to get too intense."

In those years, a diploma from Milton practically guaranteed admission to Harvard College. And so, on a clear fall day in 1950, Ted Kennedy arrived in Cambridge.

2. Halls of Academe

Since the day he was born, Ted Kennedy had been programmed for Harvard.

Joe junior went there, scored fair grades, played freshman baseball (though he never made the varsity) and graduated in 1912. Each of his brothers went, too, because their father was impressed not only with Harvard's educational standards but the prestige that came with it. There was never any doubt that Teddy would go, too.

Ted chose to room at Winthrop House, a venerable red brick structure overlooking the Charles River between the Weeks Memorial and Anderson Bridges. Selection of a house is important to a Harvard man because it governs his social, cultural and athletic life during his upper-class years. The Harvard "house plan" divides the main college into nine smaller, self-contained ones. After freshman year in a dormitory, a student picks a house, each accommodating about 350 students and each named after a former president or revered son. While varsity sports are college-wide and most classes are held outside, all other activities of undergraduate life are centered around the houses. Students take their meals there. House teams compete in rowing, football, baseball, squash, golf, tennis, swimming, basketball, and the rivalry is keen. Dances, smokers, teas, special dinners, concerts, lectures, forums, debates — all are planned and carried through by student committees in the houses.

Winthrop was Harvard's "jock house," mecca for the school's

athletes. "House of the Mesomorphs," it was called, a meso-
morph being defined anthropologically as an individual with a
heavy muscular frame or, as one of Ted's roommates put it in
less academic language, "guys who are built like brick shit
houses."

At Harvard, Ted's closest friends were, like himself, the mesomorphs. (At six-two and weighing between 200 and 210 pounds,
he qualified.) He found them more congenial than the book-
worms of the socially elite even though jocks as a group did not
rate high with the student body. There was always a faint touch
of snobbery at Harvard toward athletes, which has grown
stronger since the close of World War II. E.J. Kahn, Jr., has
noted in his book, *Harvard*, that athletes are even looked upon
as "social inferiors" and, indeed, the eminent sociologist Dr.
David Reisman once rallied to their defense. "I hate snobbery
toward jocks," he said. "The jocks at Harvard are no threat to
anybody. They don't even get the prettiest girls." (There are ex-
ceptions. Joe Kennedy Jr. got more than his share of beauties;
Jack didn't do badly, and Ted didn't let the family tradition
down. Only shy Bobby fared poorly.)

Certainly wealth and social position counted for nothing in
Ted's choice of friends. Dick Clasby, the superb athlete, was the
son of a policeman. Bill Frate, another close buddy and excellent
tackle and guard, came from a small town in Connecticut where
his parents ran a small retail store.

While Ted would invite these and others to his grand home at
Hyannis Port, he would also accept invitations to theirs. On a
number of occasions, Dick Clasby would take Ted home to
dinner at his folks' small house in Natick, just outside Boston,
where they'd sit around a table in the tiny dining room. "And
when we were finished," Clasby recalls, "mom would toss us dish
towels and we'd both dry the dishes."

One of Ted's roommates at Winthrop was George Anderson,
who now lives in Maine and manages two television stations.
"There were four of us in one suite of rooms, separated by a fire
door from four other guys," he recalls. "The fire door was always open, though, contrary to rules, and the eight of us were
together a great deal." When they weren't on the playing fields or
studying, the eight expended a good deal of creative energy de-
vising stunts and making small bets on the outcome of almost
anything.

At dinner one evening Ted challenged Anderson: "Bet I could hit a golf ball across the river with a seven-iron." Anderson took him on and, clubs in hand, they went out to the Weeks footbridge. Ted swung first, connected squarely and sailed his ball 150 yards to the opposite bank of the Charles.

"Then," says Anderson, "it was my turn. In the middle of my backswing, Ted called out: 'Double or nothing!' He timed it perfectly, startling me just enough to lose the groove. My ball dribbled five yards."

Another time Ted Kennedy took Edward (Ted) Carey of Westfield, Massachusetts, to the same spot and bet him ten dollars he could put the ball across the river. He won and Carey was given the option of paying the money or shining Kennedy's shoes for a month. He chose the latter.

Once Ted spotted the actor Monty Woolley dining in a Boston restaurant. He bet a friend that he wouldn't have the nerve to sneak over and tug his beard. The friend did have the nerve. The astounded Mr. Woolley let out a whoop, the friend dashed off — and Ted paid.

For sheer size and scope, few stunts in which Ted, or any other Kennedy, was involved could match the Big Cairo Caper. One evening in the rooms, Kennedy and Carey began needling each other about the way they had handled themselves in a touch football game a few hours earlier. Finally, Kennedy jokingly said he wished Carey would go somewhere, preferably far away, and that he, Kennedy would love to send him. "As a matter of fact," Kennedy said, "I'd like to send you to Africa — but I'll bet you won't go."

Carey, who would pick up a bet as fast as Kennedy, replied the hell he wouldn't. Just get him a ticket and he'd take off. Right away, too. And so the wager was made: Kennedy would supply Carey with a one-way airplane flight to Cairo, providing he left that Friday — it was already Tuesday — and that he made it back to Cambridge on his own. Carey didn't even blink: he accepted. The amount of the bet has long since been forgotten by the parties involved, but all agree it was small. ("I hadn't the faintest idea how I'd get back," Carey admitted recently. "I only had a few bucks. I figured maybe I'd get on a freighter and work my way back.")

Next day, Carey showed up at the Harvard infirmary and, pleading that his uncle had just died in Cairo and he had to rush to the funeral, got himself pumped full of shots. He repeated the story to the passport-issuing office in Cambridge, which hurried through his papers. The passport was ready on Thursday.

Carey announced he was ready to depart. Kennedy, surprised that Carey hadn't backed down, bought a one-way plane ticket to Cairo on a credit card, muttering: "If my father gets wind of this, I'm done." At 6 a.m. Friday morning, Carey came down to breakfast wearing a towel like an Arabian mantle and headdress; then he, Kennedy and a half-dozen others piled into cars and drove to Logan Airport. Carey carried with him a paper bag holding a toothbrush, camera and an extra pair of underwear. The camera was needed to prove he was there: he had to have a photo taken of him in Cairo.

By this time, Ted Kennedy began getting serious second thoughts. At the field, he said to Carey: "Okay, Ted, you won this one. You got us over a barrel. Let's go back." But Carey looked down at his arm, all puffed from the shots, and replied: "No sir, I'm going." Ted began to worry. (George Anderson says: "He could just visualize the headlines. 'SEN. KENNEDY'S BROTHER SENDS HIS ROOMMATE TO AFRICA.') Carey could not be dissuaded. He yelled goodbye, boarded the plane and took off for New York where he was scheduled to change for an overseas flight.

At Idlewild (later to be renamed Kennedy International Airport) Carey heard himself paged. Ted Kennedy was on the telephone from Cambridge, making frantic pleas for Carey to return. "Okay," he said. "Enough is enough, you win, come on back." But Carey didn't give in, though by that time he had no intention of going to Cairo. He caught a plane to Hartford, went to his home in Westfield, remained there overnight and finally showed up at Winthrop House on Saturday to Ted Kennedy's enormous relief.

Recalling the story years later, Kennedy smiled ruefully and admitted: "I sure lost that one!"

In 1953, Kennedy bet Carey $500 that his brother John, then Senator from Massachusetts, would one day be President of the United States. Carey accepted. They sealed the terms of the wager into an envelope, which they gave to Joe Kennedy to hold.

When Kennedy defeated Nixon in 1960, Carey offered to pay off but Ted refused, saying: "Let's make it double or nothing on Bobby."

Two years after Bobby's assassination, when Ted Kennedy ran for reelection to the Senate, Carey, by that time established as a mechanical contractor in Westfield, paid off the $500 in the form of a campaign contribution.

If Ted dropped the ball on the Cairo incident, he and Dick Clasby made a smashing success with a mind-reading act that astounded and puzzled Harvardians for three years.

Bill Frate: "They had everyone crazy. Clasby would hand a deck of cards to somebody, who would pick a card. Then he'd tell Kennedy to go ahead and guess — and Ted would never miss. The football team picked it up in the locker room, where they pulled it again and again. The basketball team heard about it and then it spread all through the school.

"The funny part was that Clasby and Kennedy insisted that you could only 'read minds' if you conditioned your body in certain ways. They said it could be done if you'd tear off your clothes in five seconds, take an ice-cold shower and then call out the first card that came into your mind.

"They were so convincing that guys would actually do this. Obviously, these fellows who jumped into the shower weren't coming close to reading minds, but Clasby and Kennedy pretended that the card they came up with was the one they picked.

"One guy did it ten times and they had him believing completely in his ability to read minds. One night this fellow went to a dance at a girls' school, told them about his incredible power and proceeded to demonstrate. He ripped off his clothes, took an icy shower — and of course was wrong. He couldn't understand why."

Clasby and Kennedy never divulged their secret but if Harvardians of the early 1950s are still befuddled — and for those who may want to pull their own mind-reading acts — here is how they did it:

The card suits are referred to in the following order:

Spades are *one*, hearts are *two*, clubs are *three* and diamonds are *four*.

The cards were divided into four groups:

1. Ace, 2, 3 and 4.
2. 5, 6, 7 and 8.
3. 10, Jack, Queen
4. King by itself.

Now pay attention. Clasby would offer the deck to a subject who would select a card and show it to him. Kennedy, the "mind-reader," would ask if the fellow has received the card. *Clasby's responses to this innocuous question would give Kennedy the clues he needs.*

A "yes" answer meant card suit *one*, or that the card is a spade. "Right" meant suit *two* or hearts. "That's right" indicated suit *three* (clubs) and "okay" suit *four* (diamonds).

Thus at this point the "mind reader" would know the suit. He would then ask an innocuous question, such as "Are you holding the card?" or "Is it a red card?" Clasby again would make one of the four replies — yes, right, that's right, okay — only this time the answers would refer to the card groupings.

"Yes" would mean the card lies in group one, or that it is an Ace, 2, 3, or 4. "Right" would mean group two or 5, 6, 7 or 8. And so on.

Just one more piece of information would be needed to pinpoint the card. The "mind reader" would ask another simple question to elicit a reply. This time, the answer would refer to the order of the cards within the grouping. For instance, if Kennedy knew the card was a spade and lay in group one, a "yes" answer would inform him it must be the Ace. "Right" would mean it's the second card along, or the 2, and so on. If the card would be a club and lie in group three, or the 9, 10, jack or queen, the same rule holds. An answer of "yes" would mean it's the first card, the 9; "right would mean the 10, etc.

Often victims surmised the clues lay in the responses, so Clasby and Kennedy devised non-verbal answers. For example, Kennedy, when guessing a card, might furrow his brow and, looking occult, say slowly: "I ...... think ...... it's ...... a ......" At a certain point, Clasby would emit a puff of smoke, place his tongue in his cheek, wink or make some other imperceptible sign. Timing was the key — if the sigh was given when Kennedy uttered the first word, "I," the clue was No. 1. Given on the second word, "think," means No. 2, and so on.

Kennedy and Clasby were also innovators in another area: they started a "rate the girls" game which eventually spread to the other houses. An "A" girl was a smash, someone on the beauty level of Elizabeth Taylor. A "B" girl the the equivalent of Debbie Reynolds, and so on down to grade "E," which was not considered very desirable.

Clasby: "If either of us got the other a blind date, we would describe her quickly by referring to her by grade. We'd even rate the important women of the day, including some of the Kennedy women."

(Clasby would not divulge the ratings given to them: "I've got courage, but not that much.")

At Harvard, Ted Kennedy had credit cards, charge accounts and a checkbook, but he didn't use them much. The small allowances of his childhood years — he was up to $1.50 a week at Milton — and his father's continual reminders that he must understand the value of a dollar had borne fruit. He drove an ancient Pontiac, a hand-me-down from Bobby, for several years, though he acquired a Thunderbird in his final year. He bought only the clothes he needed and frequently not even those. He wore Ted Carey's shirts so often his roommate once demanded in exasperation: "What's the matter? Can't you afford to buy your own?"

Once after a football game at Princeton, Ted arranged for his friends and their dates, eighteen persons in all, to have dinner at a fine French restaurant in New York. Everyone expected Kennedy to foot the bill — after all, it had all been his idea. But at the end of the evening, Ted was standing outside with a pencil and a sheet of paper, totaling each diner's tab. "Okay, Hank, you owe $18. George, yours comes to $18.75 — you had the extra drink."

Joe senior quickly discouraged all extravagance, even after Ted turned twenty-one. In the summer of 1954, Ted was making arrangements to spend the summer in Europe. Quietly, he arranged with his father's New York office to check his newly-acquired Thunderbird aboard ship, urging the secretaries to keep the matter from his father's attention. When he invited some of his roommates to dinner at Hyannis Port, he cautioned them against mentioning the car.

"But you don't keep things from Joe Kennedy," George Anderson recalls. "He had found out. And he raked Ted over the coals for it, telling him how expensive it would be to transport and use in Europe."

As for the girls, one family friend observed: "Ted wasn't a real ladies' man at college, at least not like his brothers Joe and Jack." He had plenty of dates, blind and otherwise, but there never was anyone special in the Harvard years. "He never went out too many times with the same girl," Clasby says.

"There'd be some pretty good parties," one classmate recalls, "but a hell of a lot of dull ones, too." Mostly, Ted and his friends went to the mixers and other social affairs at the many girls' schools in and around Boston. Once Ted and George Anderson took a couple of girls from Bradford Junior College to dinner, bringing a Monopoly game with them. "After eating, we set the game up on the table and started to play," Anderson says. "But they kicked us out because they didn't want any gambling on the premises." (None in the foursome saw anything especially funny about watching Ted Kennedy buy and sell vast properties with paper money at the same time that his father was transacting similar business with the real thing.)

Ted would drink beer with the boys at parties but not too much and never anything else. One might suppose that Joe Kennedy kept a well-stocked bar at Hyannis Port, but all that was available was a small cabinet with a few bottles. Ted Carey says :"If you wanted to tie one on, you couldn't do it up there."

On one memorable occasion, Ted pulled a stunt that almost made Bill Frate swear off beer for the rest of his life. One April, Kennedy went to Bermuda with a Harvard team to participate in the International Rugby Festival held each year on the island. The government put them all up in barracks in a militia camp. After a game, all the boys went out on the town. Frate, who consumed a considerable quantity of the local brew, had to be taken back to camp in a condition generally described as feeling no pain.

He woke the next morning to find a cow tied to the foot of his bed, staring at him out of soft brown eyes. Kennedy had found her in a pasture and brought her to the barracks.

Ted was selected for membership in Hasty Pudding-Institute of 1770 and Pi Eta, two of Harvard's more exclusive social clubs. All four Kennedys belonged to Hasty Pudding. Joe junior, John and Bobby were members of Spee. None made the ultra-exclusive Porcellan or Fly clubs, which accept only the "best" young men from the "best" backgrounds. Apparently, the Kennedys' humble beginnings did not qualify them.

The Pi Eta crowd gave Kennedy an especially rough initiation. ("They all knew who he was so they made it tough," says a classmate, "but he took it beautifully.") Ted was blindfolded and led into a room, where he was "banged around," Bill Frate recalls. "Beer was poured all over him, he was pushed onto the floor and soon he was swimming in about a foot of the stuff." He was ordered to go to Radcliffe and return with a size 42 brassiere. He did. For a finale, he was instructed to go to Boston without a cent in his pockets and bring back the most typical-looking prostitute he could find. An hour and a half after he set out, he came back victorious — "a real knockout," a classmate remembers, "but there was no mistaking her profession. We talked with her for a while and finally sent her home."

At Harvard, Ted Kennedy's great passion was football. He was no Red Grange, but he was good at the game and wanted to be better. This great interest was to bring him much personal satisfaction, a coveted Harvard letter and even a measure of acclaim.

But it was also to be responsible for a serious mistake that would rise to haunt him many years later.

3. The Spanish Test

At Harvard, all undergraduates enrolled in a bachelor's degree program must demonstrate proficiency in a foreign language. This requirement can be met in one of two ways: by presenting acceptable evidence upon entrance; or passing with a letter grade an appropriate full course or two half-year courses in the language at Harvard.

To fulfill the requirement, Ted Kennedy enrolled in a Spanish course in his freshman year. The first semester presented no trouble; the second did. He began having problems, and the problems could interfere seriously with his athletic hopes.

Football was a family obsession. While Joe senior did not play at Harvard, all his sons did. Joe junior was right end on the freshman team in 1934 and made the forty-man varsity, though not as a first-stringer. John, who was also on the freshman team, fought hard for varsity status but had to be content with the junior varsity. Bobby practiced doggedly for hours every day to perfect his skills and, though he was a bench-warmer most of the time, managed to win his letter, the big crimson H awarded to team members who, however briefly, play in a Yale game.

One may also speculate that, as all sons, Ted wanted the approval of his father. Joe Kennedy prized athletic success highly. When the Yale coach failed to send Joe junior into the Harvard game in his senior year, his last chance to win his letter, Joe senior, white-faced with rage, stormed into the locker room to berate him. Throughout the children's growing years, their father had given ample evidence that *winning* was what counted.

Ted made the freshman team and was an outstanding end. But by spring, he began to worry about the language course. Final exams were coming up soon.

George Anderson: "He was scared that he was not going to pass, which would have meant he would have been put on probation and would not be able to play football the following fall. Ted talked it over with another fellow, who was also a football player and happened to be pretty good in Spanish.

"They talked and talked, and then they did the deal."

The "deal" was a simple ploy. Final exams at Harvard are generally given in huge rooms that can accommodate between 200 and 500 students. Five or even more separate groups could be scheduled in one hall at the same time, each taking different tests. Moreover, course instructors hardly ever show up for finals, which are proctored by graduate assistants or other faculty members.

Thus it would be a fairly simple matter for a student to slip into a seat, take a test, put another's name on the familiar blue-covered exam booklet and leave without anyone being the wiser. Ted arranged for his teammate to be his proxy at the Spanish final.

But the plan backfired. One of the proctors in the examination hall knew the stand-in. When the latter turned in his paper, the proctor greeted him, then glanced at the booklet in his hand. On it was written the name of Edward Kennedy.

Brought up before the dean, both boys were asked to withdraw from the university. They were told they could seek re-admission at a later date if they conducted themselves during their absence as responsible young citizens.

The name of the teammate who took the test for Ted has never been divulged. Now a successful businessman, he told this author:

"It's something that happened twenty years ago, something that could have happened to any guy eighteen years old in school at that time."

One thing troubles him. Allegations have been made through the years that he had been paid by Kennedy for taking the test. "It's not so," he says. "Not one penny changed hands."

Ted Kennedy left school and enlisted in the Army in June, 1951, serving in Europe as an infantryman until his discharge in March, 1953. He re-applied to Harvard in 1953, was admitted to the sophomore class, and graduated in 1956. The teammate also returned and was graduated.

There matters rested until early in 1962 when Robert L. Healy, a Boston newspaperman, began checking out rumors that had been floating around the city. His efforts to dig out the story took him to the highest levels of government. He had no fewer than four conferences in the office of the President of the United States on the Case of Ted Kennedy and the Spanish Test.

The circumstances had all the elements of high drama. The personalities involved were important, the backdrop exciting, the stakes high.

Healy at the time was political editor of the *Boston Globe*, an independent newspaper. Everyone was expecting Ted Kennedy to announce his candidacy for the Democratic Senate nomination, opposing Edward J. McCormack, Jr., then Massachusetts attorney general and the favorite nephew of John W. McCormack, the Speaker of the House. Thus, two dynastic figures were on a collision course. Ted's bid at the age of thirty was to focus national attention upon him and the campaign itself would be one of the most fiercely fought encounters even in the rough world of Massachusetts.

The issue of the Spanish test could well destroy young Kennedy's political career before it got started, and everyone in his camp knew it.

After weeks of digging, Healy believed he had uncovered the true reason why Ted Kennedy had left Harvard for two years, but the records were in Harvard's archives and the university refused to unlock them. Through an intermediary, Healy got word to President Kennedy: he wanted to see the President to verify the story.

One day a call came from the White House inviting Healy to come down. He did. He talked with the President for an hour, and then three times more on subsequent occasions. Once he saw him alone, the other times in the presence of McGeorge

Bundy, Kenneth P. O'Donnell and Theodore C. Sorensen, special assistant to the President. Once Arthur M. Schlesinger, another aide, was called in.

Bob Healy, now executive editor of the Globe: "They asked me how much I knew about it and I told them I knew the story and that it would doubtless come out. I said I wanted the story and that the only way I could get it completely was from Harvard.

"The President asked me, if they would confirm it for me, how would I use it? I told him I would use it straightaway, as a news story. Then he asked me: Could I use it in a profile? (A profile is a special feature article describing a personality which does not receive headline treatment. Using the Spanish incident as part of a profile would be burying the story and Healy knew it.)

"I told Kennedy: 'No, I couldn't do that.'

"So we had three other meetings on the subject, going over the same ground each time. These meetings were held about every week and lasted about an hour each time. Finally, I was able to convince the President that I wasn't going to bury anything like that, and he wasn't going to have any influence over how I would use it.

"At one point the President turned to Bundy and said: 'We're having more trouble with this than we had with Cuba.'

"To which Bundy replied: 'And with about the same results.' (The Bay of Pigs fiasco was a recent and bitter memory.)

"It was like a union negotiation; they were trying to get what they could. The President wasn't trying to defend Ted; it was strictly a business session. I knew what he wanted and I knew he wasn't going to get what he wanted, and he knew he wasn't going to get what he wanted. So finally they let me have the information and they held their breaths."

Bundy called the dean at Harvard and arranged for Healy to talk with everyone concerned, with no strings attached. Healy believes the final decision on opening the records was put up to Ted by the President. "Ted realized that sooner or later he had to come to grips with it. It wasn't pleasant for him, but he just knew he had to come clean on it. And he did."

Healy's story, including a statement from Ted Kennedy, was published in the *Globe* on March 30 and made headlines throughout the country. "What I did was wrong," Ted said after admitting that the facts were correct. "I have regretted it ever since. The unhappiness I caused my family and my friends, even though eleven years ago, has been a bitter experience for me, but it also has been a very valuable lesson."

When the news broke, the Kennedy political machine feared the worst. Bobby, for one, was certain Teddy would be soundly defeated. But few people in Massachusetts were especially upset by the disclosure.

Early that June, at the Democratic state convention in Springfield, Teddy easily won the party's pre-primary endorsement. Typical was the attitude of a delegate who was also a school teacher: "I see this all the time. I punish children by flunking them for the term, but I believe that for the next term — if a person proves that they're learning by a mistake, have improved by a mistake, I'd never hold it against him." Mostly, people accepted Teddy's action as a "boy's prank." Many expressed the view that things like it have happened before, and will again. *

The story mattered so little, in fact, that McCormack did not even bring it up during the long, rough campaign. Persons with long memories recalled that Jim Curley once took a civil service test for a friend back in 1904, was sent to jail for two months and ran for reelection as city alderman, conducting his campaign from his cell. He won.

The voters may have forgiven Teddy but the incident has not been forgotten: it has surfaced on more than one occasion. In 1970, Senator Kennedy was involved in a sharp exchange with Sen. Strom Thurmond of South Carolina over Supreme Court Justice William O. Douglas's involvement with the Inter-American Center for Economic and Social Studies, an affiliate of the Albert B. Parvin Foundation. Thurmond assailed the center as a "socialist" organization and introduced the name of

*One Harvard classmate told the author: "The practice wasn't exactly commonplace but it wasn't unknown either, at Harvard or anywhere else. I myself took a swimming test, required by the physical ed department, for a guy who couldn't swim."

Exactly twenty years later, in 1971, the following news item went out over the wires of the Associated Press:

Cambridge, Mass., May 20 (AP) — Harvard has meted out university discipline to two history students who turned in identical term papers written by a commercial concern, Dean Archie Epps said yesterday. A graduate student was suspended for one year, Dean Epps said, and an undergraduate was dismissed. *Plus ça change.* . . .

President José Figueres, the former president of Costa Rica. as a member. Almost offhandedly, Kennedy corrected Thurmond's pronunciation of the Latin leader's name. Thurmond became furious at Kennedy. "Are you holding yourself out as an expert?" he demanded. "Are you correcting my Spanish? What was your record at Harvard?"

For Ted Kennedy, the hardest part of the incident was having to face his father, and here we should mercifully avert our eyes. A close family friend says: "Mr. Kennedy, who loved Teddy so much, was so grieved, so hurt. And then, of course, he was furious, too. Ted really caught it from his father that time."

But Joe forgave his son, and the incident left its mark in another, rather strange way. In September, 1960, *Newsweek* noted the following: "He [Joe Kennedy] can coldly demand a business associate's life insurance as security for a loan. Yet when eighty-four West Point cadets were expelled in the cribbing scandal of 1951, he quietly helped thirty-one of them who had not cheated but merely failed to report other cheaters, to enter other colleges; he paid their tuition, too."

Ted's military career was uneventful. In Paris, he was attached to a Military Police unit at SHAPE headquarters, was offered a chance to go to officers candidate school, turned it down and returned to civilian life having advanced to private first class.

In the fall of 1953, Ted Kennedy was back on campus, back at Winthrop House — and back in a football uniform.

4. No. 88

With his height and weight, Ted had the beef to be a good blocking end. His coordination was excellent and, like his brothers, he was a battler. His one disadvantage: he lacked speed.

But he worked hard and was able to improve, though he never became a flash. His inability to outrun Dick Clasby rankled. One day Ted told him: "Dick, sometime in the next ten years, I'll bet I beat you in a race." Nine years later, when Clasby — who had married Mary Jo Gargan, Ted's cousin — was a house guest at Hyannis Port, Kennedy suddenly told him he was ready to take him on. Clasby looked blank and Kennedy reminded him of the wager. There, on the playing fields of

Hyannis Port, Ted at long last beat the redoubtable Clasby in a foot race.

During the season, Ted was a stickler for training rules: he ate the right foods and went to bed early. On more than one occasion he would howl out to his noisy roommates when he wanted to sleep: "Hey, knock it off!" Some Sundays, he would invite a half-dozen team members to Hyannis Port for a day on the beach — and more football.

Once during a game with Brown University Ted leaped into the air to make a spectacular catch of a pass thrown by Clasby. In the years following they loved to re-enact the play.

Clasby: "Many times we'd be tossing a football around and one of us would call for the 'Brown play.' Ted would run out and I'd overthrow the ball as I did in the original game, way out ahead of him, and he'd race ahead, make that gigantic leap and catch it.

"One day his father was watching at Hyannis Port. I threw, but this time Ted misjudged and didn't leap high enough. He landed headlong in the rose garden, emerging with all sorts of scratches. His father commented: 'Too little and too late!' Then he gave us both a stern warning not to perform the Brown play any more near his roses."

As first string right end, a huge white 88 fore and aft on his crimson jersey, Ted acquitted himself well. And he had a few moments of glory, too.

The greatest of these occurred during the Harvard-Yale classic on November 19, 1956, played during a snowstorm before 56,000 frozen spectators in New Haven. It was a bruising match from start to finish, tempers growing shorter as the snow swirled faster; several times the referees had to wade into players, who were whaling away at one another with their fists.

In the third quarter, with Yale leading 14 to 0, Harvard began to move, advancing 79 yards in ten plays. On the eleventh, Walter Stahura, Harvard's huge sophomore tailback, who had been playing a tremendous game, tossed a short pass. Ted Kennedy caught it on Yale's seven-yard line and carried it over for a touchdown. The Harvard side went wild.

It was the only score of the game, which Yale won, 21 to 7. Joe Kennedy sat through the whole game, chilled to the bone but glowing with great pride. Next day, *The New York Times* report of the game singled out Ted Kennedy for special praise.

A few weeks earlier, during another stormy afternoon, Kennedy had shone brightly in the Columbia game at Baker Field in New York. He caught a 20-yard pass from Jim Joslin, Harvard's left tailback, for a touchdown. This time, Harvard won, 21-7.

Teddy graduated with honors in some courses though his overall scholastic achievements were modest. His field of concentration was government, the same as his three brothers. And like them, he studied under the brilliant Dr. Arthur N. Holcombe, Eaton Professor of the Science of Government.

John Kennedy's scholastic performance, described as excellent in biographies, turns out to be somewhat less than brilliant. When these and other records became available at the John F. Kennedy Library, temporarily housed in Waltham, Massachusetts, we learned that he ranked only a little above midway point in his graduating class at Choate, 65th among 110. In his freshman year at Harvard in 1936, he earned only one B, in Economics, and three Cs, in History, French and English. As a sophomore, his record was even worse: he racked up four Cs, a D and a B. As a junior, he drew five Bs and a C, considerably better, and was a straight B student in his final year. Thus, his overall average fell midway between a B and a C.

In mid-1971, Dr. Holcombe was the only living person who taught all five Kennedy males at Harvard. Retired and living in Germantown, Pennsylvania, he has had the unique opportunity of viewing their developing careers. "I like to talk about the Kennedys," he admits. "They were all extraordinary people."

It was Professor Holcombe who first sparked the interest that led John Kennedy to work under two other professors on an honors thesis that eventually led to a best-selling book, *Why England Slept*. "Jack got very much interested in research work," Dr. Holcombe says. "During his Christmas vacation, he went down to Washington to continue his work."

Of Edward Kennedy, Dr. Holcombe says:

"He took two courses with me, Government I, which was the general introduction to American government, politics and contemporary government generally, and my more advanced course in the government of the United States.

"His work was always satisfactory, and I have no doubt that he could have graduated with high distinction if he had wanted to devote the time to his studies.

"He had more than average capacity for study, but I don't know how much more because he was thinking about athletic activities and about social activities. I think academic activities came out third.

"He did just what was necessary to remain in good standing."

Dr. Holcombe has watched his last Kennedy's progress since graduation and, as the senator launched upon his second term, evaluated him thus:

"I give Edward Kennedy a high rating now, higher than I would at the time he graduated. My opinion has been revised upward as his career developed. At the outset, I say frankly I didn't think he was in the same class with his older brothers, but that was merely because I didn't have any evidence to form a high opinion of him.

"But ever since he met disaster, which is a test of what a man is and can be, it seems to me he has shown remarkable capacity to make the best use of his opportunities. I'm much impressed with his leadership record."

V

Can You Support
My Daughter?

1. The Meeting

It isn't often that a father is asked for both his daughters' hands in marriage on the same evening.

Harry Wiggin Bennett, Jr., a wealthy advertising executive, and his wife Virginia had two beautiful daughters — 19-year-old Candace, a brunet, and blond Virginia Joan, twenty-one. Both were active in the elegant suburban social whirl of Westchester and New York. They had grown up in Bronxville in a fine twelve-room Mediterranean-style home at 14 Eastway, were launched as debutantes and had gone on to college. Now two young men were coming to call on Mr. Bennett, Candy and Joan on their respective minds.

First on this spring evening in 1958 came tall, slender Bob McMurrey, who had been dating Candy, the dark-haired one. She was waiting upstairs. Bob told Mr. Bennett he was in love with Candy and wanted to marry her. Mr. Bennett cleared his throat and explained that since Candy was just out of junior college, and Bob himself newly graduated from Yale and had law school ahead of him, perhaps it might be best to wait. (They were disappointed, but they waited. A year later, Mr. Bennett gave his blessing. Now Mr. and Mrs. Robert M. McMurrey live in Houston, Texas, with their three sons, where Bob has a law practice.)

Two hours later, the tall Kennedy boy showed up, unaware that Bob had preceded him. He had telephoned earlier at the Joseph Katz advertising agency, where Mr. Bennett was president, for an appointment. The two men sat in front of the great stone fireplace in the living room and chatted about the weather. Kennedy crossed and uncrossed his long legs. Mr. Bennett offered him a soft drink which was politely refused.

Finally Ted got it out: Could he marry Joan? Mr. Bennett grinned and broke up the session and Ted simultaneously with a remark that is still a family joke:

"Do you think you could support my daughter in the style to which she has been accustomed?"

Eight months earlier, on a brisk Sunday afternoon in late October, a long black limousine glided down Purchase Street in Westchester County, New York, to the walled-in campus of Manhattanville College of the Sacred Heart. It turned in between the two great stone pillars marking the entrance and came to a stop in front of Reid Hall, the massive granite structure that houses the administrative offices. Ted Kennedy alighted first and helped his mother Rose from the car. His father followed.

Manhattanville's 250-acre campus was alight with fall coloring. The hard maples blazed in fiery reds, the soft maples glowed golden, the oaks, birches and sycamores added russets and yellows to the pageant. The day, October 27, 1957, was an especially important one in the history of the college and, as it turned out, in the life of Edward Kennedy.

Two new structures were to be dedicated on the campus — the Kennedy Physical Education Building, for which the family had contributed generously along with many other alumnae, parents and friends of the college, and Spellman Hall, a new dormitory for 331 students. Present for the ceremonies were a host of dignitaries, including Francis Cardinal Spellman, Mother E.M. O'Byrne, president of the college, and a number of assorted Kennedys, including Jean, Eunice and Ethel. Ethel had brought along several of her children and had burst out with some characteristic *Wows!* when she toured the new gym and saw the 75- by 35-foot swimming pool, the two bowling alleys, basketball and tennis courts, the fencing salle and the rest of the equipment.

The Kennedys had been linked with Manhattanville for

many decades. Rose herself is a graduate; Ethel Kennedy and her sister-in-law Jean Smith (Ted's sister now married to Stephen E. Smith) were roommates; Eunice, married to Sargent Shriver, went there. In 1952, the college moved to its Westchester site from the Morningside Heights section of Manhattan when its urban campus was purchased by the College of the City of New York. Later, the college shortened its name to Manhattanville College; in 1972, it opened its doors to boys after 131 years as a girls' school.

At three o'clock, the ceremonies got under way on the floor of the new gym, a buff-colored brick building in the northwestern corner of the campus. On behalf of his parents, Ted, then a student at the University of Virginia Law School, made a short, gracious speech. In a light grey suit and narrow tie, the youngest Kennedy looked uncommonly handsome as he stood on the podium smiling shyly, grasping the lectern with both hands, a stray lock of hair falling across the right side of his forehead.

After the dedications, the entire audience walked over to the Benziger Building for a reception in the enormous white-walled Prom Room where graduation exercises, all the big school dances and major affairs were held.

Nearly all of Manhattanville's 700 students were there — except Harry Bennett's eldest child. She was across the road in her room at Founder's Hall, her hair in curlers, wearing an old skirt and blouse, nipping her lower lip as she typed out an English theme.

Attendance at the ceremonies and reception had been compulsory but Joan Bennett, though she appreciated the new gym and all that, had gone to a football game the day before and now there was this paper due that week. Besides, music and literature were her fields; politics and its practitioners mattered little or nothing to her. Totally unlike the Kennedys, the Bennetts had never talked politics at the dinner table. And Joan had not even heard of the Kennedys.

Shortly before five, however, her roommate Margot Murray, daughter of the atomic scientist Thomas E. Murray, raced up with the warning that one of the nuns had missed her. She had better get down right away or she'd catch it. Joan slipped off the curlers, put on a cleaner skirt and blouse and, without bothering about makeup, went to the reception.

Jean, who had married Steve Smith the year before, was a friend of Joan's and she stopped to say hello. Jean, the least-known of the Kennedys — she rarely gives interviews — is vivacious, an excellent mimic and, apparently, an incurable fixer-upper. A roommate of Ethel Skakel at Manhattanville, she plotted to bring her together with her brother Bobby and eventually succeeded. Now she had something in mind for Ted.

"I'd like you to meet my little brother," Jean told Joan, and she introduced them. They spent the rest of the afternoon together. That evening, Margot, who had a car on campus, drove Ted and Joan to New York so he could catch a train to Charlottesville.

A fews days later, Ted telephoned from Virginia though it was not until Thanksgiving recess a month later that he could come up to see her.

They dated regularly all that year and into the next. Joan went to Charlottesville for school functions; Ted showed up regularly at Manhattanville. They would have dinner in New York, attend football games and the theater, go sailing and skiing. Joan visited Ted at Hyannis Port and promptly got labelled "the dish" when John Kennedy saw her. Ted came to Bronxville for dinner many times and, on a fine spring evening, asked her to marry him.

Joan told her parents and her sister. Says Candy: "She had never once let on things were getting serious or how she felt, though I kind of suspected this was special." Ted gave Joan a huge emerald-cut diamond engagement ring which Joan calls her "skating rink" and, on September 21, the betrothal was announced officially.

2. The Wedding

The night before the wedding, a furious storm struck West-chester. Winds of near-hurricane force, accompanied by the heaviest rainfull in years, toppled trees, tore down power lines and flooded streets. In Bronxville, more than 1,700 homes were blacked out and telephone service was disrupted. Over on Pondfield Road, a large plate glass window of a fashionable shop blew out and showered shards all over the street in front of the Gramatan Hotel.

By morning — it was Saturday, November 29, in 1958 — an

icy wind had plummeted temperatures to seventeen degrees for the coldest day of the year. Joan Bennett, in her ivory satin gown, had to lift her full skirt as she stepped over the debris on the way to the car that would take her to St. Joseph's Roman Catholic Church a block down from Pondfield Road in town. The streets were still cluttered with small trees and branches and the driver had to keep a wary eye out for fallen power lines across the road.

At about the same time, Cardinal Spellman was driving up from New York City from his residence behind St. Patrick's Cathedral to perform the ceremony. Joan would have preferred the Rev. John Cavanaugh, the former president of Notre Dame University, but the Cardinal had pulled rank and insisted on officiating.

A large crowd was gathered on Kraft Avenue near the main entrance to the large stone church. They saw Ambassador and Mrs. Joseph Kennedy and, soon after, the handsome young Senator Kennedy and his pretty wife Jacqueline. Cars discharged dozens of political notables — senators, congressmen, judges.

Robert Kennedy, then chief counsel for the Senate Rackets Committee, came with Ethel, already the mother of six children. They brought five of them along. Robert, busy in Washington with his investigation of corruption in the union management field and his explosive confrontations with Teamster boss James R. Hoffa, had missed all the wedding rehearsals. The Rev. William J. Kenealy, then assistant pastor, started to brief him on his functions as chief usher, but Robert interrupted: "I've been through this many times, Father, don't worry about me."

If Robert felt at home, John Kennedy did not. Before the ceremony, he changed into the striped pants and frock coat that had been rented for the male members of the party and found the outfit much too small. He was extremely uncomfortable. So he examined all the other men carefully, finally cornering Dick Clasby.

Clasby had donned his suit and thought he looked "pretty good," but Jack prevailed upon him to swap. "His was too obviously the wrong size," Clasby recalls, "so he took mine, and I was bigger than he was. We went to the back of the church and changed. I came out with a suit that could fit a kid of twelve."

Among the ushers were K. LeMoyne Billings, John's roommate at Choate who has been one of the Kennedy family's most loyal friends through the years; Joseph Gargan, Ted's cousin who was to figure prominently eleven years later in a tragic episode in Ted Kennedy's life; and a lanky youth with a wide toothy smile, John Varick Tunney. In 1970, Tunney was elected to the United States Senate.

By eleven, all 475 guests had been seated and Cardinal Spellman, in red cassock and white chasuble, had emerged to stand before the white marble altar, now banked with fall chrysanthemums. Behind him was a great stained glass window of the Crucifixion; around the church, other windows depicted the mysteries of the Rosary.

The bride, in her long-sleeved fitted-bodice dress and veil of rosepoint lace, a cascade bouquet of white roses and carnations in her hand, came down the aisle on the arm of a proud Harry Bennett. Candy was maid of honor. One attendant was Margot Murray, who rustled her out of the dorm that day; another was Jean Kennedy Smith, whose "little brother" advanced to meet her and to kneel with her before the cardinal for the nuptial mass.

Floodlights lit the scene, making eerie shadows on the high vaulted ceiling. Cameras ground; microphones concealed in the clothing of the principals caught every word as the ceremony proceeded. As a gift to the bride and groom, a friend of Mr. Bennett had arranged to have a professional motion picture made of the entire wedding from start to finish. While waiting for the ceremony to begin, Ted and Jack tossed a football to each other outside, forgetting they had been wired for sound. Their dialogue was duly recorded and is now a part of Ted and Joan Kennedy's permanent record of the day.

Afterward, the couple and their guests drove two miles down Pondfield Road to the exclusive half-century old Siwanoy Country Club for the wedding reception, a modest one by Kennedy standards.

The wedding of John and Jacqueline on September 12, 1953, was acknowledged to be the most spectacular Newport had seen in thirty years. About 3,000 persons came by chartered buses to stand behind police lines in front of St. Mary's Roman Catholic Church. At Hammersmith Farm, the 75-acre estate of Hugh D. Auchincloss, Jackie's stepfather, the bride and groom stood for two hours in the receiving line greeting their 800 guests. Three years earlier, on June 17, 1950, Bobby and Ethel were hosts to 1,500 persons on the grounds of the Skakel mansion in Greenwich, where a vast tent had been erected.

In contrast, Teddy and Joan invited only 158 guests, including all the Kennedys. A receiving line was set up in the club's large, square lobby, which becomes a ballroom when the rugs are rolled and the soft chairs removed. Later, in the dining room overlooking the ninth hole, the guests were served breast of chicken Eugénie under glass, chicken with white sauce and mushrooms with a slice of ham on toast.

Cardinal Spellman, unable to attend the reception because of pressing church business, had returned to the church rectory where he breakfasted on eggs and coffee, explaining to the housekeeper that he was watching his waistline.

Wedding day or no, the Kennedys' enthusiasm for football could not be restrained. After the guests had been greeted, the receiving line broke for cocktails and conversation. Soon, though, Rose Kennedy, in a mauve velvet dress, missed her sons and asked where they had gone.

The senator, the rackets prober and the new husband were in the men's grill watching the Army-Navy football game on television from Philadelphia! They missed the finish because Rose summoned them back to the guests.

The honeymoon lasted only three days. Ted and Joan flew down to Nassau where Lord Beaverbrook, the British press lord, had loaned them his estate. On Wednesday morning, the bridegroom was back at classes at law school and the bride was unpacking in Charlottesville.

3. Law School Days

As a law student, Ted did not live frugally. Before his marriage, he and his closest friend at school, Varick John Tunney,* son of the former heavyweight boxing champion, shared a two-story, three-bedroom red brick house on Barracks Road. Neatly trimmed bushes lined the long driveway; pine trees

---

*On advice of John Kennedy, the handsome, athletic Tunney transposed his first two names when he entered politics. As John V. Tunney, he was elected to the House of Representatives from California in the Johnson landslide of 1964 and, in 1970, won a Senate seat.

planted in rows grew tall in the spacious front yard. From the screened-in rear porch the view was breathtaking: green valleys dipped and rolled for miles until they met the Blue Ridge Mountains, hazily visible on most days. The only other occupant was a large German shepherd who would accompany Ted on long solitary walks across the countryside.

Here the two young men set up housekeeping, with part-time help. They would go off to the stores and come back with shopping bags stuffed with food loaded in the rear seat of Ted's Oldsmobile convertible. Their neighbors and friends, the William Battles who lived three houses away, were appalled at the size of their grocery bills. Battle, an attorney who now heads a mill in North Carolina, says the young men were not "the most discreet shoppers." But they could afford not to be, for by this time the cash available to Ted had increased by quantum leaps. And young Tunney was also wellheeled. On many weekends, he flew off to the Netherlands to visit his beautiful blond fiancée, Mieke, returning Sunday evening. (Tunney married Mieke before he graduated from law school.)

After his wedding, Ted rented a three-bedroom split-level on four acres of wooded land in Bellaire, a residential section a mile from Charlottesville, across the road from a small, lovely lake. Like her sister-in-law Ethel, who had been hopeless in the kitchen as a campus wife on the same campus eight years earlier, Joan came unprepared for domestic duties. "I moved in," she said, "with a cookbook and no experience." It would take her an hour to clear away the breakfast dishes and by then it was lunchtime. With preparation and cleaning up, Ted figured Joan spent some eight hours daily in the kitchen. But there were other hours, and she filled these by enrolling at the university and taking courses in sociology and American history. For recreation, they took long walks, swam and, most often, played tennis at the Farmington Country Club.

Kennedy and Tunney played tennis twice a week, sometimes more often. Joan would come down daily for tennis lessons from Mike Dolan, the pro and coach. "Joan didn't go in for many sports before she got here," Dolan recalls, "but by the time she left she was playing a really nice game." Dolan had also played with Bobby and Ethel who had come to the courts even when she was in the final weeks of pregnancy with her first child.

Dolan says: "Around the tennis house we were afraid she was going to have the baby right on this court."

Joan made friends with other students' wives, attended school-related functions and, with Ted, went to the usual student parties. She impressed all who met her as being shy but, as one said, "down-to-earth, a really great girl." E. Gerald Tremblay, a Charlottesville attorney who was in Bob Kennedy's law school graduating class and had come to know the Ted Kennedys, says: "Joan was her own person. She had enough on the ball so that she didn't have to try to be a Kennedy."

As for Ted, his laughter boomed out at parties, where he told jokes and did imitations of political notables of the day. He was jovial, gregarious, the Irish sense of fun bubbling within him. He would always be having, says Tremblay, "a hell of a good time."

But there couldn't be many parties because the work was hard at law school and there was plenty of it.

At 8 each morning, opening time, Kennedy and Tunney would come to the library lugging heavy briefcases stuffed with books. They would walk up the steps, enter the 100-foot-long, high-ceilinged reading room and sit at their accustomed table just outside the office of Frances Farmer, the law librarian and former law professor. Flanked by two huge murals — Moses holding the Ten Commandments on one wall, Spartan youths in a colloquy on the other — the two young men would study for hours, go to class and return to put in more long hours in the library.

Ted wasn't a quick student. "I've got to go at a thing four times as hard and four times as long as some other fellow," he would say afterward. He remembered those days at law school. "Up early and late, hitting the books. I had to, just to keep up with some of the other guys."

Kennedy's grades at law school were as unimpressive as ever. Professor Neil Alford, who taught both Kennedys, feels that while records might show Bobby "a little smarter," both were "very able — and I'd hate to compare the two." Professor A. J. G. Priest, who taught Ted corporation law and parliamentary law, remembers Ted as "handsome, good-mannered and a hell of a nice boy," but "he didn't have the best grades."

However, Kennedy's work outside class earned him special

distinction. In his senior year, he was elected president of the Student Legal Forum, a post Bobby had held eight years earlier. The Forum invited prominent persons to the university to speak on national and international issues.

The Forum had been a dying thing when Bobby took hold and, with his and Joe Kennedy's connections, he was able to bring a stream of important speakers to Charlottesville. One was Joe Kennedy himself; another the Communist-hunting Sen. Joseph R. McCarthy, whom Joe liked and on whose staff Bobby was to work for a brief time after graduation. Others were Ralph Bunche, the United Nations official, later winner of the Nobel Peace Prize; Supreme Court Justice William O. Douglas; and the young congressman from Massachusetts, John F. Kennedy. The invitation to Bunche caused a furor: no Negro had ever been permitted to speak inside the university halls; there was, in fact, a statute forbidding the mixing of races in public places. Bobby took his case up to the president of the university himself, arguing that the Supreme Court had exempted higher education meetings from such statutes. He won and Bunche came down to address a mixed audience.

Ted was equally successful in corralling important speakers. He brought down Walter P. Reuther, then the international president of the United Automobile Workers and vice president of the AFL-CIO; Supreme Court Justice William J. Brennan; and Sen. Hubert Humphrey. He planned to balance off the United Arab Republic ambassador to the United States, with the Israeli ambassador; the UAR ambassador appeared but the Israeli was hurriedly summoned home the day he was scheduled to speak, leaving a gap in the program.

Hurriedly, Ted called his brother Robert who, as chief counsel to the Senate Rackets Committee, was making national headlines with his dogged pursuit of corrupt labor leaders, in particular the Teamster bosses Dave Beck and James R. Hoffa, both of whom were subsequently sent to jail. After his brief service with the McCarthy communist-hunters and a boring few months with ex-President Herbert Hoover's commission studying the reorganization of the executive branch, Bobby had leaped at the chance to tangle with labor racketeers. Busy as he was, he rushed down to Charlottesville as a replacement for Mr. Eban.

Introduced by his younger brother, Bob proceeded to needle Ted for a traffic mess that had earned him a fair amount of publicity. Ted had been ticketed for reckless driving, for which he subsequently paid a $35 fine. "My mother," Bobby told the audience, "wants to know what side of the court my brother is going to appear on when he gets out of law school, attorney or defendant."

The law school enlisted Ted's influence on another occasion to bring Bobby down. In 1958, for the first Law Alumni Day, graduates were invited to a day-long reunion to be climaxed in the evening with a banquet. The alumni day committee asked the then Senator John Kennedy to make the principal address and he agreed to come. Then Miss Farmer, the law librarian, had an idea: why not have all three Kennedy brothers at the dinner? They had Ted there already; all they needed was Bobby, But this wasn't easy: Bobby was so busy with the Rackets Committee, the alumni committee couldn't even get him on the telephone.

Miss Farmer, a member of the committee, volunteered to try her luck. She knew Bobby well; in fact, she had flunked him in his first year in a course on library bibliography. Bobby had to repeat the course and he, too, remembered Miss Farmer, to whom years afterward he sent an inscribed photograph and recalling the incident.

Returning from the committee meeting, Miss Farmer saw Ted in his customary spot in the library. She called him into her office, and asked if he'd help get Bobby. He would. In less than two hours, he was back. "I've talked with my brother," he told Miss Farmer, "and he'll be delighted to come down." He did; so did John and Jackie, and the evening was a huge success.

In his senior year, Ted Kennedy and John Tunney were winners of one of the law school's most coveted honors, the Moot Court competition — equal in prestige, says Professor Alford, who was co-chairman of the competition at the time, to editing the *Law Review*. In Moot Court contests, law students argue hypothetical questions before "judges." They enter in teams of two during their second year and, through eliminations, head for the finals, which are held toward the close of the third and final year. From the semi-finals on, the competition is judged by actual jurists.

Kennedy and Tunney beat out fifty teams. The finals were argued on April 17, 1959, before an audience of 500 in the ballroom of Newcombe Hall on the University of Virginia campus.

The team represented the defendant in a case concerning the legality of contributions by banks to political campaigns. Kennedy and Tunney argued that the statute involved, Section 16 of Title 18 of the United States Code, which makes it unlawful for corporations to make certain types of contributions to campaigns, infringed on the rights of free speech granted under the First Amendment, and hence was unconstitutional. Professor Alford recalls: "Ted Kennedy definitely showed the abilities he was later to put effectively into use as a public figure. His argument was very persuasive, quite professional and quite polished."

Sitting in judgment were Supreme Court Justice Stanley Reed, since retired; Lord Kilmuir who, as Lord Chancellor, was England's chief judicial officer; Alexander W. Parker, president of the University of Virginia Law School Association; and Judge F. Clement Haynsworth Jr. of the fourth U.S. Circuit Court of Appeals. *

4. Political Baptism

When Ted graduated from law school in June of 1959 in the middle of his class, about the same standing as Bobby, he was a rich and handsome young married man, undoubtedly heading for a successful career someplace but possessed of no special distinction. Although he had won the Moot Court competition, few who had taught him were predicting a brilliant legal career. He had left a favorable impression upon his professors but only a faint one. He possessed, they all thought, a good mind but not an exceptional one.

That summer, he and Joan took a belated six-week honeymoon to South America, where Ted continued Joan's athletic education. He had already introduced her to skiing in Vermont; there, in the Andes, he gave her further lessons. She found the skiing easier than in New England — "there weren't so many trees to crash into." Back in Boston, they bought a three-story brick house at 3 Charles River Square at the foot of Beacon

---

*Twelve years later, as senators, Kennedy and Tunney were to sit in judgment on Judge Haynsworth after President Nixon nominated him for the Supreme Court. Both voted against confirmation.

Hill. Ted was admitted to the Massachusetts bar and, soon after, was plunged thigh-deep in politics.

Late in October of 1959, at a major strategy session in Robert's Hyannis Port home, the Kennedys and their closest advisers decided that Senator John would go after the Presidential nomination the following year. Everyone was there who counted in the Kennedy machinery: Steve Smith, Ted Sorensen, Larry O'Brien, Ken O'Donnell, Pierre Salinger, John Bailey, an important political figure in Connecticut, and of course the candidate and Bobby. It was decided that Bobby, who had left the Rackets Committee, would be campaign manager. Plans were made to call upon the full resources of the fabled Kennedy-organization to defeat the other challengers, chief of whom were Hubert Humphrey and Sen. Stuart Symington of Missouri, and the 1952 and 1956 standard-bearer, Adlai Stevenson.

Ted, the young new lawyer, was assigned the job of coordinating eleven western states, and at once set out to prove he could be considered a major resource too. Tirelessly, from fall until late spring, he crisscrossed his territory, flying from Arizona to Nevada to Idaho, up to Alaska, down to Washington and Oregon, speaking in his brother's behalf, helping to create local organizations, firing enthusiasm. He spent seven weeks in Wisconsin alone, helping to strengthen JFK's defenses against Hubert Humphrey's challenge.

Meanwhile, Joan had returned to her parents' home in Bronxville to await the birth of their first child, Kara Anne, born on February 27. Ted had little time to become acquainted with his new daughter before he was off again. Indeed, a month after Kara's birth, Joan herself had joined her husband on the campaign trail. Everywhere he went, he drew throngs who were entranced by the almost uncanny resemblance to his older brother: he had the same flat tones, the same shock of hair, his hand chopped the air in the same gesture. He never got angry, never grew weary. He made friends; he did well for John. Once in Wyoming, a delegate to the forthcoming convention embraced him and blurted: "I wish you were running."

On Wednesday, June 13, at seven minutes after ten p.m., after Kennedy, Lyndon Johnson and Adlai Stevenson had been placed in nomination, the clerk at the Sports Arena in Los Angeles began calling the roll of states. A total of 761 of 1,520 votes was needed for a majority. By the time Washington State was reached, Kennedy's total was 710; after Wisconsin, it stood at 750. Wyoming was next. Teddy Kennedy was standing at the elbow of the chairman of the delegation, a wide grin on his face. Watching on television, seeing his brother's happy smile, John Kennedy said to his aides: "This could be it."

And it was. Wyoming cast all of its fifteen votes for John F. Kennedy and from then on all the states swung onto the bandwagon.

With only a brief rest, Ted, given the title of Campaign Coordinator for the Rocky Mountain and Western states, rented a house in San Francisco and barged off once again. He was home for only thirteen of the 100 days between the first of August and Election Day, leading Joan to sigh that, while there was a certain excitement in being the wife of a campaigner, "it has its drawbacks."

The Rocky Mountain and Western States Coordinator was an important asset to his brother, even though he eventually failed to deliver more than one of the eleven states to which he was assigned. Nobody blamed him because they had been all but lost to the Democrats anyway. And Teddy had made many friends, especially among the professional politicians who count the most. His exuberance and enthusiasm, followed by the inability to capture any brass rings, reminded the family of his bold foray two years before into two other enemy camps. They chuckle as they retell it:

There are two tiny communities in Massachusetts called Mashpee and Washington which have a minor political reputation. For decades, these towns have opened their polls very early in the morning, completing their balloting by about 10 a.m. Not much of a feat considering their tiny populations. By afternoon, the results are always published in the Boston newspapers as "first returns" which, though not political bellwethers, nevertheless let Bostonians know who's ahead.

For years, these towns have gone down the line for Republican candidates. Ted thought he would change this trend. If the Boston papers would publish the fact that the two had gone Democratic for the first time in years, he reasoned, the psychological impact would be enormous. So he went to both communities. Bursting with good humor, he made friends with everyone. He walked into shops and soon had clumps of people around him, enjoying his sallies. He talked with the town leaders. He knocked on doors, introduced himself, was invited in to tea and charmed the antimacassars off the sofas. He returned to Boston, certain he had done the trick for his brother.

On Election Day, the Boston newspapers, as usual, published the first returns from Mashpee and Washington. There were two votes for Kennedy, 349 for his GOP opponent, Vincent J. Celeste!

In January, 1961, Ted rode a bus to Washington for the inauguration and, once there, danced in an Irish jig at one of the inaugural balls. He also sang "When Irish Eyes Are Smiling" passably well and went home to Boston carrying a cigarette case, a gift from President Kennedy, inscribed with the line from Matthew: "And the last shall be first."

At this point in his life, Ted Kennedy fought an inner battle for independence from his brothers and family, but lost.

At least once before, he had tried to move out from under their influence. After graduation from Milton (where he went, he said, "because Bobby liked it and thought I would"), he wanted to break with family tradition and attend Stanford University in Palo Alto, California, but somehow he never made it. Now, with his brother elected President, he thought seriously of cutting all ties with the East Coast. "In other places," he said in Washington as he helped wind up business at national campaign headquarters, "I might be accepted more on my own than I would be right here where Jack is." And Joan, too, said: "Teddy has always been interested in the West, and during 1959 and 1960 when he was campaigning in the Western states, he just about decided to move out there. His idea was to practice law for a while after Jack's election and then, in maybe five or six years, run for office himself. He took me with him to New Mexico and Wyoming during the campaign so I could see what it was like. His main reason for wanting to move was a feeling that in a new state he would have to succeed or fail on his own."

In the end, though, he was unable to make the break. "Eventually," Joan declared, "we both decided you can't run away from being the President's brother no matter where you go." In February, 1961, Ted purchased a summer home at Squaw Island, a mile from the family compound at Hyannis Port. It had some significance in light of his announced intention to move out from the family's shadow, though not much. Joan said:

"It's close enough to go down to the big house for movies and yet far enough away not to be in the midst of the family. Ted loves his family, but there are times when we enjoy being alone." Besides, there weren't any homes for sale closer to the compound.

Having decided to remain, Ted took a job as assistant district attorney of Suffolk County in Massachusetts, which takes in all of Boston plus three communities to the north and east — Winthrop, Chelsea and Revere. It was his first public office but he wasn't to remain in it for long.

VI

The Chutzpah Issue

1. Father Knows Best

On a humid day in early September of 1960, three men flew down from Boston for a conference with Joe Kennedy in his office on New York's Park Avenue.

One was Joseph Duckworth Ward, whose campaign for the governorship of Massachusetts wasn't going well. He was opposing the Republican John A. Volpe and the trouble was he had run out of money. Ward was accompanied by Sheriff Howard Fitzpatrick of Middlesex County, an important party leader, and Francis X. Morrissey, a Boston municipal court judge.

Morrissey, an old and loyal political workhorse for the Kennedys, had suggested to Joe Ward that perhaps Joe Kennedy might be willing to make a contribution that could perk up Ward's lagging drive. Ward agreed to go, made an appointment and came down to see the ambassador.

This little known story is important because it shows that even while John Kennedy was running for President in 1960, his father was working to shape the political futures of his other two sons.

Kennedy's six years as United States Senator from Massachusetts were to expire in 1964. According to the law, the governor of the state would be called upon to name an interim successor until congressional elections were held in 1962 to fill the un-expired term. Then, two years afterward, a new full-term senator would be chosen.

Joe Kennedy had a candidate for the seat: his son Robert. Nearing thirty-five, Bobby had resigned as chief counsel to the Senate Rackets Committee to manage John's campaign. After the election, he'd be out of a job but he had no time to worry about that. Joe, however, *was* thinking about his son's coming unemployment and, without even telling him or asking, was making some plans.

The three Boston Democrats — Ward, Fitzpatrick and Morrissey — were ushered into Joe Kennedy's office. After a few moments, an inner door opened and the ambassador entered.

Mr. Ward: "Somebody in our group said that I would like to have John Kennedy's endorsement in my campaign and Joe said: 'Hasn't he had it? Of course Jack should give it and right away. He's the Democratic nominee and I'll see that he gets it.'

"Then Joe asked: 'How's it going?'

"I said, 'Not too well, not too badly. But we need campaign money desperately.'

"He said, 'We want to help you. I want to ask you a question. If you are elected Governor and my son Jack is elected Presi-dent, what will you do?'

"I said that I didn't quite follow his question and he an-swered: 'I'm not interested in you. I'm not interested in who's governor of Massachusetts. I'm not interested in anyone except my son Jack. I want him to be President of the United States and I'm interested in my son Bobby. I want him to be the next United States senator from Massachusetts. Will you appoint him?'

"I said, 'Is Bobby interested in being the senator from Mass-achusetts?'

"He said, 'I haven't asked him. It doesn't make any differ-ence. I want to know — will you appoint him if he wants the job?'

"I told him it seemed to me that, if Jack were elected, Bobby should be close to him in Washington in the administration, that he could do more good there than he ever could in the Senate. But Joe insisted on getting an answer from me on the question of naming Bobby.

"Finally I said: 'If Jack is elected, he and I will have no serious difficulties, but I want you to know I already have a candidate for the Senate seat, a man who has helped me considerably to raise money and a man I believe has also been tremendously helpful to Jack. I think he should be rewarded.'

" 'Who is he?' Joe asked.

" 'He's Howard Fitzpatrick,' and I pointed to him beside me. Fitzpatrick, who hadn't known my intention, was astounded. The ambassador exhaled sharply. 'Howard,' he said, 'is a wonderful friend of ours and Jack's. Howard would be our second choice.' I argued that Fitzpatrick would be loyal to John Kennedy on every major issue and Joe agreed he would, but said that wasn't his concern. At last he said:

" 'Is that your answer — that you'll appoint Howard Fitzpatrick?' I said it was, even though Fitzpatrick insisted he wouldn't take the job unless Jack Kennedy wanted him to have it, and that he was embarrassed at my bringing it up in the first place.

"The ambassador placed his finger tips on the table, stood up to his full six-one and said, 'This conference is at an end,' and walked out.

"We went back to the airport, where I picked up a newspaper. I began reading when I heard an odd noise. I looked up and saw Frank Morrissey crying. I said, 'Frank, what on earth is the matter with you?'

"He said through his sobs, 'Joe, you've just blown the governorship of Massachusetts. Kennedy had $40,000 in his desk drawer which he intended to give you if you gave him the answer he wanted to hear.' "

Despite his father's wishes, Bobby did not look with favor on being appointed to the Senate. "The only way I'll go to the Senate," he told intimates, "is run for it." The President, however, preferred to have his brother close to him in Washington. Soon after his election, John Kennedy suggested the fourth most important post in the cabinet for Robert — the attorney generalship. At first, Bobby was not interested; he had planned to take a lengthy vacation to chart his own future which, he felt at the time, probably would not be in government. Perhaps, he thought, he might buy a small newspaper or manage his father's business interests. "I've been chasing bad guys all my life," he said. "I'd like a change." But the President insisted, though agreeing that the charges of nepotism would be thunderous. He suggested wryly they might be able to duck them by announcing the appointment some dark midnight. Finally, after seeking the advice of Sen. John McClellan of Arkansas, Supreme Court Justice William O. Douglas and other friends, Bobby at last agreed — though still reluctantly — to take the job.

Nonetheless, since the Kennedys had come to regard the Senate post as something of a family seat, steps had to be taken to make sure it would be waiting — for Bobby or anyone else the clan wanted to put up in 1962. Kennedy asked the lame duck Massachusetts Governor, Foster Furcolo, to Washington for a conference about an interim appointee, and thereafter had several long phone conversations with him. Furcolo made a number of suggestions, among them Rep. Torbert Macdonald and Howard Fitzpatrick, but all were turned down by the President.

Finally, in a telephone call from the White House to the Boston State House, Kennedy suggested someone named Benjamin A. Smith. Furcolo was incredulous. Smith was a manufacturer of wooden boxes who had served as mayor of the seafaring city of Gloucester, twenty-eight miles northeast of Boston, and had been a roommate of John Kennedy's at Harvard.

Why Ben Smith?

Furcolo: "It dawned on me as I talked with him that the President-elect wanted two things — someone who would be friendly and would do as he wished, and someone who could not be powerful enough to get elected on his own in two years. In other words, the Kennedys wanted a seat warmer who would step aside when they wanted him to."

The Governor, who also harbored hopes of naming himself, now saw the way the wind veered. He could hardly buck the President and the nation's leading Democrat, and so he named Ben Smith.

Smith went to Washington to keep the seat warm — but for whom? If it wouldn't be Bobby, Joe Kennedy had another candidate picked out; early in 1961, he told the new President and the attorney general. It would be Teddy.

Joe Kennedy's wishes were not easily disregarded. Now 72, he had seen a son elected President and another named to a high cabinet post. Now he was determined that his third son should

also assume a prestigious political position. He was proud of
what he was able to accomplish with the two older ones. "I
got Jack into politics," he had said back in 1957. "I told him
Joe was dead and that it was his responsibility to run for Congress. He didn't want to. He felt he didn't have the ability and he
still feels that way. But I told him he had to." Afterward, John
Kennedy had remarked: "It was like being drafted. My father
wanted his eldest son in politics. 'Wanted' isn't the right word.
He demanded it. You know my father."

John, the President, and Robert, the attorney general, understood their father when he told them in the White House that
winter of 1961: "You boys have what you want and everybody
worked to help you get it. Now it's Teddy's turn. I'm going to
see that he gets what he wants."

And by that time, Teddy wanted the Senate. He had had a
taste of politics and he loved the excitement, the fun of the game,
the challenges. But there was more: Like a racehorse bred for
racing, Ted Kennedy had been groomed all his life for public
service. His earliest memories were listening to political talk —
talk about national and domestic issues and problems — at the
dinner table. He had been required to study newspaper clip-
pings his mother had pinned to a bulletin board and answer
questions about them at mealtime. All through his growing
years, he had been told he "must make a contribution." He had
seen one brother and then another move into the political arena.
Competitive, eager to begin, confident of his ability to handle the
job, he wanted to move too.

He knew he was too young and he would be considered un-
speakably brash. But he was also a realist. With his father's
considerable influence and his own political talents, he felt he
could succeed.

But even though the President-elect and attorney general-
designate listened to their father respectfully, they worried about
Teddy's youth and inexperience, and so did the White House
staff. At twenty-eight, he couldn't even qualify legally for the
Senate until 1962 when he would turn thirty. And they could
already hear all those cries of "too many Kennedys!" As one
aide put it: "We'd have everything to lose and nothing to gain."
Lawrence O'Brien and Kenneth O'Donnell, two presidential
assistants, were particularly dubious. What, they asked, would

happen to JFK's prestige in the event that Teddy lost? Why not start him somewhere lower down, perhaps the House or as Massachusetts attorney general?

As winter drew to a close, Kenny O'Donnell put a suggestion on the table: Conduct a private poll to see how well Ted Kennedy would make out in a Senate race.

He would be up against two formidable opponents in two consecutive titanic struggles. First, everyone knew that Edward J. McCormack, then thirty-eight and the attorney general of Massachusetts, wanted the Democratic nomination. Would Teddy be able to beat him in the primaries? Ed McCormack was a seasoned political veteran who was, moreover, the favorite nephew of John W. McCormack, the Speaker of the House. Ed was an able man, with powerful support who had come up from the ranks and knew his way around.

But even if Teddy could beat Ed, he would face a second battle, this time against George Cabot Lodge, who would probably be his Republican opponent. Lodge, too, came from a family distinguished in state and national politics: his great grandfather was the scholar-statesman, Henry Cabot Lodge, who served thirty-two consecutive years in the Senate; his father was the former Sen. Lodge who had been U.S. representative to the United Nations.

The poll was taken — and the results astonished everyone. Teddy would easily defeat Ed McCormack and go on to win the election. Joe was elated. As far as he was concerned, the debate was over: Teddy would run.

The President was the last to be convinced. He and Bobby studied the poll results carefully and, though John knew the attacks on the family would be bitter and vicious, he finally withdrew his objections. The deciding factor was that Lodge would probably defeat any other opponent, and the President could hardly risk the humiliation of having a Republican wrest his old Senate seat from the Democrats.

Analyzing his decision, a close friend of the President commented:

"When it comes to a showdown like that, the Kennedys are willing to ignore the politicians and the newspapers and take the big gamble that eventually the general public will back them up.

"Remember how the pols and press experts told Jack in 1959

that he'd never make it with his youth and his Catholicism. He wouldn't have run for the Presidency if he'd listened to them. The same ones warned him against making Bobby his attorney general. That turned out to be all right. He was criticized for putting his brother-in-law Sargent Shriver in charge of the Peace Corps and the Peace Corps became one of his most popularly approved programs. This young Teddy is a hard and conscientious worker with a more easy-going way with people than the President or Bobby. Who knows? Maybe Teddy will be a big hit in the Senate."

The decision made, Ted's political handlers began training their man for the battle.

After taking the assistant attorney job, he set up residence in Boston. Anyone hoping to become an elected official of Massachusetts must reside in the state.

Next, he took to the speaking and traveling circuits. He appeared at church suppers, synagogue dinners, communion breakfasts, testimonials to retiring businessmen, politicians, judges and doctors, at veterans' affairs and fund-raising functions, before men's clubs, women's clubs and chambers of commerce. He went everywhere.

In May of 1961, he and Joan flew to Italy on a "goodwill mission" to participate in the centennial observance of Italian unification, was received by Pope John, met President Gronchi, visited orphan homes and hospitals and was photographed with Sicilian fishermen. His journey was recorded on an elaborate color film called "Ted Kennedy in Italy," privately produced; with a voice-over by a professional announcer, it was exhibited many times after his return. Later in the summer, he visited South America with Prof. John N. Plank, Harvard University Latin-American expert, on a private fact-finding tour during which he held conferences with many key political leaders.

Boston pols buzzed with speculation that Ted was being primed for *something*. But only Ted, Frank Morrissey, who accompanied him on most of his speaking engagements, Joe Kennedy, and a few in the White House knew what all the exposure and image-building was about.

He had written on his application to the Massachusetts bar that his "ambitions lie in the public service of this state," and this was a clue. He was even more ambiguous in his replies to newsmen: "There is a great deal of luck involved in politics," he once said, "in being at the right place at the right time. You can't make your breaks. You must let things develop."

Teddy was in Boston on December 19 when news came that his father had suffered a stroke. All political activity was suspended as the family converged on Palm Beach and waited and prayed for Joe's recovery. Ted was a regular visitor during the long months of convalescence and therapy at the New York Institute of Physical Medicine and Rehabilitation and, later, at Hyannis Port.

The patriarch's illness made Ted's bid for the Senate almost a crusade for him. One close friend says: "Like a football game, Ted wanted to win it for the old coach. It's embarrassingly corny when you put it that way, but that's precisely the way events turned out." And he was right. The old man, who had loved his son fiercely and wanted to see him in high position, was now unable to walk or speak. Sometimes tears of frustration would come to his eyes when he tried to say words and only unintelligible sounds emerged. Ted knew, however, what was expected of him and he would try all the harder to make it all come true.

Sick though he was, Joe Kennedy could still think of ways to help Teddy. He received thousands of letters, cards and telegrams from friends, business associates and admirers. A completel ist of their names and addresses was typed up and sent to Teddy's Boston headquarters as good prospects to tap for campaign contributions or other assistance.

Soon after 1962 opened, Massachusetts and the rest of the nation finally learned the reason for Ted Kennedy's unusual activity. On February 22, he became thirty years old. Then, on March 14, he called a press conference to make a momentous statement.

2. Brickbats

On March 14, constitutionally eligible by twenty days, Ted announced his candidacy for the Democratic Senate nomination from the living room of his town house at 3 Charles River Square in Boston. With Joan at his side, he stood before a nest of microphones as TV cameras whirred and said:

"I make this decision in full knowledge of the obstacles I will face, the charges that will be made, and the heavy responsibilities of the office to which I aspire. . . . I am aware that my brother is the President and my other brother attorney general. I am convinced, however, the people will choose the candidate they consider most effective." He insisted that neither of his brothers would stump for him in Massachusetts, but added with a grin that the Kennedy sisters might "come for a visit." A few days later, the President would be asked at a news conference if he planned to support Ted. "My brother is carrying this campaign on his own," he was to say, "and will conduct it in that way." But few doubted that Kennedy power in the form of cash and manpower would be plentifully available, or that arms would be twisted in his behalf all the way from Washington.

Kennedy's qualifications at that stage were minimal, perhaps non-existent. For his campaign brochure, his managers could come up with nothing more impressive than that he had been named one of the ten outstanding men of the year by the Boston Chamber of Commerce, awarded the Order of Merit by Italy for "interest and achievements in behalf of Italian culture and progress," and received a citation for being chairman of one of the most successful American Cancer Society campaigns in Massachusetts history.

Among a dozen more "accomplishments" listed were the chairmanship of the United Fund Health and Fitness Fair, work as trustee and member of the executive board of the Massachusetts chapter of the Arthritis and Rheumatism Foundation, and service as judge advocate of the Polish American Veterans Post of Boston, and chairman of the Massachusetts delegation to Italy in commemoration of the First Centennial of Italian Unification in May, 1961. Nor, indeed, was it certain, his opponents were to point out, which of these positions were working jobs and which "in name only."

Ed McCormack's record in state and city government emphasized Kennedy's thin list of credentials. He graduated first in his class from Boston University Law School and was editor-in-chief of the *Law Review*. In 1953, he was elected to the Boston City Council and thereafter served a total of three terms, the last as president. In 1956, he was elected attorney general and, in 1961, reelected by a plurality of 430,000 votes. As the attorney general, he had performed outstandingly: his Division of Civil

Rights and Consumers' Council, which he created in his office, had been adopted by other state governments and his record in originating and supporting civil rights legislation was outstanding.

As the nephew of the Speaker who openly championed his candidacy, the attorney general himself was open to charges of nepotism. But his vulnerability was nothing compared to that of Teddy who, as the campaign progressed, was to be the target of furious onslaughts from many quarters, including supporters of President Kennedy.

Mark De Wolfe Howe, professor of law at Harvard who had been an adviser to Sen. John Kennedy, wrote scathingly: "His academic career is mediocre. His professional career is virtually non-existent. His candidacy is both preposterous and insulting." Professor Howe incorporated his views into a letter he sent to 4,000 Massachusetts educators. The National Committee for an Effective Congress, whose leaders included Arthur Schlesinger, Jr., a presidential aide, and the poet Archibald MacLeish, said in a statement that "Teddy's undistinguished academic career has not been followed by a record of serious personal accomplishment. . . . Teddy's candidacy is an affront to the Senate."

That Ted's start at the top of the ladder would cause a fallout of resentment against the entire Kennedy administration was a key theme of many critics. Already, supporters of the President were grumbling at some of his appointments, which included too many friends of the family and family itself. Professor Howe, writing in *The Reporter*, pointedly observed that his backers "have not always found it easy to justify the inclination toward nepotism" suggested by a number of JFK's selections to important posts. Since a Senate seat is regarded as a choice plum awarded to those who work hard for it in the House, no legislator would be likely to think highly of, or feel like cooperating with, a President who transgresses the folkways, or unwritten rules, under which the House and Senate operate.

Columinists, editorial writers and cartoonists dipped arrows into vitriol and shot them at Ted and the Kennedys. The Chicago *Tribune* looked into the future and saw this list of White House occupants: "President John F. (1961–69), President Robert F. (1969–77), President Edward M. 1977–   ), and before you know it we are in 1984 with Caroline coming up fast and John F. Jr. just behind her." Inez Robb, writing for the Hearst newspapers, invented a character she described as a typical Massachusetts pol and had him say it was "sporting" of Ted to wait until his thirtieth birthday instead of seeking a constitutional amendment lowering the qualifying age for the Senate to twenty-five or perhaps even twenty-one.

James Reston, then chief of *The Times* Washington bureau, charged that John Kennedy, in allowing Teddy to run, had jettisoned his own high standards for persons serving the public. Reston, assailing the candidacy as "an affront and a presumption," wrote that the Kennedys "have applied the principle of the best man available for the job to almost everybody but themselves," and warned that the race may turn out to be the first Kennedy blunder in years. "In politics," he said, "nothing fails like success after a while. One Kennedy is a triumph, two Kennedys at the same time are a miracle, but three could easily be regarded by many voters as an invasion." *The Times* in its editorial columns offered the withering observation that Ted was "just old enough for the Senate, but has few other visible qualifications."

The cartoonist Herblock drew a politician in the act of introducing Ted to guests at a dinner. He was saying: "It is my great privilege to present a man who — uh — has a brother who —."

Hungerford of the Pittsburgh *Post-Gazette* pictured the three Kennedy brothers as Revolutionary War fife-and-drummers marching over a political battleground with the Capitol in the background. John was in the middle, Bobby on his left. On his right was little Teddy banging on a small drum. The cartoon was captioned: "Spirit of '62."

As for Ed McCormack, he dug in for a hard three-month campaign which would culminate in the state Democratic convention that June. As criticism of Ted Kennedy mounted, his confidence grew.

"I think," he said, "that I'll win on the *chutzpah* issue alone."

VII

Ted and Ed

1. Round One

The first major test of strength came June at the Massachusetts State Democratic convention in Springfield, where the
party met to endorse a candidate for the September primaries. It
was not sudden death for either Ted or Ed. The loser could, if
he chose, oppose the winner at the September primaries. But
party backing was an important leg up and both fought for it
hard.

Some 1,700 delegates packed the hall which, lacking air-
conditioning, soon became miserably hot, smelly and steaming.
Well-intentioned party chieftains sought to soothe both factions
by hanging huge likenesses of the two leaders, President Kennedy and Speaker McCormack, above the rostrum. It only
underscored the dynastic aspect of the confrontation, which
hardly needed additional promotion. The entire nation was
already watching. Normally, only the Massachusetts press
would have covered the state convention, but this one attracted
200 correspondents from all over the country, including famous
Washington columnists, and radio and television networks.

Campaigning continued until the last moment. McCormack
supporters appeared on the convention floor with one arm in
slings, the other waving signs reading: "Don't let them twist
your arm." Other signs read: "Mommy, can I run for the

Senate?" Loudspeakers outside blared the message: "Don't be pressured. Stay with Eddie McCormack and we'll win." Kennedy people were equally busy buttonholing delegates and making certain they controlled the important committees. McCormack charged "manipulation" of committee appointments "to provide the necessary complement of puppets who will do his bidding in committee and on the convention floor."

Ted himself had received a tumultuous greeting when he arrived in Springfield the day before in a motorcade that snaked through the city behind a brass band. Confidently he predicted a first-ballot victory to newsmen; to insure it, he barged around town in a last-minute burst of politicking. He even made a speech from the steps of the convention hall before retiring to his suite at the Sheraton-Kimball Hotel.

There, his brother-in-law Stephen Smith was supervising the superbly-trained Kennedy forces. Dr. Murray B. Levin, professor of government at Boston University, in a detailed study of the campaign, reported on the extensive electronic preparations:

"Two hundred and forty floor workers, six for every delegation, met frequently with Smith during the forty-eight hours prior to balloting, checking and re-checking Kennedy's strength in every delegation. Six Kennedy aides equipped with walkie-talkies reported switches and rumors from the floor while Smith communicated with Kennedy workers through a multi-circuit switchboard at the Sheraton-Kimball.

"A second Kennedy headquarters was set up in the room allotted the candidate backstage. In addition to a twelve-circuit switchboard, this communication center contained a diagram of the auditorium seating plan and the position of delegations, and the names of Kennedy walkie-talkie aides who covered the floor and the delegations they were responsible for. Communications between headquarters and the field were so good that one Kennedy coordinator remarked, 'I felt as though I were back in the army. They want to know where you are all the time.' "

The two candidates, barred by rules from appearing on the convention floor before a choice had been made, watched the proceedings on television from their hotel rooms.

Rep. Edward M. Boland of Springfield, nominating Ted, said the designation for the office of senator "should not be given as a reward for service rendered. It should be given to the man who will best perform the work that must be done." Ed's name was put into nomination by a labor leader, Salvatore Camelio, who stressed: "Nobody starts at the top. If you want leadership, responsibility, you start at the bottom and work your way through the chairs. . . ."

Shortly after 8 p.m. on Saturday, the balloting began. First to be called was the delegation from Berkshire County, which cast 27 votes for Kennedy, 31 for McCormack. At once, a Kennedy supporter demanded a roll-call, which did not change the count but gave a McCormack backer an opportunity to make a devastating remark into the microphones. When his name was called he rose and yelled: "I'm too old to get a post office, so I'll cast my vote for McCormack!" The convention erupted into wild applause and loud boos; it was minutes before the chairman could restore order.

As the voting proceeded, Ted Kennedy steadily drew further ahead. McCormack was urged by his supporters to withdraw, but he said he would hang on just a while longer. By midnight, after twenty-four districts had been polled and Ted was leading 691 to 360, McCormack capitulated.

McCormack entered the smoky auditorium and, cheered loudly by his backers, made his way to the rostrum where he announced: "I respectfully request my name be withdrawn from further consideration at this convention, and I will now take my case to the people."

Ted expected it, and now it was official. He had won the Democratic endorsement. But Ed McCormack was going to fight him for the nomination in the September primaries.

2. Round Two

Ted proved to be a superb campaigner. He was gifted with the charm, the blarney and the friendliness of Honey Fitz which, combined with his good looks and an inexhaustible energy, were enormous assets.

He loved people. He went to subway, rapid transit stations and bus terminals during the rush hours, to the gates of big industrial plants when the shifts changed, into large shopping centers and housing developments — everywhere he could find them. He rarely missed anybody. Once he leaned into an open manhole on Commonwealth Avenue to shake hands with sewer workers; a few feet farther on, he climbed a ladder to greet a painter on a ledge. In one day, he would shake 5,000 hands.

He would start at six in the morning. Always he would be accompanied on these walking tours by several aides who, like carnival shills, would button-hole passersby and say: "Ted Kennedy's down there at the subway entrance and he wants to say hello." Few would decline. As he shook hands, the candidate smiled and said how glad he was to have this chance to say hello to him (her). If he greeted someone he knew, he would invoke the White House, saying: "The President was asking about you the last time I saw him."

In the evenings, his trucks would draw crowds by criss-crossing searchlight beams in the sky and playing *oom-pah* music over loudspeakers. He would deliver short, homey talks and move on.

Honey Fitz used to do the same kind of thing and the voters loved him for it. Like him, Ted could enter a bar, throw his arm around the nearest customer and call for drinks for everyone in the house. In South Boston, a flavorsome, fiercely independent, Irish-dominated region, he would climb on a bar table or the top of a sound truck and, in a strong baritone not always on key, bellow a Boston Irish number called "Southie is My Home Town," (written in 1935 by a local song and dance man named Benny Drohan) which extolled the virtues of the section and its inhabitants. He would also honor requests for Honey Fitz's theme melody, "Sweet Adeline."

The applause and the shouting would last for minutes. Those who watched Ted in action said that, as good a campaigner as John Kennedy was, he could not come close to this. "It was an effort for Jack to slap backs and be jovial," says the writer, Joe McCarthy. "He could never call out for drinks for everyone in a bar. But this kid wasn't like that at all. He was a big, bluff, hearty Irish politician type, and they loved him for it."

John Kennedy may not have gone to Massachusetts to campaign for his brother, but he helped him with his homework. When Ted was scheduled to appear on "Meet the Press" on March 11, John rehearsed him for a full hour, tossing rapid-fire questions at him on every subject he felt the reporters would ask.

The Kennedy women went into action. Experienced after the campaigns for John, they knew what to do and did it with consummate skill. Led by Rose and financed by the Kennedy organization, which supplied bottomless vats of coffee and endless supplies of cake, they held innumerable little parties all over the state, chatting cozily with housewives about children, school and other problems. As in the earlier campaigns, these parties commanded considerable attention in the local society pages. Ted, of course, would attend as many as he could. As many as nine or ten might be held in a single day. The Kennedy women would also stake out sections of Boston and other cities and ring doorbells, giving out Ted Kennedy buttons and pamphlets. Rose herself made countless appearances before all sorts of women's groups and was once more the tireless campaigner she had been in her other son's hurrahs. But now another Kennedy woman moved into the center stage: Ted's beautiful wife Joan.

By his side at rallies and many street corner speeches, she captivated audiences from Provincetown to North Adams. "She's a gold mine," an old pro said as he watched her smiling radiantly during a press conference one day. The Massachusetts novelist John Phillips, not kindly disposed toward the Kennedy candidacy, was moved to write in *Commentary:* "For an instant they seemed just too young to be Mr. and Mrs.; they belonged in a 30s movie, a technicolor musical with a campus setting, holding hands on the 50-yard line. . . ."

Joan was soon being compared with Jackie as a political asset, and indeed, she soon became known as the "Green Jackie," green being Boston-ese for Irish Catholic.

For his part, McCormack needled Teddy on his youth and inexperience and on his relationship to the President. His campaign literature listed twenty-six of his own not inconsiderable qualifications, including the fact that he had been elected to public office five times. In the space devoted to his opponent's qualifications he named but one: "Brother of the President." He charged that the Kennedy organization was dangling offers of postmasters' jobs before delegates in return for votes. He scoffed at Teddy's claim that he had voted regularly since he became of age, producing records showing Kennedy had voted in one primary and two regular elections.

McCormack supporters, running their man as "The Qualified

Candidate," circulated a parody of the folk song, *Billy Boy*
which struck gleefully at the issue of Ted's White House rela-
tionships:

> Would you like to run for Mayor, Teddy
>   boy, Teddy boy?
> Would you like to run for Mayor, charming
>   Teddy?
> I don't want to run for Mayor; life in
>   Washington is gayer.
> I'm a young thing and want to join my
>   brothers.
>
> Then for Governor will you run, Teddy
>   boy, Teddy boy?
> Then for Governor will you run, charming
>   Teddy?
> No, for Governor I won't run; life in
>   Washington's more fun.
> I'm a young thing and want to join my
>   brothers.
>
> Oh, to Congress will you go, Teddy boy,
>   Teddy boy?
> Oh, to Congress will you go, charming
>   Teddy?
> No, to Congress I won't go; John McCormack
>   runs the show.
> I'm a young thing and want to join my
>   brothers.
>
> Would you like the White House more,
>   Teddy boy, Teddy boy?
> Would you like the White House more,
>   charming Teddy?
> Let us not be premature; I shall wait
>   till '84.
> I'm a young thing and will not rush my
>   brothers.

The story of Ted's expulsion from Harvard following the
Spanish test episode, which had broken in March, had little
effect. The general attitude was that it was little more than a
prank, at worst a youthful misstep, and one couldn't hold this

kind of thing against a man for the rest of his life. Kennedy's frank admission and his expression of regret made a good impression. ("He was man enough to admit it.") Curiously, some even felt that the cheating incident made Ted seem more human, proving that a Kennedy, like anyone else, could be caught up in the kind of worries and mistakes that can plague anybody else. It mattered so little, in fact, that Ed McCormack never once brought it up during the campaign.

The campaigning got rougher, the tempers shorter as the summer wore on. One late afternoon, while Teddy was touring Boston, someone in his party mentioned that Knocko McCormack, his opponent's father, was in a backyard near by. Edward J. McCormack, Sr., brother of the Speaker, was a Runyonesque character, a huge man brought up in the rough and tumble game of Boston politics who was as loyal to his son as Joe was to Ted. Ted had never met him.

In the yard, he found Knocko in shirtsleeves, hammering together two-by-eight-foot signs for his son's campaign. Ted approached him and said: "Hi, I'm Ted Kennedy."

Knocko didn't pause in his sign-making. "I know who you are," he said.

Ted looked at all the signs the old man had put together. Trying to make conversation, he said: "You must be tired doing all this work."

Knocko kept hammering. "No," he replied, "not at all. Every time I drive a nail, I just think I'm driving one right into your ass."

Once near the docks Ted shook hands with a huge longshoreman who was not a Kennedy fan. At once the young candidate realized the man was trying to crush his hand to make him cry out in pain. He returned the pressure. For two and a half minutes, the two big men stood face to face, talking to each other with slight strained smiles, all the while squeezing one another's hands with all their strength. Beads of sweat popped out on their reddening faces, but the smiles remained and the squeezing continued. Finally the longshoreman clapped Ted on the back with his free hand and told him: "You're a pretty good fellow, and you're a tough guy too." Ted's hand was sore for a week.

Ted's campaign slogan, "He can do more for Massachusetts," with its strong implication that somebody up there will help deliver political patronage, was criticized by his opponents as carrot-dangling. As one politician put: "We've all heard that it isn't just what you know, it's who you know. But this is the first time I've seen a man run for the United States Senate on that platform." And, as the publication *Business Week* observed: "When he tells businessmen and labor groups that he can be effective in seeing that the state gets its share of government contracts, he doesn't have to draw them a picture." Over and over, Ted's campaign speeches stressed a jetport to be built in Worcester, a federal highway through the Berkshires, new industries for his state. "I have promised to go out and visit the major corporations of the country and tell them the advantages of Massachusetts." Facts being facts and Teddy being the President's brother, nobody doubted that company heads would listen closely to what Ted had to tell them.

McCormack's forces blasted away, but it seemed that fewer people were listening. By early July, Kennedy had gathered so much strength that a quick and clean knockout at the polls was being forecast. On July 25, McCormack made one last effort to stop the steamroller: he challenged Ted to a series of eight televised debates.

Kennedy was not enthusiastic. Debates, he and his aides felt, were great for a trailing candidate but could harm a front runner if something went wrong. But, since his brother had debated Richard Nixon in 1960 and had taken the position thereafter that candidates for public office should meet face to face on a platform, he could scarcely turn down the invitation. Nor, indeed, was there any special reason to fear McCormack in a debate. Ted was good with an audience. He thought fast on his feet, articulated well, and was thoroughly well briefed on national and state problems. Gerard Doherty, his campaign manager, voiced the sole reservation: Even a championship ball team could have a disastrous day and Ted was courting some slight risk that his might come on the platform during a debate.

The sides agreed to the confrontation, which called for two debates, one on August 27, the other September 5, each with the same ground rules: Opening and closing statements by the candidates, and questions from a panel of newsmen. Each candidate would have two and one-half minutes for a response and a minute and a half of rebuttal.

Nobody realized that a fuse had been lit for a devastating explosion.

3. Round Three

On a sticky Monday evening, Ted and Ed, in dark suits and blue shirts, walked onto the stage of the South Boston High School near Dorchester Bay. Ted had refused to wear makeup but Ed's face was so plastered with it he looked to one observer as though made up for an early Lon Chaney movie. McCormack's supporters took one look and shook their heads. Getting the message, Ed went to a corner and wiped some off. The Boston *Globe* commented that he was still so deep in carmine that "whenever he looked off into middle distance while Teddy was speaking, he suggested the juvenile lead in a silent film scanning the horizon for Clara Bow."

Erwin D. Canham, the respected editor of the *Christian Science Monitor*, had been chosen moderator; and the panelists included Leo Egan, a television newscaster from WHDH-TV; Abraham A. Michelson of the Berkshire *Eagle* in Pittsfield; C. Edward Holland, managing editor of the Boston *Record-American;* and David McNeil, a radio news analyst of station WCRB. The debate was sponsored by the Boston Young Democrats.

Ted rose first for his opening remarks. His mood was somber, his manner dignified. In his statement he touched all bases, deftly linking national issues to the problems of Massachusetts, making the point that decisions made in Washington in the coming few years would have a decisive effect on the economic growth of the Commonwealth. "If America is to make progress," he said, "Massachusetts must make progress. If we are to beat the Russians to the moon, we must do it in part with the help of the electronics firms on Route 128." Route 128, which forms half of a parenthesis around Greater Boston, cuts through an important industrial area.

He talked about Honey Fitz but stressed important differences between those years and 1962. "When my grandfather was mayor of Boston," he said, "the city and town made their own determinations about their future. This is not as true in 1962. For the United States Senate will make determinations whether Boston will have the urban renewal that it needs. Whether Pittsfield will have the air transportation that it needs. Whether Fall River will have the industrial development that it needs."

To counter the opposition's efforts to cast him as a tool of wealthy and ruthless power seekers, he said: "I believe that people who have sought public office for money and power have had their day in Massachusetts. I believe that it is time to elect people who want to serve."

He sat down to loud applause. Gerry Doherty, who had watched intently, said half to himself: "He looks good."

Less than 30 seconds after he was introduced, Ed McCormack unleashed a personal assault that, for vehemence and vitriol, was rare even in Massachusetts politics.

Born and raised in South Boston, he had gone to school in that very building and grown up with the residents of tenements that surround it. He was proud of his close ties with the district. "These are hard-working people here in South Boston," he said. "They are deeply religious and they take their politics seriously and they want the issues discussed fully . . ." He grasped the lectern with both hands, his voice rising, cords forming in his neck. Those issues, he said, were not political, for the Democrats basically agreed on the Administration program. They centered, rather, on the qualifications of the candidates.

McCormack seldom became angry in his campaign speeches. Usually his style was mocking, needling; but now his face was dark and unsmiling as he turned to young Kennedy.

"What are your qualifications?" he demanded. Answering his own question, he turned to the audience and said: "He graduated from law school three years ago."

Turning once more to Ted, he said scathingly, his voice now shrill with anger and scorn:

"You never worked for a living. You never ran for or held an elective office. You are not running on qualifications, you are running on a slogan, you can 'do more for Massachusetts.' And I say to you, 'How?' Because of experience? I say 'no!'

"This is the most insulting slogan I have seen in Massachusetts politics because this slogan means, vote for this man because he has influence. He has connections. He has relations. And I say no.

"I say that we do not vote on influence or favoritism or connections. We vote for people who will serve.

"This is a slogan that insults the President of the United States. He can do more — that means that the President is not now doing enough. Or that the President will discriminate against someone other than his brother if he is the senator from this state."

Turning to Ted's voting record, McCormack recalled his opponent's words: "I want to serve because I care." Bitingly, he said: "You didn't care very much, Ted, when you could have voted between 1953 and 1960 on sixteen occasions and you only voted three times." He attacked Kennedy, too, on civil rights: "While I was fighting to eliminate black belts and ghettos, you were attending a school in the south, totally segregated, at the University of Virginia."

His final blow before he sat down:

"We need a senator with experience, not arrogance, and the office of United States senator should be merited, not inherited."

A second of silence was followed by screams, foot-stompings and loud applause from the McCormack adherents. Canham admonished them: "You are not aiding the dignity of Massachusetts and the cause of this debate by these demonstrations."

Twice during Ed's violent attack, Ted had leaned forward as though to interrupt but checked himself and remained silent. He had turned pale and his lips were a tight line but otherwise showed no sign that he was affected. During the question and answer period, he had said nothing, though Ed continued to make references now and then to his lack of expertise.

At one point, McCormack ridiculed Ted's trips abroad as political, asserting his opponent had visited eleven European countries in 24 days, nine Latin American countries in 27 days and nine African countries in 15 days. "Well, he said, "certainly spending one or two days might not make you or I experts but" — the sarcasm was heavy — "he picks things up more quickly than perhaps I would."

There were no surprises in the question and answer segment. The candidates addressed themselves to such subjects as revision of the tax structure, disarmament and nuclear weaponry, the Massachusetts shoe and leather industry and proposals for strengthening the United Nations. Kennedy was serious and unfailingly polite: it was always "Mr. McCormack." As though to emphasize his opponent's youth, McCormack constantly referred to him as "Teddy."

From his silence, many had supposed Ted would ignore the attacks and taunts but, as he rose for his closing remarks, it became apparent they had cut deeply.

He stood stiffly in front of the lectern and talked in general terms about the problems of peace in the world and whether Massachusetts would move forward or stand still. The leap from world tensions to Bay State problems was dizzying; Ted's mind, it appeared, was on another subject, and it finally emerged.

"We should not have any talk about personalities or families," he said. "I feel we should be talking about the people's destiny in Massachusetts."

A great burst of applause came from the audience. Ted's voice broke with his long-suppressed feelings. Those closest to him said his eyes misted over and tears glistened in them. "The camera did not show a closeup at this moment," reported Dr. Levin in his study of the campaign, "so it was difficult to determine whether Kennedy actually wept. Many viewers, however, thought so. It was obvious, nevertheless, that Kennedy was in a state of some shock."

But Ed McCormack had tasted blood. In his closing statement, he turned once more to the subject of qualifications. "Now it is all right for my opponent to say that we keep families out of it and we stand on our own two feet," he said. "I favor this. I stand on my own two feet. I stand on a record. . . . I'm not starting at the top."

His voice reedy and quivering with his anger, his coppery hair glinting in the television floodlights, Ed McCormack hurled at Ted Kennedy the most savage attack of the evening.

"I ask that since the question of names and families has been injected," he cried, "that if his name were Edward Moore, with his qualifications — with your qualifications, Teddy — if it was Edward Moore, your candidacy would be a joke." As he spoke, his right index finger was pointing accusingly less than a yard from Ted Kennedy's head.

Ed turned to the audience. "And nobody is laughing," he said, "because his name is not Edward Moore; it's Edward Moore Kennedy!"

Ted's face was white and his body had stiffened. He looked straight ahead through glazing eyes, seeming to stare at the back of the hall. The audience gasped as the ferocity of the attack and then suddenly it was all over and they filed out into the hot night.

The opponents did not shake hands nor bid one another good night. Ed grinned and joked with his supporters, accepting their congratulations. "He wiped up the floor with him," one said.

Ted, quickly surrounded by his aides, looked shaken. Wordlessly, he left the building.

4. The Decision

The second debate, held on September 6 in the War Memorial Building in Holyoke, produced no fireworks. The Boston *Globe* headlined it: "Round 2: No Rough Stuff This Time." It was, the newspaper reported, "a kid glove affair . . . the fire of personal exchange replaced by polite restraint." Robert Healy, the reporter who had broken the Spanish test story, wrote: "Ted Kennedy nearly fell off the stool when McCormack came charging across the stage before the debate and gave him a great big handshake." He charged across once more at the end for a goodbye handshake. He and Ted chatted for a minute, broad smiles on their faces.

"One thing was quite clear here," Healy wrote. "McCormack was not going to risk another big attack on Kennedy." Though he still stressed he was the "qualified candidate," his voice did not rise in anger, his finger did not jab accusingly, he never referred to his opponent's candidacy as a joke. And he called Ted "Mister."

In the final eleven days, the Kennedy blitz was all-encompassing. Ted whirled faster around the state. The Kennedy women poured more cups of tea, handed out more cakes and smiled more bewitchingly than ever. Supporters, paid and unpaid, made phone calls on his behalf from morning until late evening; radio and television carried "elect Ted" commercials dozens of times daily.

Nothing was left to chance. On the Sunday before Election Day, Joe Kennedy invited Richard Cardinal Cushing, Boston's beloved prelate and a close friend of the Kennedy family, for a ride on his yacht. A photograph of the two appeared in the newspapers next morning. One columnist observed it was bad enough that Ed had to run against the father and son — now he was competing against the father, the son and the Holy Ghost.

On September 18, Democrats went to the polls and gave Ted Kennedy a magnificent victory, 69 per cent of their votes. He received 559,303 to Ed's 257,403, sweeping every ward in Boston and even capturing McCormack's home precinct in Dorchester.

What were the ingredients that helped create Teddy's spectacular victory?

Money was a prime factor. Officially, Kennedy's managers reported expenditures of $121,535 for the primary campaign, against $78,765 by McCormack. But Newton H. Fulbright was to write in the New York *Herald Tribune:* "People with an eye for campaign costs maintain that Mr. Kennedy . . . spent around $1,000,000." Dr. Levin quoted a Kennedy staff man as saying: "I have had different percentages quoted. But let us say that Mr. McCormack spent in the vicinity of $200,000. And it would not be unfair to say we outspent him six or seven to one."

In his study of the campaign, Professor Levin said the Kennedys bought time on nine TV stations, more than fifty English-language radio stations and twenty foreign-language outlets, more coverage than all the other candidates combined. In addition, they purchased advertisements in all the major Massachusetts newspapers and dozens of smaller ones and acquired prime billboard space throughout Massachusetts.

"They provided automobiles on election day throughout the state to drive voters to the polls, and when convenient they rented airplanes to transport the candidate," says the Levin report. "They purchased or were provided with space for headquarters in twenty locations in the city of Boston and in most cities and towns in Massachusetts where substantial numbers of Democrats and Independents live. . . . Special project groups created to work with labor, the elderly, Jews and various ethnic and religious groups were established, and special mailings were prepared for each group. Area coordinators were recruited for every senatorial district, leaders for every major city, virtually every ward, and thousands of precincts. In some large cities where streets run for several miles, block leaders were enlisted to contact voters in apartment houses and housing projects, block by block."

Kennedy's staff made 300,000 phone calls to push his candidacy, bought a half million bumper stickers and mailed 1,500,-000 pieces of campaign literature. An eight-page, two-color publication, "The Ted Kennedy Story," was distributed throughout the state. Little was left to chance.

Ed McCormack's sledgehammer personal attack turned out

to be a major blunder. Telegrams and letters pouring into campaign headquarters and newspapers disclosed that Kennedy had actually scored a big victory that August evening. Thousands saw that Ted had conducted himself with the decorum and restraint befitting a United States senator. One Kennedy supporter said McCormack had come on "just like a ward politician speaking out of the side of his mouth and just didn't seem to grow in stature." The Boston *Herald*'s political editor wrote: "His [McCormack's] assault on Kennedy, and the latter's refusal to be drawn into an army base brawl, apparently created unfavorable reaction to the attorney general among many viewers, especially women."

Moreover, while McCormack's own record as attorney general was spotless and, indeed, he had successfully prosecuted many large-scale wrongdoers, he was a victim of guilt by association. He was identified in the public mind as a politician who had held office in the years when corruption was rampant in Massachusetts. Rascals were busy in bookmaking, land appraisals, unemployment compensation frauds and a number of other areas.

During those years, the tangled affairs of Bernard Goldfine, the Boston textile magnate, were unwound in the courts. Mr. Goldfine's gift of a vicuna coat to Sherman Adams, Eisenhower's assistant, and Mr. Adam's subsequent resignation in the wake of charges of favor-seeking, made choice headlines for months. On the other hand, Teddy himself had no political past and his family was above reproach when it came to corruption. One Bostonian summed it up thus: "The Kennedys won't steal because they already have plenty of money."

But perhaps counting for most was the name, image and appearance of Kennedy himself. On the platform, with the familiar chopping gesture and the flat, unmistakable Bay State accent, he recalled the other Kennedy, now the President. On the streets, the high-powered charm was irresistible. He had the kind of sex appeal which appealed to bobby soxers and mature women alike.

At McCormack headquarters on primary night, a young staff worker told Joe McCarthy that her mother had shaken hands with Teddy a few evenings before at a delicatessen in Dorchester. "She called me up today at the bank where I worked and she said to me, 'Marcia, even though Teddy may not be qualified, I had to vote for him because ever since I met him personally, he's been my ideal.' "

"Imagine!" the McCormack aide said in a shocked voice. "My own mother!"

5. "I'm Not Sorry"

Nearly ten years later, Edward McCormack was practicing law in a large suite of offices on Congress Street in downtown Boston. In 1966, after defeating Ken O'Donnell for the Democratic nomination, he ran unsuccessfully for governor against John Volpe and then retired from politics. At forty-eight, his hair was still coppery-gold, his face youthful.

I asked him: "Looking back, do you regret tearing into Ted Kennedy so furiously that evening?"

He replied: "I'm not sorry. And I probably would say those same words if I had it to do over again."

"But why? The analysts have concluded that the severe attack boomeranged and lost you many votes you would otherwise have gotten."

"I don't agree with the analysts. I think my remarks gave the people who latently were going to vote for Teddy an excuse for going with him, but they would have voted for him anyway."

"Did you have to be so rough in your personal attack?"

"Those remarks were not spontaneous but deliberate. They were said deliberately to shock people, to make them think to themselves, 'Those are very dramatic statements.' But then they would, after the first shock had passed, add: 'Yes, they are dramatic, all right, but they are also very true!'

"There are two types of contests in which one engages in an election. One is a very gentle type in which you try to outdistance your opponent as in a foot race. The second is to try to have a confrontation in which you dramatically emphasize your opponent's weakness. In 1962, the contest was really not between Edward McCormack and Teddy Kennedy at all, but between the McCormacks and the Kennedys. I was running against the President and the attorney general, as well as all the good things the family had done.

"The only way we had a chance of winning was to shock the people into the realization that this was a young man just out of college who was presumptuous in aspiring to such high office. It was essential, I felt, to sever Teddy in the voter's minds from the majesty of the Presidency, the glamor of the First Lady, the importance of the U.S. attorney generalship, the great contributions of the Kennedys. They were *they*, but Teddy was still only Teddy, a very young man who had accomplished nothing.

"Well, I did one thing anyway. I made his middle name famous."

Ed McCormack has long since healed the breach with Kennedy. "We're friends now," he said. "I'm not bitter. If you go into politics, if you're going to be a professional at the game, you've got to accept the fact that you win some and you lose some."

After all those charges of youth and inexperience, what did he think of Ted's performance as a United States Senator?

Ed McCormack answered: "If you look at the whole man, examine his record over the years, consider his dedication to public service, you have got to say that this is a remarkable young man who concerns himself with problems that are the problems of our day, our generation. He tries to understand them and come up with approaches to their solution. Importantly, many of these are problems he himself does not experience personally but he identifies with those who do. I happen to like him. I happen to admire him. I think he's been a good senator."

6. . . . and George

The election campaign itself was another dynastic struggle, but it did not produce the excitement of the Ted versus Ed fight. The Lodges and Kennedys had tangled off and on for almost half a century, ever since Honey Fitz failed by only 32,000 votes to unseat the great senator in 1916. (During that brief but bitter campaign, Honey Fitz delighted his audience with the assertion that the Brahmin Lodge traveled in the lofty circles where the Lowells spoke only to Cabots who, in turn would speak only to God. Not so with Honey Fitz. "I dwell in the homes of Massachusetts," he would bellow, "the abode of Democracy, where the Lord speaks to Jones in the very same tones as he uses with Johnson and me!") George's father, running for reelection to the Senate, had been defeated by John Kennedy in 1952 and once again in 1960 when he was Richard Nixon's vice-presidential running mate.

Curiously, a third member of an eminent American political family had entered the race — H. Stuart Hughes, professor of modern history at Harvard, the grandson of the former Chief Justice Charles Evans Hughes. He ran as an independent candidate.

Young Lodge, who was thirty-five, had a little more experience in government service than Ted, though not much. Having served only as an assistant secretary of labor for international affairs under President Eisenhower, he was vulnerable to the barb leveled by his opponent for the Republican nomination, the sixty-eight-year-old Rep. Laurence Curtis, that "the Senate is no place for on-the-job training." Curtis argued, with some validity, that if the Republicans chose Lodge they would throw away their greatest issue — Ted's youth and inexperience — by nominating someone with the same liabilities.

Nonetheless, Lodge was named and the campaign opened.

Ted, with scarcely a pause, renewed his bouncy drive.

He made jokes in high good humor: In Natick, when the president of a temple brotherhood was introduced, he jumped up to acknowledge the applause. "Oh, I'm sorry," he said in elaborate apology. "I thought the toastmaster said 'the brother of the President.'" The audience howled.

He was friendly, unpretentious. "Gimmy that, buddy," he said heartily grabbing the greasy hand of a foundryman who had been reluctant to soil Ted's palm. At a banquet in honor of Casimir Pulaski, the Polish military commander in the Revolutionary War, he whirled around the floor in a polka with sixteen partners.

He was old-fashioned and cornball in his appeal to voters. In Jewish areas, he would open his brief talks with a funny Yiddish remark. In Italian areas, he had an Italian opening. In the Irish sections he shamelessly allowed a brogue to enter his speech. Stewart Alsop wrote: "Here is the grandson of Honey Fitz, enjoying the smell and feel of the crowd, as another grandson of Honey Fitz never has." And the crowds loved it. Alsop concluded: "After covering many campaigns, a reporter comes to recognize whatever it is that makes a great natural politician — call it what you will. Whatever it is, Teddy Kennedy has it. His older brother was quite right when he remarked that 'Teddy is a better natural politician than any of us.' Teddy Kennedy was designed by his Maker to be a politician."

Lodge, too, campaigned Kennedy-style, meeting the voters at their work, on the streets, wherever they could be found. Three buses loaded with enthusiastic volunteers accompanied him around the state, whooping up enthusiasm, singing campaign songs, tossing around campaign buttons and handing out bumper stickers.

With an attractive wife, Nancy, and six children, a quiet charm and unquestioned intelligence and grasp of problems, George Lodge made a good candidate, but he lacked Teddy's verve, vitality and sex appeal. His speeches were always brief and serious, always on the issues of importance — farm subsidies, the question of American aid to Yugoslavia, emerging Africa, solving the unemployment problem in depressed areas of Massachusetts and the rest of the nation. He was tall and ruggedly handsome but, as Alsop remarked, no bobbysoxer would be likely to squeal and pronounce as "cute" a man who stood six feet two inches in his stocking feet.

Like Ed, George was contemptuous of Ted's inexperience and unfamiliarity with the issues, but he did not make Ed's mistake of attacking him personally. "We've got to keep George bland," his campaign manager Paul Grindle once said. "He can't offend anybody, and that includes anyone who might be offended by an attack on Teddy."

On November 6, Massachusetts went to the polls and elected another Kennedy. Ted received 1,143,020 votes to Lodge's 836,460. Hughes, the independent, polled 49,102.

Rose and Joe Kennedy watched the results on television at Hyannis Port. After Lodge conceded, the patriarch received a telephone call from Ted who told reporters: "He was very excited." Ted spoke to his father before he called either of his brothers in Washington.

On January 15, Ted Kennedy boarded a plane at Logan Airport and flew to Washington. He was met at the field by a staff aide who drove him to the Constitution Avenue entrance to the

Old Senate Office Building. He entered by a side door, went into a small elevator to the fourth floor and walked halfway down the corridor to his suite.

On the door was a small sign, "Mr. Kennedy," and beneath it the State seal of Massachusetts.

The new senator went inside to begin his career as a public official.

VIII

Young Senator Kennedy

1. Model Freshman

At noon on Wednesday, January 9, with Joan and the children, his mother and Ethel in the special relatives gallery, Ted Kennedy was sworn in as a United States Senator. It was the first time in history that a President's brother had served in that body.

Almost everyone in Washington expected a brash young jock who would make a considerable noise, throw his weight around and be talked about, in print and in whispers. Nor could they be blamed much, for the capital knew him only as a member of the very modern, sometimes madcap New Frontier social set and, candidly, considered him somewhat of a cipher. He was the young man who, in an excess of exuberance, had leaped fully clothed into Bobby Kennedy's swimming pool at Hickory Hill during those much-publicized dunking episodes. He was photographed in night clubs and frequently got his name in the gossip columns. Except for this and what it had read of the political goings-on up in Boston the past year, Washington knew little else about him. One Republican senator put it this way: "It's kind of hard to predict what a senator will do when all you know about him is that he likes to go swimming with his clothes on and plays pretty good football."

Kennedy amazed everyone. From the beginning, his behavior

was exemplary. With some surprise, one journalist called him "the model child of the Senate family."

Ted Kennedy: "It's been said that the President briefed me on how to handle myself in the Senate. He never did, not in the sense of sitting me down and offering me instruction, though we did have some talks about the Senate and the responsibilities of its members.

"In our family, nobody briefed anyone on how to conduct himself in a job. We just picked things up by watching and absorbing. That's one advantage of being a Kennedy — there were so many of us, doing so much. You just soaked up things as you went along.

"There's no school for senators. You learn the job by listening to other senators, observing and studying the great institution and how to make a contribution to it."

Kennedy succeeded as well as he did precisely because he was aware that one must learn to be a senator. "The amateur," wrote Dr. Donald R. Matthews in his study, *U.S. Senators and Their World*, has a great deal to learn. "Many able men have wrecked their legislative careers because, through arrogance, stupidity or both they did not conform to . . . unwritten rules of the game as played on Capitol Hill."

"The new senator," wrote Dr. Matthews, "is expected to keep his mouth shut, not to take the lead in floor fights, to listen . . . . Freshman are also expected to show respect for their elders and to seek their advice. They are encouraged to concentrate on developing an acquaintanceship in the Senate."

Woe to the fledgling legislator who breaks the rules. Once when the redoubtable William E. Borah, Idaho Republican, celebrated his birthday, senator after senator rose in the chamber to praise his accomplishments. Borah beamed with pleasure. Then, when a freshman senator asked for the floor, his smile disappeared. As the newcomer, in a fine speech, added his tribute to those of his colleagues, Borah lowered his great round head and began muttering through his clenched teeth: "That son of a bitch, that son of a bitch!" Borah had no personal animosity toward the orator, nor did he quarrel with the panegyric he was uttering. He was angered because the man, only four months in the club, was taking the floor too early.

Young ambitious senators who strain at the bit to get going are slapped down by the elders. The story is told that John

Kennedy, a short time after his election to the Senate, moved from his rear row seat to an unoccupied desk closer to the rostrum so that he could join in an on-going floor debate. Next to him was the legendary Carl Hayden of Arizona, who was to establish a record as the first man to serve in Congress for a full half century. During a lull, Kennedy asked Hayden what changes had taken place in the Senate during his many years of service. Replied Hayden frostily: "New senators didn't speak in those days."

Hayden had another rule: "If you want to get your name in the papers, be a show horse. If you want to gain the respect of your colleagues, keep quiet and be a workhorse." He meant that the real work of the Senate, like an iceberg, is below the surface. Flashy debating and pronouncements can grab headlines but painstaking work in the home or office on the business of legislating, which involves careful examination of endless pages of dull documents, wins the admiration of colleagues.

There were other rules: Do unto other senators as you would some day like them to do unto you. That is, vote for something he wants and, some day, he will reciprocate. A thorough understanding of, and willingness to go along with, this traditional system of logrolling is crucial to anyone who hopes to make it in the Senate. Be unfailingly courteous to your fellow senators in public, even if you privately consider him an idiot. Alben W. Barkley of Kentucky, for many years a senator and the endearing "Veep" in the Truman administration, once offered this advice to a beginning senator: "If you think a colleague stupid, refer to him as 'the able, learned and distinguished senator,' but if you *know* he is stupid, refer to him as the '*very* able, learned and distinguished senator.' "

If you are ambitious for higher office, hide it. And above all, do nothing that will upset the traditions of "the greatest deliberative body in the world" or bring disrepute upon it. A prime example of one who did was the late Sen. Joseph R. McCarthy, the Communist-hunting maverick who violated the unwritten rules by abusing his colleagues on and off the floor. He was, as Sen. William E. Jenner, Indiana Republican, once told him, "the kid who was invited to the party and peed in the lemonade."

Kennedy had no intention of contaminating the lemonade or anything else the Senate holds dear. He knew what was required of him: that the senior members expected him to serve an apprenticeship of at least two years, that he would get the least desirable office space and, like the youngest in any family, a spot at the far end of the table in committee rooms. He was also aware that he would be given, as one Senate aide put it, "all the shit details," such as sitting in the Vice President's chair as President Pro Tem during the tedious debates, serving on the Calendar Committee of the party.

He made friends with his colleagues on both sides of the aisle, read until far into the night to be familiar with the bills, resolutions and other matters coming up for consideration, and, perhaps most important of all, he was *there*. Whenever Kennedy heard the buzzer announcing a quorum call, he would dart off from wherever he was like one of Pavlov's conditioned dogs and head for the floor to answer to his name.

He made only one mistake. It is customary for freshman senators to pay courtesy calls on their elders when they report for work. Ted dropped in on sixty-one-year-old Mike Mansfield and received some fatherly advice; he then visited the venerable Richard B. Russell of Georgia where the young initiate led with his strong, firm chin.

Russell began with usual counsel to move slowly because the Senate does not take kindly to first-termers who come on too strong. Ted listened respectfully, then casually observed that the Georgia Democrat had also been elected to the Senate at the minimum constitutional age.

"That's true, son," Russell replied gently. "But you see, before I came here, I had already been Governor of my State." *

Ted refused almost all invitations for speeches and opening-of-Congress parties. He asked for no special favors, attended mostly to Massachusetts business and issued no pronouncements calculated to win headlines. He talked only with Massachusetts newsmen, avoiding as much as he could all other correspondents, especially network television people. He did consent to make a brief talk before the Women's National Press Club at its annual dinner. There is no better way to disarm critics than by recognizing the main thrust of their arguments and turning them good-humoredly against oneself, and this Ted did with superb skill.

"I was down at the White House this afternoon," he told

*At 23 Russell was a member of the Georgia legislature, at 29 Speaker of the Georgia House, at 33, Governor.

the women journalists, "with some suggestions for the State of the Union address, but all I got from him was, 'Are you still using that greasy kid stuff?' "

And again: "I want to stay out of the limelight, out of the headlines — and out of the swimming pool."

And once more: "There is no reason to think that I am emphasizing the fact that the President is my brother just because I had a rocker installed in my Senate seat this afternoon."

A number of apocryphal stories aimed at the nepotism issue and Ted's personal ambitions went the rounds in Washington. Rep. Thomas P. (Tip) O'Neill of Massachusetts, an old friend of the Kennedys, told one of the best at the White House one day and had the President roaring.

Ted, he said, went down to court one day and asked the judge to change his name. "Kennedy is so well known politically," he explained. "One Kennedy is President, the other a high-ranking cabinet member. Your Honor, I want to become a success on my own."

The judge, sympathetic, asked him what other name he would prefer. "Well," Ted replied, "I think Teddy is all right as a first name, but I'd like to change the last name. "To what?" asked the puzzled judge.

"How about Roosevelt?" Ted replied.

Ted Kennedy was especially careful to avoid any incident in his private life that might be misunderstood or exaggerated. Only once in the early months was there anything approaching an "incident." In February, Joan and Ted, accompanied by Bobby and Ethel, went to Smuggler's Notch in Stowe, Vermont, for a weekend of skiing. One late afternoon, a photographer for a local newspaper asked Ted if he could take his picture with a local beauty contest winner who was at the resort. Ted refused, but the cameraman took the picture anyway. The senator snatched the man's camera and confiscated the film. Later, Kennedy apologized to the photographer.

He was named to the Labor and Public Welfare Committee, where the President had served, and placed on the subcommittees on Labor, Veterans' Affairs, Migratory Labor and Employment and Manpower. He was also placed on the Judiciary Committee, and named to the Subcommittees on Immigration and Naturalization, Antitrust and Monopoly, Constitutional Rights and trading with the Enemy. Finally, he got a place on the Special

Committee on Aging, mandated to investigate the problems of old people but with no powers to report legislation. He worked hard and uncomplainingly on his assignments, earning the approval and even admiration of his senatorial elders for his alertness, conscientiousness and, in one instance, his ability to toss off a snort of bourbon right after breakfast. When he paid a courtesy visit early one day to Sen. James O. Eastland, chairman of the Judiciary Committee, the Mississippi Democrat, with true Southern hospitality, poured him a good-sized hooker which — so the story goes — Kennedy tossed into a wastebasket when the senator wasn't looking.

Meanwhile, Joan had conferred with Jackie and Ethel on where to live in Washington. Both had assured her that if she had any hopes of seeing her busy husband now and then, she had to be in Georgetown, the exclusive residential section on the Potomac. It is a quaint and gracious area of narrow, tree-lined streets and eighteenth-century homes, most of them small and very expensive, where many government officials live. Jackie had lived there when John was a senator; Ethel and Bobby moved from one house to another as their family kept enlarging until there was nothing big enough and they went out to Hickory Hill. Joan found a four-bedroom red-brick home at 1336 31st Street, which she rented for $600 a month, $200 more than Ethel and Bobby paid for their first Georgetown lodgings. Later, the Kennedys moved to a larger home on 28th St.

While Teddy made no national waves, his efforts to "do more for Massachusetts" elicited some grumbling from those who didn't want to get less so that the Bay State could get more. Kenneth B. Keating, New York's white-haired Republican senator, was especially incensed when Kennedy took a trip to the Grumman Corporation on Long Island to get some of their work for Massachusetts firms. Grumman at the time was constructing the lunar module, the funny-looking bug-like ferry that would take astronauts from their command ships down to the moon's surface, and then back again. Kennedy urged Grumman to subcontract some of its work to Massachusetts firms, explaining that many of them possessed special technology and skilled people to do the best possible job.

Keating charged Kennedy with making a "pirating" foray and warned he might just go up to Massachusetts and retaliate in kind. But if New York's senator was angry, Kennedy's constituents applauded. Wrote the Boston *Traveler:* "If making a pitch for new industry makes Teddy a pirate, let's all salute the Jolly Roger."

Kennedy voted with the administration on all key matters that first year. He backed the vain attempt to have the filibuster rule — Rule 22 — amended. He voted for a mass transit bill, a wilderness preservation measure, a feed-grain bill, a bill to aid distressed areas. The worst defeat he suffered was for a proposal he made in the spring to send the U.S. frigate *Constitution,* the almost holy "Old Ironsides," down to the New York World's Fair the following year. The 44-gun frigate, launched in 1797 at Hartt's Shipyard in Boston, was — and still is — America's most famous and revered fighting vessel: the victor over the British warship *Guerriére* off Cape Race in 1812; the bane of French privateers infesting the Caribbean, and of the Barbary pirates off the shores of Tripoli.

The ship, many feared, was too fragile to withstand a voyage to New York. A Boston newspaper said she was "too sacred a relic of our heritage to make it a road show." Leverett Saltonstall, the senior senator from Massachusetts and a Republican, was opposed; so was Boston's Mayor John Collins, the Greater Boston Chamber of Commerce and the Navy Mothers.

Kennedy defended the idea but in late August the U.S. Navy had the last word, and it was "no."

2. Thirty-Nine Hours of Life

Shortly after noon on Wednesday, August 7, Kennedy was presiding as President Pro Tem — a chore assigned to all new men — when Mike Mansfield, the majority leader, asked to be recognized. Mansfield, a broad smile on his usually taciturn face, announced that President and Mrs. Kennedy had just become the parents of a third child, a son. The senators rose in their seats at the news and applauded. Ted Kennedy, on the rostrum, beamed happily.

But the next day, after talking by telephone to his brother Robert, he flew to Boston to be with the President. For the new baby, Patrick Bouvier Kennedy, was dangerously ill and not expected to survive.

It was hot on Cape Cod, 83 degrees and sultry. Jacqueline Kennedy, who was spending the summer in a rented home on Squaw Island, had taken her children, Caroline and John junior, to Osterville, seven miles from Hyannis Port, for an outing. At 11 on Wednesday morning, she had felt pains and started back for Squaw Island by car. A Secret Service man notified Dr. John Walsh, her obstetrician. Jackie was not expecting her baby for another five weeks, but Dr. Walsh was taking his vacation at the Cape to stand by for emergencies such as this.

At the house, Dr. Walsh advised Jackie to fly at once to Otis Air Force Base hospital, near Falmouth, where a four-room suite had been prepared. Mrs. Kennedy had planned to have the baby at Walter Reed Army Medical Center but, in view of the First Lady's history of miscarriages, Otis had been alerted to be ready. With Dr. Walsh and a Secret Service man, Jackie flew by helicopter to Otis where, at 12:15 in the afternoon, a four-pound, ten and one-half ounce baby boy was delivered by Caesarian section.

At 11:50, Dr. Janet G. Travell, the White House physician who was also on the Cape, got word to the President that his wife was about to have her baby. Seventeen minutes later, Kennedy was on a helicopter bound for Andrews Air Force Base where he boarded a Lockheed Star jet (his two Presidential planes were out of the country) for the flight to Otis. While aloft, he learned by radio that he had become a father for the third time.

But soon after the boy was born, he showed signs of respiratory distress, alarming enough to convince doctors to rush him by ambulance to Boston Children's Hospital Medical Center an hour away.

The President, after seeing his wife, flew, to Boston. On the fifth floor of the Farley Building, in white gown and surgical mask, Kennedy watched his new son struggle for life.

Patrick was suffering from hyaline membrane disease which claims the lives of 25,000 infants each year. Unable to breathe because protein deposits clog up their tiny lungs, they usually succumb in a few days. All day and through the next, the President with his brother, Robert, and Dave Powers shuttled between the hospital and the Ritz-Carlton Hotel. In a desperate effort to ease his breathing, the baby was placed in a hyperbaric chamber to force oxygen into his lungs but, at four minutes past four on Friday morning, after living for only 39 hours, Patrick Kennedy died.

The agonized President, watching intently through the glass of the high-pressure chamber, struck the wall with his clenched fist, then went through a door into a boiler room where he sobbed for ten minutes.

On August 10, with Ted and Robert at his side, the President wept once more at his baby's funeral. At Holyhood Cemetery in Brookline, John Kennedy touched the tiny coffin and whispered "goodbye," then knelt and touched the earth. "It's awfully lonely here," he said softly.

Ted went to his brother's left side, Robert to his right. Powers, who had witnessed the graveside scene, moved back.

"In moments of sadness," he says, "they always want to be alone."

IX

You'd Better Call
Your Mother

1. Last Happy Party

Throughout the summer and fall of 1963, Kennedy continued in the role he had created for himself: to listen carefully, say little as possible and learn the business. He stayed away from the White House, aware he must not appear to be John Kennedy's "ears" inside the Senate. Acquiring a reputation as a spy for the Administration would, he knew, bring the wrath of the Senate upon him and damage, perhaps destroy, his chances of acceptance, and his effectiveness as a legislator. Politics being politics and Kennedys being Kennedys, few seriously doubted that Edward and the President conferred, but nothing surfaced to indicate that the new senator was bearing tales. As Senator Javits said: "Obviously, the President's going to get some inside information from Ted. The point is, how much, how often and how it's used."

On the weekend of November 16, Ted and Joan flew to New York for a gala affair which brought together the New Frontiersmen and their ladies. Only the President was absent: he was busy in Washington trying to get his tax cut and civil rights measures through a balky Congress.

On Sunday, November 17, an enormous throng gathered behind police lines at the Warner Cinerama Theater on Broadway near 47th Street, to watch the glittering personalities arrive for the premier showing of the film, *It's A Mad, Mad, Mad, Mad World*. More than 1,500 persons had paid $50 each for the performance, which was a benefit for two charities established by the Kennedy Foundation — the Kennedy Child Study Center for Retarded Children in New York, and the Lt. Joseph P. Kennedy Jr. Institute in Washington. Eva Gabor and Milton Berle were roundly applauded, but Bobby and Ethel Kennedy were cheered. And Joan, beautiful on Ted's arm, drew gasps.

Rose Kennedy came and was cheered too. Eunice and Sargent Shriver, Jean and Stephen Smith, Patricia Lawford were there. Ted Sorensen, Ken O'Donnell, Arthur Schlesinger, Lawrence O'Brien and all the others who followed John Kennedy's banner were applauded. Afterward, guests were transported by special buses to the New York Hilton, where a supper dance was held in the grand ballroom. Ted danced with Joan, then with Ethel. There was much food, much bantering, much laughter.

It was the last happy party to be attended by the Camelot courtiers in the lifetime of the President.

A few days earlier, Kennedy himself had flown to New York to address an AFL-CIO convention and terrified the Secret Service by driving into the city from the airport without a motorcycle escort. When his limousine stopped for a traffic light in midtown Manhattan, a young woman dashed up and snapped a picture at close range. A police official who observed the scene said despairingly: "She might well have been an assassin."

Edward Kennedy flew back to Washington on Monday.

2. "Your Brother, the President..."

Friday was a sunless day in Washington, though warm for late November. The grass in the Plaza opposite the Capitol had long since browned and the great elms were in the last stages of their autumnal coloring. Inside the Senate chamber, Edward Kennedy was once again in the Vice President's chair, flanked by the sergeant-at-arms on his right and the secretary of the Senate on his left. Once again, he had drawn the KP chore handed out to senatorial rookies, presiding officer at the routine sessions.

At 1:30 p.m., the Senate was deep into consideration of S. 2265, a bill to amend the Library Service Act to increase the amount of federal assistance to urban areas. Wayne Morse of Oregon pleaded that "school after school the country over does not have a library" and urged immediate passage. Jennings Randolph of West Virginia said that "the inquiring mind and the search for the truth are compensations which come to the boy and girl who use the facilities of our libraries." H. A. Williams of New Jersey said 199,000 persons in his State had no public library service. Winston L. Prouty of Vermont was grateful that large new bookmobiles purchased under the act now reach many people who would otherwise have no readily accessible library facility. Only eight senators were present and some fifty spectators were scattered throughout the galleries.

Off the Senate chamber, reached through two great doors on either side of the rostrum, is the Senate lobby which leads to the President's Room where newsmen can meet and interview the legislators who come in from the floor. Usually there is a good deal of traffic in and out of the room and lobby but that afternoon it was empty. William Langham Riedel, a six-foot-two, 200-pound press liaison officer, was in the room, reading a newspaper account of President Kennedy's visit to Texas.

Suddenly Tom Pellikaan, Riedel's assistant, burst in from the lobby. A young research assistant to Senator Morse had just read a bulletin on the Associated Press news ticker that the President had been shot in Dallas.

Riedel rushed to the machine and saw what had been printed on the yellow pre-folded paper from the black crackle-finish machine:

"President Kennedy was shot as he rode in a motorcade in Dallas. Two shots rang out. Blood was seen streaming from his head."

It was 1:42 p.m.

Riedel: "I rushed out onto the floor. The first person I saw was Spessard Holland (Florida Democrat). I told him: 'The news ticker says the President has been shot.' He looked at me amazed. Then I saw Dirksen (Sen. Everett M. Dirksen, the minority leader) and told him. He stared at me.

"Then I looked around, back where I had come from, and I saw it was Ted Kennedy presiding. He was looking down at the desk, busy with a portfolio filled with correspondence. I ran up to the rostrum and leaned over the desk. 'Senator Kennedy,' I said, 'your brother the President has been shot!'

"He looked stunned. Then he asked me how I knew and I told him.

"By this time, Senator Holland had come over behind me. Kennedy hurriedly left the rostrum and Holland slipped into the chair to take his place. I walked off the rostrum toward the lobby with Kennedy, my hand on his shoulder, saying how sorry I was and hoping it was not serious. In the lobby, he picked up a telephone just outside the Vice President's office to call the White House."

Bill Riedel, now retired to Centreville, Virginia, sits on his terrace and gazes at the Blue Ridge mountains in the distance. He can look back on many famous personages and customs in the Senate, to the days when Ellison D. (Cotten Ed) Smith would take pinches of snuff several times daily from the lacquer boxes the young page filled each morning, when shiny brass cuspidors were spotted throughout the Chamber for tobacco-chewing lawmakers, when Charles McNary of Oregon would initiate each new page with an order to rush to the Document Room for a bill-stretcher. He had seen great debates, tense votes and violent conflicts, watched the suffragettes and the bonus marchers, witnessed the defeat of the League of Nations, the creation of the TVA, the personal report of Winston Churchill on the progress of the Battle of Britain in 1941, the declaration of war against Japan and Germany. Still he can say: "In the forty-seven years I worked in the Senate, my whole working life, that was the most dramatic occurrence I had ever witnessed. Never in my lifetime had the Senate been in session when a President died. The Senators were all so shocked, so stunned; they wandered around the floor and in and out of the cloakroom and lobby aimlessly, helplessly, gathering around the radio, watching the news tickers, hoping and praying to themselves, until at last the word came that the President had died."

By this time, all Washington was telephoning and switchboards were flooded. Kennedy, unable to reach the White House, went to his office and tried again, with no success. In a borrowed car, accompanied by two aides, he drove to his house in Georgetown, listening to news bulletins on the radio. He told Joan, who had been in a beauty parlor having her hair done, and finally found a working telephone in a neighbor's house.

In an upstairs library at Hickory Hill, Bobby had heard the news of the President's death from Capt. Tazewell Shepard, the

President's naval aide, on the direct line from the White House. With Ethel at his side, Bobby had gone downstairs to tell John McCone, the director of the CIA, who had just arrived, and others who were beginning to gather at the house. When Ted called he picked up the ringing phone himself.

"He's dead," Bobby told his brother. "You'd better call your mother and our sisters."

The news had not yet reached the Senate chamber. As the Senators stood with bowed heads, Chaplain Frederick Brown Harris prayed for the President's life: "Our Father, Thou knowest that this sudden, almost unbelievable news has stunned our minds and hearts as we gaze at a vacant place against the sky, as the President of the Republic goes down like a giant cedar, green with boughs, goes down, with a great shout upon the hills, and leaves a lonesome place against the sky. We pray that in Thy will his life may still be spared. . . . Hold us, we pray, and the people of America, calm and steady and full of faith for the Republic in this tragic hour of our history. . . ."

In their brief conversation, Bobby had set the role his younger brother was to play that sorrowful weekend. As the new head of the family, Robert Kennedy would remain in Washington and supervise the arrangements for the burial of the President. He met Air Force One, the great blue and white Presidential jet when it landed at Andrews Air Force Base with the body, rushed up the ramp and embraced Jacqueline who whispered to him: "Would you come with us?" He was at her side as they drove to Bethesda Naval Hospital where the body was prepared for burial, throughout the low funeral mass in St. Matthew's Cathedral and the burial ceremony on the grassy slope across the Potomac in Arlington National Cemetery.

Ted finally got through to Hyannis Port where his mother, only moments before, had been awakened from an afternoon nap by loud squawks coming from the bedroom of her niece, Ann Gargan, down the hall. Miss Gargan, a selfless woman who had devoted her life to caring for her invalided uncle, was dressing for a visit to her sister and brother-in-law, the Richard Clasbys, then living in Detroit. A maid had heard the news on a radio and screamed upstairs: "Someone has taken a shot at the President!"

Ann and Rita Dallas, who was helping her get ready, turned on the television set. Without realizing it, they had switched the volume to full loudness and the voices of the commentators were blaring through the house.

"Please turn the TV down," Rose said in the doorway. "I'm taking a rest." Instantly Ann and Rita snapped to awareness and tried to blank out the set, but Rose had already seen and heard.

Moments later, Ted called and told her what he knew.

"I'm worried about your father," Mrs. Kennedy said. Joe Kennedy was napping. "I'll come right home," Ted replied.

Rose, her face pale, her body quivering, sat for a few seconds, looking frail and shrunken. "I've got to keep moving," she said, and returned to her room to pace the floor. After a while, she went outside and released her tensions by walking for hours on the lawn and beach.

Ted stopped in briefly at the second floor family quarters of the White House to see the President's children, Caroline and John, who had not yet been told. That night, nurse Maude Shaw was to enfold Caroline in her arms and tell her that her father had been slain; John would hear the next day. Then, with Eunice, Ted drove to National Airport where they boarded a plane for Hyannis Airport in Barnstable, arriving at 5 p.m. He was met by a band of reporters and photographers, one of whom said to him: "Senator, we apologize for being here at this time of tragedy." It was a rare and much appreciated display of courtesy. "I understand gentlemen, I understand," Kennedy told them as they snapped their pictures. He entered a waiting car with Eunice and was driven to the big house at the end of Scudder Avenue.

For almost a day, at Rose's plea, the tragedy was kept from Joe Kennedy. It was a grim game. Ted eviscerated a television set so that his father could not see and hear the continual flow of news about his dead son. To divert him, Nurse Dallas played classical music and showed part of a movie in the basement theater. She put a heavy sedative in his milk which took hold after a while and gave them a few hours more. In the morning, *The New York Times*, with its three lines of 72-point type and a black-bordered two-column picture of the slain President, was not at its accustomed place beside his plate. Ann Gargan told him that the family chauffeur didn't have time to get it that morning. At that moment, he saw Rose through the window. Just returned from St. Francis Xavier's Church in Hyannis, she was wearing a mourning veil. He moved convulsively. Watching him, Ann Gargan was convinced he knew that some great tragedy had come once again upon them.

When Ted at last blurted out the story soon after breakfast, they both wept. That "Kennedys don't cry" is one of the most enduring myths about the family. Though they appear in public under tight emotional control, in the privacy of their own homes they cried, Ethel and Rose and Jacqueline cried, and father and son cried on that leaden, rain-threatening morning in the ambassador's bedroom. A few doors down, out of the ambassador's sight, Dr. Russell S. Boles Jr., a Boston neurologist, and several special nurses were standing by, ready to rush to his aid if the shock proved too much for his weakened heart. But Joe was still strong enough. There was no need for the doctor.

With his mother and Eunice, Ted attended the 8 a.m. mass at the white clapboard St. Francis Xavier Church. He and Eunice sat in a pew; Rose prayed in a side chapel, before an altar dedicated to her firstborn, Lt. Joseph P. Kennedy Jr. Later in the day, Rose, Ted and Eunice drove to the Hyannis Airport for the flight to Washington. Here Ted spoke briefly to newsmen, expressing appreciation for the outpouring of thoughtfulness and prayers that had come from all Americans. "This has been a source of tremendous consolation to both my parents," he said, "and they wanted me to express their great thanks to all of the people who have been so kind in remembering them now."

The next day, with Jackie and Robert, he marched the five blocks at the head of the procession toward St. Matthew's, behind the flag-draped casket on the caisson drawn by three pairs of matched greys, the right row saddled but riderless. Directly in back of the casket, a saddled horse — boots reversed in the stirrups as a sign of the rider's death — stepped skittishly. Ahead of the caisson, the drums beat the cadence, 100 steps to the minute; behind them massed 200 kings, queens, emperors and prime ministers from more than 100 nations, the greatest assemblage of world dignitaries ever to gather in the nation's capital.

At Arlington across the Potomac, after fifty F-105 military jets had flown by, after Air Force One roared past, dipping its wing in final farewell, after a 21-gun Presidential salute, after the sounding of taps and the benediction by Richard Cardinal

Cushing, after the presentation to Jacqueline Kennedy of the folded flag that had covered the coffin, the President's body was committed to earth.

There was one final moment. A lighted taper was handed to Mrs. Kennedy to ignite the eternal flame she had requested at her husband's burial place. She brushed it against the tubing through which propane gas flowed and it blazed up. She handed the taper to Bobby, who touched the light.

Ted was the last to take the slender rod and hold it to the flame in a symbolic gesture to keep it burning.

Nobody on the silent hillside that crisp and clear afternoon could foresee that, before the decade had run its course, this final gesture by the youngest Kennedy could have profound meaning.

3. Comeback from Grief

Less than four months later, Edward Kennedy marched through South Boston in the annual St. Patrick's Day parade, his step jaunty, his smile bright. He waved to the crowds lining the curbs and they shouted back their greetings. Later, he mingled with the local pols at campaign manager Gerry Doherty's annual open house, joking with them and tossing off one or two to honor the Saint on his day.

A few hundred miles away, in Scranton, Pennsylvania, his brother Bobby also marched in a parade, then addressed 1,200 members of the Lackawanna County Friendly Sons of St. Patrick. For the conclusion of his brief talk, Bobby had chosen to recite a ballad written by the Irish-American poet and journalist John Boyle O'Reilly about the death of Owen Roe O'Neill, the great seventeenth century fighter for Irish independence.

For hours in Washington he had rehearsed the lines, not heeding a warning from his press aide, Edwin O. Guthman, that he'd never get through it without breaking up. "I can't yet," Bobby had admitted, "but I will by the time I speak."

In his flat, nasal tones, before a hushed audience, Bobby spoke the lament written by O'Reilly:

> Oh, why did you leave us, Owen?
> Why did you die?

Your troubles are all over,
You're at rest with God on high,
But we're slaves and we're orphans, Owen!
Why did you die?

We're sheep without a shepherd,
When the snow shuts out the sky —
Oh! Why did you leave us, Owen?
Why did you die?

The actions of the brothers on the same holiday dramatizes the differences in their recovery from the assassination of John Kennedy. After the funeral, Bobby was plunged into a melancholy that deepened as the months went on. Margaret Laing, a biographer, wrote: "With the death of John Kennedy every personal and public pleasure, every personal and public hope, every personal and public ambition, seemed to have come to an end for his brother." He would sit in an armchair and stare for hours out of a window; he would come to work at the Department of Justice, remain a few hours, then abruptly depart. "His eyes bore a haunted look," Nick Thimmesch and William Johnson wrote. A close friend reported that he was even wondering about the existence of God. So deep was his gloom that he could say to his family and co-workers that "in a few weeks the Kennedys will be forgotten in this country."

Ted was equally distraught in the first terrible weeks. On the day the President died, Luella Hennessey, the Kennedy nurse, had gone to the White House to be with Jackie and to help Maude Shaw with Caroline and John. She saw Ted when he went to the nursery.

Miss Hennessey: "He was so overwhelmed, so shocked he could barely speak. He came to me and kissed me and he said 'Lulu, it's nice to have you here.' His face was so white and so drawn. I got the feeling that if he said any more he would break down and cry."

Immediately after the rites Bobby went into seclusion at Hickory Hill, but Ted flew to Hyannis Port to be with his parents and the children for a sorrowful Thanksgiving Day dinner. The following day, he planned to take the children, including Caroline and John, skating at the public rink the Kennedys had donated to Hyannis Port as a memorial to Joe junior. A heavy rainstorm, however, washed out the idea;

instead, he took them all for a short drive into the country. In the afternoon, the family gathered in the large living room as the fog shrouded the house and the rains lashed the panes, alone with their sorrow.

By mid-December, Ted was back at work in Washington, dining with Bobby often and, when he did not see him, talking with him on the telephone. He, along with Ethel and other close friends, became increasingly worried at his older brother's ominously deepening depression, which was to last until early summer and from which, according to Jack Newfield, the liberal journalist, he was never to recover completely.

Two factors account for Ted's faster recovery:

His nature is essentially sunny, Bobby's was more intense and emotional. "Bobby tended to react to events with his guts, Teddy with his head," one friend says.

Bobby had submerged himself totally as he became involved in his older brother's work and career. William V. Shannon wrote: "They were almost like two bodies with a single brain," and the closeness was even more apparent within the family circle than outside it. One friend put it this way. "When you hit Jack, Bobby winces." Richard N. Goodwin, a speech writer for the two elder Kennedys, says: "His brother John was, while he lived, his teacher, friend, and idol, the center of his life." It is not surprising that, because of this total involvement, the cruel and sudden loss would leave Bobby shattered. Ted, on the other hand, worshipped John but, because of the fifteen-year gap in their ages, was not as wholly involved.

One fact seems to have gone unnoticed: The thought that all the Kennedys were foreordained to perish in some similar manner began haunting Bobby. In 1964, when he was deciding on the race for the Senate in New York, he stopped in the midst of a discussion and said despairingly: "I don't know that it makes any difference what I do. Maybe we're all doomed anyway."

Five years later, the same despairing thought was to occur to Ted Kennedy.

X

Two Triumphs

1. Maiden Speech

Like a first date, a senator's first major address on the floor is a milestone in his career that will be remembered painfully or fondly depending on the warmth of the response.

For Ted Kennedy, the event occurred in the midst of a busy springtime. Not only was he flying to Massachusetts frequently to work on the organization of his fall campaign for reelection, but he was accepting more and more invitations for speeches in other parts of the country. In March he made a swing through the midwest, covering five states in four days. In April, he made Jefferson Day and Jackson Day addresses, traditional Democratic fund-raising occasions, in Philadelphia and Indianapolis. He was scheduled for talks in Wyoming and Oregon in early Summer. The step-up in activity aroused speculation that he was, this early, establishing a political organization. Kennedy replied that such talk was without foundation, that he was merely responding to requests by the National Democratic Committee and by friends running for office.

Some Kennedy biographies have erroneously stated that Ted's maiden speech was devoted to a denunciation of the Civil Aeronautics Board for cancelling Northeast Airlines's temporary certification to fly between New York and Miami. Since the airline employed some 1,200 Massachusetts constituents, the speech was denounced as an effort to keep getting more for Massachusetts. While Teddy did indeed make a statement on the airlines's behalf, it was but one of several brief talks he made on the floor. His first major address, delivered on April 8, 1964, fourteen months after he became a senator, was on behalf of the Civil Rights Bill, the most far-reaching measure of its kind in American history. Sent to the Hill in June of 1963 by President Kennedy, it would outlaw discrimination in public accommodations and allow all who were denied service to bring suit in a Federal court; it would strengthen voting rights by barring unequal application of registration requirements, authorize the Department of Justice to file desegration suits against schools and colleges, ban discrimination in federally assisted programs and establish a Commission on Equal Employment Opportunity to investigate all complaints.

Presenting the measure to Congress, the President had written: "I . . . ask every member of Congress to set aside sectional and political ties, and to look at this issue from the viewpoint of the nation. I ask you to look into your hearts — not in search of charity, for the Negro neither wants nor needs condescension — but for the one plain, proud and priceless quality that unites us all as Americans: a sense of justice."

By the time Kennedy left for his journey to Dallas, the bill was still in the House Rules Committee. After the assassination, President Lyndon Johnson put his full strength behind it but the going was rough. Eventually the House passed it, but a bitter floor fight began on the Senate floor. After Hubert Humphrey, floor manager for the bill, had argued for three and one-half hours for the "long overdue legislation;" after California's Thomas Kuchel, the Republican whip, had pleaded from the other side of the aisle that the issue should not be "a partisan fight but an American fight," the young senator from Massachusetts spoke. Joan, Ethel, Jean Smith and some of their children were in the gallery as he began:

"Mr. President, it is with some hesitation that I rise to speak on the pending legislation before the Senate. A freshman senator should be seen, not heard; should learn, and not teach. This is especially true when the Senate is engaged in a truly momentous debate. . . .

"I had planned, about this time in the session, to make my maiden speech in the Senate on issues affecting industry and employment in my home state. . . . But I could not follow this debate for the last four weeks — I could not see this issue envelop the emotions and the conscience of the nation — without changing my mind. To limit myself to local issues in the face of this great national question, would be to demean the seat in which I sit. . . . "

The basic problem, he said, was adjustment to the realities, that Negroes "are going to be members of the community of American citizens, with the same rights and responsibilities as every one of us." Massachusetts, he asserted, has been making this kind of adjustment for 300 years, absorbing "every nationality group from Puritans to Poles to Puerto Ricans," and "we have not suffered from the effort."

"In 1780," he said, "a Catholic in Massachusetts was not allowed to vote or hold public office. In 1840, an Irishman could not get a job above that of common laborer. In 1910, a Jew could not stay in places of public accommodation in the Berkshire Mountains.

"It is true, as has been said on this floor, that prejudice exists in the minds and hearts of men. It cannot be eradicated by law. But I firmly believe a sense of fairness and good-will also exists in the minds and hearts of men, side by side with the prejudice; a sense of fairness and good-will which shows itself so often in acts of charity and kindness toward others. This noble characteristic wants to come out. It wants to, and often does, win out against the prejudice. Law, expressing as it does the moral conscience of the community, can help it come out in every person, so in the end the prejudice will be dissolved."

Toward the close, he cited some personal reasons for his deep interest in passage of the bill. "As a young man," he said, "I want to see an America where everyone can make his contribution, where a man will be measured not by the color of his skin but by the content of his character. . . . I remember the words of President Johnson last November 27: 'No memorial oration or eulogy could more eloquently honor President Kennedy's memory than the earliest possible passage of the Civil Rights Bill for which he fought so long.' "

At this point, the young senator's voice broke. He lowered his head and paused for several seconds. In the gallery, Joan Kennedy leaned forward as she watched him intently. The chamber was hushed.

Kennedy resumed speaking but his voice, until this point strong and clear, was low and strained.

"My brother was the first President of the United States to state publicly that segregation was morally wrong. His heart and his soul are in this bill. If his life and death had a meaning, it was that we should not hate but love one another; we should use our powers not to create conditions of oppression that lead to violence, but conditions of freedom that lead to peace.

"It is in this spirit that I hope the Senate will pass this bill."

When he finished speaking, several senators rose and went to his rear-row desk to congratulate him. Paul H. Douglas of Illinois took the floor to call the address "magnificent." Douglas said: "I have never heard an address of a more truly noble and elevated tone. . . . Not only should the whole State of Massachusetts be grateful for what he has said, but I believe the whole nation also is grateful to him." Morse of Oregon, calling it a "truly great speech," said Kennedy "has moved us deeply, both emotionally and intellectually. When the news of this great speech goes across the nation, it will move the American people deeply too." Humphrey commended and thanked him, "not for his speech but also for his steadfastness of purpose and his willingness to be present during these difficult, trying days in handling the chores of managing certain parts of the Bill, which continue day after day."

As the senators rose, one after the other, to commend Kennedy, Joan was weeping openly in the gallery.

2. Sentimental Journey

Late in May, Edward made a private nine-country European swing to raise funds for the proposed Kennedy Library, which was to be built in Cambridge. On May 29, the forty-seventh birthday of the President, he arrived in Ireland. It turned out to be a sentimental journey, sorrowful and joyful, recalling in the wild enthusiasm of the crowds the visit his brother had made eleven months earlier to the land of the family's origins.

The President had literally wowed the Irish with his charm and good-humored sallies — insisting that Dave Powers looked more Irish than his own cousins, archly wondering if the Scotch salmon that kinswoman Mary Ryan was serving for luncheon had been caught illegally, introducing Monsignor O'Mahoney, who accompanied the Presidential party, as the pastor of a "poor humble flock in Palm Beach, Florida."

Ted was no head of state but he was a Kennedy and the brother of the dead President. When he spoke, it was with the voice of the President, the same flat, New England tones they had heard and cheered the other springtime. For the Irish, Ted Kennedy was transformed for the twenty-four hours of his visit into the President himself, and they poured out their emotions to him.

Kennedy was met at the Dublin airport by Prime Minister Sean Lemass and escorted to the city behind a six-man motorcycle squad. Crowds waved at intersections as the limousine sped by, teenage girls screamed, bus drivers allowed passengers to get out and wave. A native, watching from a tavern, was moved to remark: "Aren't they treating him like a bloody Beatle, now, God love him?"

The motorcycle squad wheeled up to St. Mary's Procathedral at Cathedral and Marleborough Streets, where Kennedy was to attend a memorial mass. A vast crowd had gathered in front of the huge Gothic church. Hands grabbed at him as he emerged from the limousine and pushed, smiling, through the throng. It was five minutes before he could reach the doors. One aide said: "You could feel the emotion in the crowd. They saw in Teddy a reincarnation of the President. This laying on of hands, the incredible need to touch, was overwhelming."

It was worse forty-five minutes later when Teddy emerged. The crowds had grown and the demonstration was as wild as in any political campaign. In an impromptu speech, Ted said: "Today is a day of joy and sadness for me. Joy because I am in Ireland on a beautiful spring day, sadness because today is the President's birthday. My brother will not be able to come back and enjoy any more spring days here."

Kennedy's voice faltered and his voice broke. The crowd, seconds before shouting and screaming, fell utterly silent. Ted's eyes filled with tears. Sobs were heard in the crowd. "In all the time I've known him, I've never seen Ted as deeply moved," said William vanden Heuvel, then a special assistant to Attorney General Robert Kennedy who accompanied him on the trip. "He just stopped."

In a few seconds, Kennedy regained control and ended his brief remarks on a light note.

"Today is the President's birthday and if he were here, he

would want you to enjoy yourselves. If he were here, he would tell you that the little spaniel, Shannon, and Leprechaun, are doing very well." (The Irish people had presented the dog and pony to the President on his 1963 visit.) Laughter dispelled the sorrow; the throng cheered and Kennedy entered the presbytery for a reception.

In the gardens of the United States Embassy, Edward Behr reported in the *Saturday Evening Post*, a waiter suddenly approached Ted and, with simple eloquence, told him of Ireland's grief at his brother's passing and assured him that all their love and all their hopes had now been passed on to him. Vanden Heuvel, who saw the incident, turned away "because it was a moment so emotional that he had to have it by himself." At City Hall, he was made a Freeman of the city. Outside, he was mobbed by a screaming, jumping crowd. Next morning, on the way to Shannon airport, throngs appeared as word spread that Ted Kennedy was stopping at a pub. At Adare, in north central County Limerick, he visited his mother's family for a rousing lunch. Edward Behr reports that Ted greeted a cousin, Jim Hogan, nearing ninety, with the observation: "You look like my grandpa, Honey Fitz, only thinner." Jim replied: "You bet I'm thinner. I probably worked harder!" Later, in the city of Limerick on the Shannon River, he stood on a hotel balcony and spoke to 40,000 persons who listened quietly and, when he finished, screamed their goodbyes.

Flying home, Kennedy was plainly tired but, at the same time, exhilarated. He had seen at firsthand that his brother — whose picture hung in many homes, next to those of Pope Paul — had been virtually sanctified by the Irish.

There had now been two moments of triumph — his successful maiden speech and now this affirmation of his own place in Irish hearts.

For Kennedys, triumph is never far removed from tragedy.

While he was across the Atlantic, Joan was admitted to Georgetown University Hospital: complications had developed in her pregnancy. Soon, she suffered her second miscarriage. Ted returned immediately to comfort his wife.

XI

Flight of the Aero-Commander

1. Apple Blossoms in the Clouds

As evening fell on Friday, June 19, the great debate on the civil rights measure entered its final hours on the Senate floor before a hushed and crowded gallery.

As soon as the voting ended, Kennedy would be off. A small plane was waiting at Washington's National Airport to fly him to Springfield where the Democratic State primary convention had opened the evening before. Some 1,730 delegates and 5,000 spectators had jammed the vast Coliseum on the sprawling Eastern States Exposition grounds in West Springfield for the political battles that would determine party control in Massachusetts for the next two years.

It was an important event in Massachusetts politics, especially important for Kennedy. He was expected to be nominated by acclamation at the Friday evening session and had planned to enter the hall afterward to deliver a triumphant address. The convention was also scheduled to hear a keynote speech by Sen. Birch Bayh who was to fly with Kennedy to Springfield that afternoon.

At one o'clock that afternoon, Edward Moss, Kennedy's husky young administrative assistant, had made arrangements for the flight. Daniel Hogan, an Andover industrialist, had flown the senator to fund-raising affairs on three of the five preceding weekends in his private plane, a two-engine Aero-Commander 680. Moss telephoned Hogan in Andover and asked if he could come down to pick up the senator and take him to the convention.

Hogan, unable to come himself because he was planning to attend a 25th class reunion at Yale, sent the plane with 48-year-old Edwin T. Zimny of Lawrence, Massachusetts, a veteran pilot. Zimny took off from the Lawrence Municipal Airport, reached Washington at 4 p.m. and called Kennedy's office. He would be waiting, he said, at the Butler Aviation operations office, a half-mile from the passenger terminal.

The hours passed. Finally, at 7:40 p.m., the Senate began its momentous balloting. Ten minutes later, by a vote of 73 to 27, the Civil Rights Bill had passed. Kennedy strode back to his office where he was to meet Senator Bayh and his wife, Marvella, who was to accompany them to Springfield.

Moss got their bags together and, as they left, remarked to Kennedy: "You should make some kind of spectacular entrance into the convention."

"What do you want me to do," Ted asked, "crack up the airplane?"

"Nope," Moss grinned, "just parachute out of it into the convention." Kennedy laughed. Downstairs, a car was waiting to take them to the airport.

At 8:25, the party boarded the white, red-striped six-passenger plane and ten minutes later, Zimny took off for the routine hour and 20-minute flight to Barnes Airport in Westfield, seven miles from Springfield. Moss sat in the co-pilot's seat to Zimny's right. Kennedy was behind them, facing away as in the jump seat of a taxi; the Bayhs were opposite him.

At Washington the skies had been clear enough, but heavier weather was expected to the north. By nine, flying conditions were marginal at Barnes, with only an 800-foot ceiling, two and a half-mile visibility and a light rain falling.

Switching to instrument flight because of the murky going, Zimny flew north into Massachusetts then hooked west and south toward Barnes. Nearing the field, he established contact with the control tower where Eugene Prouix, the chief operator, instructed him to report when he was over Easthampton, some ten miles to the north. At Easthampton, Zimny radioed: "We are over the Z marker" — meaning he was precisely on course.

Five miles ahead was the runway, which had been newly extended to 9,000 feet. Ahead, too, was a hill which rose 300 feet above the landing field. Zimny began descending at the approved rate of 500 feet a minute.

To Birch Bayh, peering out, "it was flying through a black void."

Kennedy loosened his seat belt so that he could twist around and watch the pilot make the instrument landing.

The plane sat lower and lower. Bayh now saw something, white clouds on both sides.

Suddenly the craft broke through the overcast. The "white clouds" were apple blossoms, clearly visible as the plane skimmed through the tops of trees in an apple orchard, only a few dozen feet from the ground.

Zimny tried desperately to gain altitude, but the plane was too heavy to reverse direction as quickly as the emergency demanded. Rebelling against the sudden shift of forces, the plane shuddered violently. And then it fell.

To Kennedy, the last seconds felt like a toboggan slide. Realizing a crash was imminent, he tightened his seat belt and sat down, facing the Bayhs. Nobody spoke. A second later, the plane dived between two apple trees. Parts of both wings were sheared off and the top of the cabin ripped back. The plane struck the ground, somersaulted and plowed 75 yards through the orchard, finally coming to rest with its nose against one apple tree and its tail crushed against another. The impact crushed the cockpit like a tin can, bent the fuselage in two. By some eerie chance, the red tail light continued to rotate. It pointed skyward from the demolished plane, circling slowly in the wet night.

At the moment of impact, Birch Bayh, who thought the plane had been struck by lightning, was convinced "it was the end of our life here on earth."

Kennedy was thrown against the ceiling, feet first. Bayh, the first to recover, called out to his wife: "Are you all right?" She replied in a weak voice: "Yes, I'm all right." Then Bayh called Kennedy who could hear him but was unable to answer.

Kennedy lay on his back in the twisted wreckage of the cabin. Bayh, looking at him, was certain he was dead. "He lay there, inert and motionless," he said afterward. "I was sure he was gone."

Bayh, whose entire left side seemed paralyzed, pushed Marvella through a safety hatch on the right side of the cabin, then reached over and tried to pull Kennedy out but couldn't. He climbed from the cabin and, unable to stand on his left leg, hopped to the front of the plane. Zimny and Moss lay motionless and bloody, jammed inside the crumpled metal of the cockpit.

Suddenly Bayh became aware of a strong smell of gasoline. "Fire!" he thought with horror. He muttered something to Marvella about the possibility that the plane's wreckage might explode into flames at any moment. Inside, Ted heard but was unable to move. Bayh hopped back to the cabin and yelled once again to Kennedy, who had managed to crawl face down toward the window. Bayh reached in and tried to pull him out but his left arm was useless. Kennedy locked his arms, the fist of his right hand grasping the wrist of his left, encircled Bayh's neck and was slowly pulled from the cabin.

Kennedy was now conscious and able to talk. Unable to move from the waist down, realizing he might have been seriously injured, he asked Bayh to let him remain where he was.

"One of the little things I remember," Bayh said afterward, "is that a flashlight in the plane had been lighted by the crash and was shining up from a seat pocket. I got it and looked for something to cover Senator Kennedy with."

A few minutes earlier Robert Scheuer, forty years old, had backed his dairy truck from the driveway of his home on East Street and was heading down the block when he heard the Aero-Commander's engines. They sounded close but normal enough and he paid no attention until the sudden, loud thud came from the hillside.

He jammed on the brakes. Up on the slope he could see the red beacon on the plane's tail circling slowly. Scheuer leaped from his car and ran through the wet blackness toward the wreck. On the hillside, he met the Bayhs, who had just started to go for help.

Scheuer took off his raincoat and covered Kennedy who, though dazed and in considerable pain, was asking about Marvella and the others. "See that she is taken care of," he told Scheuer. Kennedy asked for water, a sign of approaching shock.

Scheuer, too, was unable to reach Zimny and Moss. He helped the Bayhs down the hill where they tried to flag down passing motorists. Ten cars roared by without stopping. Scheuer rushed 800 yards to his house where he called police and firemen, grabbed pillows and blankets and raced back to the orchard. Back on the hill, Scheuer and the Bayhs covered Ted. "He was lying there on the wet grass," Scheuer remembers, "cool as a cucumber, worrying about Mrs. Bayh and the others and asking us not to move him until help came."

Minutes later, emergency crews and ambulances began arriving.

At two minutes past midnight, the first ambulance drew up at the emergency entrance to Cooley Dickinson Hospital in Northampton, north of the apple orchard. Edward Moss, inert on a stretcher, was taken inside where a team of three nurses, two technicians and two doctors tried for four hours to save him. He died at 6:15 a.m. of massive brain injuries on the operating table. Ed Zimny was dead in the cockpit.

Seconds after Moss reached the hospital, Marvella and Birch Bayh arrived and were rushed into an emergency treatment room. Bayh, completely coherent, asked someone to call his father, a retired school teacher, in Washington, and to inform Ted's family in Hyannis Port.

"Both Marvella and I," he said afterward, "had this severe pain in the hip muscles from the seat belt when we were catapulted forward. It saved our lives." The Bayhs were to remain at the hospital only a week.

Moments later, the ambulance bearing Ted Kennedy reached the hospital. Dr. Thomas Corriden, seventy-year-old senior surgeon, and Fay Bodner, the night supervisor, were waiting at the emergency entrance. The stretcher was wheeled into Emergency Room One where Ted's clothing was cut off. By this time, his face was ashen and he had lapsed into semi-consciousness. His blood pressure was dangerously low, indicating profound shock. A transfusion was begun and anti-shock treatment started.

Inside the Coliseum on the fair grounds, the delegates had begun balloting for the candidate the party would endorse in the gubernatorial primaries. As voting progressed, a first-ballot victory for Gov. Endicott Peabody over his opponent, Lt. Gov. Francis X. Bellotti, appeared certain.

Though the hour was late, the delegates were in a jubilant mood. John E. Powers, the permanent chairman, had announced that Kennedy and Bayh were on the way and they were planning an uproarious welcome. The evening before, at the traditional convention banquet, Joan Kennedy had spoken a few breathless words, completely charming them. Ted, addressing them by phone line from Washington, had pleaded: "Don't nominate Joan until I get there!"

Almost at midnight, the first bulletin came, flashed to the city room of the Springfield *Union* where an editor called its representatives on the floor. Chairman Powers, told by a newsman what had happened, was thunderstruck. He banged his gavel for silence and, to a hushed convention, said that Kennedy's plane had crashed somewhere near Springfield and that the senator was still alive.

The announcement was greeted with shock and horror. Many women delegates and spectators began to weep. Delegates crowded ten deep around the press section, seeking information. Five minutes later, Powers had another bulletin in his hand. The first report, he said, was erroneous — there had been a plane crash, but it was not the Kennedy plane. "The Kennedy plane is still aloft," he said. The convention hall rocked with cheers.

But even as he was speaking, more bulletins were being received in the press section from newspaper offices, and Powers once again faced the delegates. "It now appears," he said, "that the first announcement was correct, that Kennedy is hospitalized, but is not in serious condition."

Governor Peabody won the endorsement, 1,259 to 377, but did not make the customary appearance on the floor. At 12:20, after a moment of silent prayer, John Powers adjourned the convention and the delegates, many in tears, filed out.

Joan Kennedy had gone to the home of old friends, Irene and Donald Dowd on Hale Street in Springfield, planning to take off for the convention site fifteen miles away as soon as Ted arrived. But so many cars were patrolling the street to catch a glimpse of her that the Dowds spirited her out to the vacant home of the Alan Biaradis not far away. Jack Crimmins, the Kennedy's chauffeur, remained downstairs while Joan went into a bedroom to rest.

Irene Dowd, who was a convention delegate, was hovering near the platform when the news came. Gerry Doherty, spotting her in the crush, pushed to her side and said: "Ted's been taken to Cooley Dick. Get Joan over there as soon as possible."

Wide World

1964. Senator Edward Kennedy with Pope Paul VI in his library in Vatican City.

1964. His face contorted in pain, Ted Kennedy is carried from the wreckage of the plane (below) after the accident which killed two and seriously injured the senator.
United Press International

United Press International

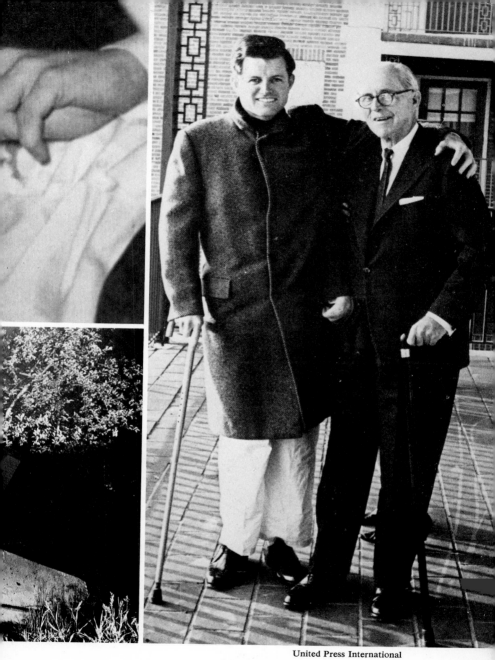

United Press International

1964. Six months after his accident, Ted Kennedy takes his first few steps in the company of his father.

United Press International

1966. Dr. Martin Luther King and Charles Evers, then Mississippi NAACP field director, greet Senator Kennedy on his arrival in Jackson, Mississippi.

1969. President Nixon shares the spotlight with Senator Kennedy at the White House. In the center is Mrs. Bruce B. Benson, national president of The League of Women Voters.

United Press International

United Press International

Ted and Joan leave St. Vincent's Church after attending the funeral mass celebrated for Mary Jo Kopechne (above) who was killed in the auto accident with the Senator.

United Press International

SINK OR SAIL

Ben Roth Agency

Ben Roth Agency

Wide World

1970. Senator Robert C. Byrd of West Virginia who, in a surprise upset, displaced Ted Kennedy as whip in the Senate. Between them is Senator Mike Mansfield of Montana.

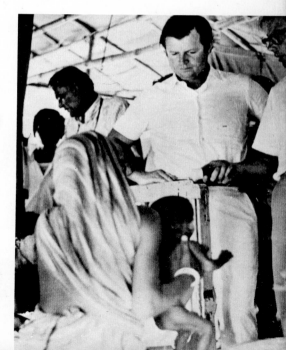

1971. A somber Ted Kennedy in India viewing the plight of East Pakistani refugees. Wide World

Wide World

1970. Ted Kennedy with his family announcing that he would stand for re-election to his Senate seat, and renouncing any aspirations for the Presidency in 1972. From left to right are Kara, 10; Ted Jr., 8; Patrick, 2; and Joan.

Mrs. Dowd: "I drove over to the Biaradi house and got there just as Joan was coming down the stairs. Jack Crimmins had heard the news on the radio and told her there had been an accident. She was white-faced but under control. She asked me if I knew any more but I had no other news. Don drove up and the four of us got into the Kennedy car and raced through the fog and drizzle to Cooley Dick, a half hour away. Joan kept repeating over and over: 'I'm sure he's all right . . . I just know he'll be all right.' Funny, but nobody thought of turning on the radio."

When Joan arrived, Ted had already been taken upstairs. "Hi, Joansie," he greeted her, "don't worry." Joan was given a room on the same floor where the Dowds and two Kennedy cousins, Joe Gargan and Robert Fitzgerald, remained with her for about an hour. Joan was dry-eyed and still under control, still telling everyone: "I know he'll be all right."

The family and close friends rushed to the hospital from all over. At Hyannis Port, Bobby Kennedy was asleep when the call came. Almost as soon as he had finished dressing, a State police car, requested by an aide, was waiting in the driveway. Bobby and his sister, Jean Smith, raced the 160 miles in silence, reaching Northampton at 4:15. Pat Lawford, who was in Pittsburgh, caught a plane and arrived at dawn. Kenny O'Donnell, in San Francisco with President Johnson, flew to the bedside.

In the morning, Joan called Cardinal Cushing who told her he already knew. His asthma had kept him awake and he had heard the news at 3:30. The cardinal told Joan he had said Mass for Ted and was planning to drive to the hospital that day. Later in the morning, President Johnson would call Robert Kennedy for a report on Ted and to express his concern. Jacqueline Kennedy would visit on Sunday, then return several more times.

By mid-morning, twenty members of the Kennedy clan had reached the hospital. Gathered in the coffee shop, they talked in low voices about the latest tragedy. Joan's face was white and drawn; she wore no makeup and her eyes were red. Bobby, hair disheveled, tie askew, sipped a bowl of hot vegetable soup and said to his sister Pat who had never made a secret of her fear of flying: "I guess you've got the right idea." To Jimmy Breslin, a journalist and friend, he said: "I guess the only reason we've survived is that there are too many of us. There are more of us than there is trouble."

Later, Bobby walked in a park adjoining the hospital with his press secretary, Edwin Guthman. "I just don't see how I can do anything now," he said. "I think I should just get out of it all." He paused. "Somebody up there doesn't like us," he said and walked silently back to the hospital.

Despite Joan's confidence, Kennedy was in grave condition. He was in deep shock. A lung had been punctured. There was evidence of severe internal bleeding. And many bones, including his spine, had been fractured.

In Emergency Room One, and later in the intensive care unit one flight up, Dr. Corriden and his staff worked to determine the extent of his injuries. The fifth and sixth ribs on the left side were broken. The second, third and fourth lumbar vertebrae, in the lower back, were cracked, along with the second, third and fourth transverse processes. Dr. Corriden explained that these were outpouchings of the spine which give it support. Ted had cuts and bruises on his legs and a six-inch gash on his right hand.

Perhaps most serious of all was the internal hemorrhaging. If organs had ruptured — the spleen and left kidney were suspected — emergency surgery, perilous in his weakened condition, would be essential.

Kennedy was given blood during the night and morning. His injured lung was collapsed to help his breathing and, with breathing tubes inserted into his nostrils, he was placed in an oxygen tent. He was in considerable pain, but for eighteen hours he had been given no sedatives because doctors wanted to trace the source of the bleeding, and pain is one of the surest indicators.

By evening, the doctors found the source of the bleeding: broken vessels near the left kidney and spleen, but not the organs themselves. No surgery would be needed. By the beginning of the second day, Kennedy learned that his broken back, though serious, would not result in paralysis. "It was my third vertebra that was hit worst," he said later. "It was pushed sideways. Fortunately, that's below where the nerves branch out to your legs. If the injury had been just an inch higher, it would have severed my spinal cord and I would have been crippled for life." After he found his legs would be all right, he said, he was never worried. "I had a goal in life," he said. "I would walk again by Christmas."

John Kennedy had suffered a similar injury, first in 1939

while playing football and later during World War II when a Japanese destroyer rammed and sank his PT-boat 109 in the Pacific. In 1964, Kennedy had almost died following a spinal fusion operation.

For almost three weeks, Ted remained at Cooley Dickinson, immobilized in a Foster frame, a metal tubing and canvas device which keeps a patient's spine rigid during the period of healing. More than 40,000 letters, 700 telegrams and hundreds of gifts came from all over the world. Pope Paul cabled a blessing and a hope for speedy recovery. Joe Kennedy, despite his disabling stroke, drove down for a visit.

For the first three weeks, the pain, as even Dr. Corriden admitted, was excruciating, but Kennedy kept his good humor, though it could not have been easy. When the doctor told him how well he was doing, he responded wryly with an old joke about a boxer who was receiving an unmerciful beating in the ring. Between rounds his handlers encouraged him with: "You're doing great. He ain't laid a glove on you!" Whereupon the fighter muttered through bloodied lips: "Then somebody keep an eye on the referee, because somebody out there is beating the daylights out of me!"

2. Life as a Human Rotisserie

On July 9, the frame was bolted to the floor of an Army ambulance and, in an agonizingly slow journey, transported 100 miles to the New England Baptist Hospital on Parker Hill Avenue in Roxbury, a Boston suburb. Doctors had offered him the choice: Boston or Walter Reed Hospital in Bethesda, Maryland. Kennedy chose his home state. "After all," he said, "I'm running for office there." Even before he arrived, four telephone lines were installed in his fifth floor corner suite.

From this command post, prone on an orthopedic Stryker frame, Kennedy conducted his campaign for the Senate. Lyndon Johnson called every week, asking: "How's my campaign doin' up there, Teddy?" It was doing fine — Joan, Rose and the other Kennedy women, jumping once more into the breach, raced up and down Boston and across the state, stumping for him.

Late in August, after having been eliminated from consideration as a vice presidential candidate on Johnson's ticket, Bobby

Kennedy announced from the steps of Gracie Mansion that he would run for the Senate in New York, a decision not unanimously cheered. Even friendly biographers Nick Thimmesch and William Johnson wrote: "It was audacious of Kennedy to run for the Senate in New York. He was an authentic carpetbagger. While his publicity proclaimed he had spent twelve of his first thirteen years in the state, he was still a son of his native Massachusetts. He waited, in fact, until the day before the Democratic National convention opened in Atlantic City before he resigned as a member of the Massachusetts delegation. He was a registered voter in Barnstable, Massachusetts, until October 15, when he removed his name from the voting lists." As a result of his quick-change tactics, Bobby was ineligible to vote in New York for himself, or in Massachusetts for his brother Teddy.

Nonetheless, on September 1, Bobby won the nomination and he was off and running hard. Ted, from his hospital bed, warned: "Bobby is going to have to run on his own. Our mother is already committed to my campaign. I asked her first." It hardly appeared, though, that Bobby would really need Rose: the polls predicted he would easily defeat the incumbent Kenneth Keating.

Life in the frame was at best frustrating, at worst barely endurable. He lay prone, able to move only his head, hands and feet. Every three hours during the day two husky attendants rotated him from one side to the other to prevent bed sores, prompting him to observe that he felt like "a human rotisserie." He ate all his meals face down, his forehead supported on a rubber bar. "Nights were the worst," he would recall afterward. "They'd turn out the lights and I'd say good night to everyone and fall right to sleep. Then I'd wake up and always be surprised that daylight wasn't shining in the window. I'd switch on a light and discover I'd been asleep for 30 minutes. . . . I would lie there for two or three hours before I drifted off, then I'd wake up again in a half-hour or so. I never really slept the whole night through."

Once in September, a nurse tiptoed into his room at 1 a.m. when a special visitor showed up and found him wide awake. Lyndon Johnson had come to call. The President remained for an hour, talking politics.

The first week, Joan remained at the hospital, thereafter

visited daily. Kara, then four, and Teddy junior, three, came frequently, bringing live frogs (in a bottle), dead caterpillars and flies, mounted leaves and, on occasion, home movies of themselves. Rose visited once a month and Bobby and the other Kennedys popped in often.

Days were never boring. He answered many of the 200 letters that arrived each morning, made an average of fifty telephone calls daily, and even took up painting from this prone position, turning out still lifes, winter scenes and sailing pictures, all from memory. He shaved, read and watched television by means of a sloping mirror above his head. He had a half-hour physical therapy session each morning with Mrs. Birte Thomasen and faithfully followed her instructions for exercises throughout the day — ankle rotating, foot-wiggling, knee-flexing. He conferred constantly with aides and gave interviews. Reporter Theodore Irwin recalls: "When I saw him in November, he was on his belly on the porch. When he spoke, he had to raise his head and turn awkwardly toward me, and I had to put my face close to his to catch his words. Yet he was amazingly cheerful and buoyant."

Kennedy showed Irwin a letter he had just received from Sen. George McGovern which, he said, made a deep impression on him. McGovern had written that he prayed for Ted's full and swift recovery primarily because he had sensed the "call to greatness that is stirring within you." McGovern wrote he always believed that personal suffering played a role in the rise to greatness of such men as Abraham Lincoln, Franklin Roosevelt and John Kennedy, adding that Ted's own recent sorrows and lengthy period of recovery "may set you upon an even finer course than would otherwise have been the case."

Early in his convalescence, Kennedy asked scholar-friends and government experts to conduct bedside seminars to keep abreast of current trends in preparation for his return to work. "Dean of the faculties" was Harvard economist John Kenneth Galbraith, the former ambassador to India who briefed him on imports and exports, money, banking, unemployment. Scientists Jerome Wiesner and Jerrold Zacharias of the Massachusetts Institute of Technology held sessions on science education. Robert Wood of M.I.T. and Samuel Beer of Harvard took the classes on government. Alain Enthoven of the Department of Defense came up for discussions on new weapons systems.

"We sent him over monster reading lists on intergovernmental relations, the balance of payments, Latin America — all the current tough ones," Professor Beer recalls. Kennedy did his homework reading faithfully in preparation for the seminars which were conducted two evenings a week from 7:30 to 9:30. The professors pulled up chairs close to the orthopedic frame and discussed the subjects with Kennedy, explaining, asking questions, receiving cogent replies. "You have to hand it to these Kennedys," Galbraith commented afterward. "They really do their homework."

Kennedy also found time to do what he called disciplined reading "to harden my understanding in fields of my interest." He asked for books on the period during the 1780s when the U.S. Constitution was ratified. He read *The Adams Papers*, Winston Churchill's *Great Contemporaries*, several books on Franklin D. Roosevelt and the New Deal, the poetry of Robert Frost. He told a reporter he did not read, nor ever would, the Warren Commission's report on the assassination of President Kennedy.

On Election Day, Kennedy, with his wife and aides filling the room, watched the returns on television. Early in the evening it became apparent that there would be two Kennedy brothers in the Senate the following January. Ted won reelection by defeating Howard Whitmore, Jr. by a majority of 719,693, fifty-four per cent of the votes.

In preparation for walking, he was shifted in November to a special kind of revolving bed, created at Walter Reed Hospital, which kept his spine rigid, as the Stryker did, but could also be tilted upward. They tilted him, a little at a time, until he was almost standing upright to bring back, slowly, his sense of equilibrium after the long months of lying prone.

On December 3, his knitted vertebrae supported by a four-pound steel and leather brace, so binding he could not stoop to tie his shoelaces, Ted walked for the first time since that June night. He took ten steps to the door and another ten back.

Nine days later he walked out of the hospital. Someone remembered that, a few days after the crash, he said he would walk again by Christmas.

XII

Brothers on the Back Bench

1. Homecoming

On January 4, the day the 89th Congress opened, and less than a month after he left the hospital, Edward Kennedy's blue Chrysler eased to the curb in front of the Department of Justice building on Constitution Avenue. Robert, who was standing on the sidewalk, hands jammed in pockets, stepped in, took the wheel and drove to Capitol Hill.

Moving stiffly because of the steel brace strapped tightly to his big frame and concealed by his dark suit, Ted climbed out of the car and entered the caucus room where the sixty-eight Democratic senators were gathering to await the noon swearing-in. Stuart Symington of Missouri grabbed his hand and said heartily: "Mighty glad to have you back, boy!" Richard Russell greeted him more quietly but with warmth and warned him to take care of his back. Clinton Anderson of New Mexico draped an arm over his shoulder, saying: "The best news of the session is having you back."

As he walked through the Senate chamber, greeting colleagues, Ted seemed to be protecting his right side. He had lost 28 pounds and it showed.

According to tradition, the Kennedy brothers were escorted to the rostrum by their counterparts from their home states. Republican Senator Jacob K. Javits shepherded Bobby, and

Leverett Saltonstall escorted Ted. In the gallery were thirteen Kennedys as the impressive swearing-in ceremony took place. Ethel was there with seven of her brood and three Kennedy sisters, Eunice Shriver, Jean Smith and Pat Lawford. In a front row on the opposite side of the galleries sat Joan Kennedy with Ted's cousin, Joe Gargan of Boston.

It was an historic occasion. It marked the first time that two brothers had taken the oath as U.S. senators together, and with that oath old Joe Kennedy became the first American to have had three sons in the Senate.

Bobby, the freshman senator, took his seat in the back of the Senate in a special row of two seats set up to accommodate him and Joseph D. Tydings of Maryland, who ranked a notch below him in seniority. It reminded old Senate hands of the days when Jack, as a senator, had also been a back bencher, sitting at a desk off the center aisle in Row Four. Asked how he liked his seat in the rear of the chamber, Robert commented: "At least I got inside the building."

For Ted, however, it was a warm homecoming, perceptively warmer than the reception he received two years earlier, for it was now clear to his colleagues that Edward Kennedy was not a restless youth in a hurry, as many had expected to find him, but a serious legislator who was growing up politically. And that year, in 1965, his record showed substantial accomplishment. He introduced a bill to set up an academy for the training of lawyers to defend and prosecute criminal cases; he sought abolition of the national origins quotas which limit the immigration of aliens from any one nation to a specific annual number; he called for the establishment of a Teachers Corps to send trained instructors on government pay into backward areas of the United States, and he called for federal aid in redeveloping industry in New England.

Edward reached another milestone when he led an effort for legislation banning poll taxes. Confronted with opposition from the White House and the Senate leadership, the measure was defeated, but it fell only four votes short of passage. And to many Washington observers, Teddy in many ways had emerged the winner in this encounter.

Supported by a group of Senate liberals, he had attempted to append to the voting-rights bill an amendment to outlaw poll taxes in state and local elections. In the battle he took on an opponent no less formidable than President Johnson, who had told TV viewers that the poll tax should be banned but that he stood firmly behind his attorney general, Nicholas Katzenbach. Katzenbach, along with Senate Democratic leader Mike Mansfield and Senate GOP leader Everett Dirksen, had openly questioned the constitutionality of the Kennedy amendment.

Some who opposed Kennedy's amendment were unregenerate southerners who never could be persuaded there was anything wrong with a poll tax. But others, though they disliked such a tax on moral grounds, were not quite convinced it was constitutional to throw it out. They argued that, under Article I, the states were permitted to create their own voting qualifications and that Amendment 24 had nothing to say about banning these taxes for *local* elections.

Ted rallied labor and church groups behind his amendment. He asked Harvard law professor Paul Freund to tutor him on the constitutional points, and conferred by telephone with his chief Republican ally, Senator Javits. He also spent long hours in Senate cloak rooms trying to drum up support.

But the other side was also active. Dirksen kept busy wooing wavering Republicans into line, using a method that New Jersey's GOP Sen. Clifford Case described as "oleaginous."

"I brought three lost sheep back into the fold," Dirksen said on the eve of the vote, "and I'll get another one tomorrow morning."

Bobby Kennedy showed no outward interest in the amendment and did not join the thirty-eight co-sponsors. But he worked for it behind the scenes.

While Kennedy and his allies were mobilizing support for the proposed amendment, Dirksen, Mansfield and Katzenbach drew up a new bill that junked the Kennedy rider. This left Ted and his supporters with one string in their bow — to take their fight to the Senate floor where Kennedy would be spokesman for about forty senators, three dozen of them rebellious Democrats. The Democratic insurgents ignored their majority leader and urged passage of the Kennedy rider.

When the crucial day came, Bobby ironically was presiding temporarily over the session, and as usual on major issues involving either brother, Kennedys filled the galleries.

Dirksen took the floor against the amendment and demanded: "If Congress can tell the states by statute this afternoon that they cannot impose a poll tax, why not tell them they cannot impose a cigarette tax or any other tax?"

Mansfield expressed concern that the amendment might endanger the voting rights bill, and said: "The choice is between the course of risk and the course of sureness."

Then it was Ted's turn. He leaned on a silver-headed cane as he stood at a front-row desk next to Mansfield's where he had moved for debate. This was the first major item of legislation that he had ever floor-managed.

"It is a settled constitutional doctrine," Ted asserted, "that where Congress finds an evil to exist, such as the economic burden in this case, it can apply a remedy which may affect people outside the evil."

In the tense roll call that followed, the Johnson forces defeated Kennedy 49 to 45, but it was an honorable defeat. The Administration was faced with the galling fact that it owed its victory to the votes of Republicans and segregationist Democrats. Ted, on the other hand, emerged as a prominent civil rights champion, a fact that won him the political support of major Negro organizations throughout the nation. He had also won valuable publicity by crossing swords with the attorney general, other senators and, indirectly, with Lyndon Johnson himself.

But 1965 was to see a far more embarrassing defeat for Edward Kennedy. In October of that year he waged an unsuccessful battle to win approval of a federal judgeship for Frank Morrissey, reportedly requested by old Joe Kennedy. Almost at once, Morrissey's qualifications were challenged: the American Bar Association and other professional groups angrily opposed the nomination on grounds that he was the least qualified candidate in memory. The Kennedy brothers worked long hours to line up support for their doubtful candidate, but almost every senator they corralled seemed embarrassed if not outright resentful.

The night before the showdown vote on confirmation, Ted Kennedy, foreseeing at best a Pyrrhic victory, informed President Johnson that he would withdraw the nomination. The next day, Gerry Doherty walked with him from his office to the Senate chamber. Kennedy was bitter and sad.

Doherty: "Let's get one thing straight. They say old Joe Kennedy alone was in favor of the appointment and that Ted didn't want it. That isn't true at all. Ted *did* want it. When I walked with him to the chamber where he was scheduled to make his speech withdrawing the name, his main concern was not for how *he* would look but for Frank Morrissey. He was telling me:

" 'Gee, here's a guy who could out-Abraham Lincoln Abraham Lincoln! If someone could just sit down at a typewriter and write the story. It's all there. He lived in a cold water flat and got up at four in the morning to sell newspapers, then went back to get breakfast because he was the oldest of twelve kids. Instead of becoming a drunk and making nothing of himself, he helped his brothers and sisters get an education and got one himself.

" 'And because he didn't go to my school, because he didn't go to Harvard, he got bombed. I just don't understand; it's a tragedy for the man.' "

But even the Morrissey fiasco won Teddy an oak leaf cluster on his established reputation for courage. When Kennedy finished his statement, Dirksen whose forces had been mobilized to try to scuttle Morrissey's nomination, crossed the floor and clasped the young senator's hand. "It takes something for a young man to subdue his pride," said Dirksen in his rumbling voice. "It doesn't bother an old bastard like me. But in a young man it takes courage."

2. Senator Bob and Senator Ted

The difference in the brothers' approach to their Senate jobs was marked. Bobby's moodiness and intensity, his shyness and at the same time his blunt manner did little to endear him to the senior legislators who found sharp contrasts between the new man and his younger brother.

Bobby was seven years older than Ted when he arrived in the Senate. However, his glamorous reputation, as majority leader Mike Mansfield pointed out provided him with "built-in enemies" and the need to prove himself, something Ted already had done.

Other differences soon became apparent. Bobby quickly showed himself to be more aggressive, more relentless and tougher-minded than his affable younger brother. It was noticeable in the Senate hearings where witnesses came to fear Bobby's probing cross-examination and his tiger attacks. In contrast, Teddy had a low-key delivery that seldom homed in on anyone, leading some critics to conclude that he lacked his brother's persistence.

Actually, Bobby was no stranger to the Senate. For years he had been seen hurrying through the corridors on Justice Department business, or during his tour as committee counsel. But even this sparked resentment. "He wasn't friendly with senators before," grumbled an old line Democrat. "He'd go by one of us a dozen times without speaking. He always seemed absorbed in something." Another Democrat from the midwest who liked both brothers personally, remarked, "Bobby doesn't need the Senate, and the Senate doesn't especially need him."

There were other incidents that irritated the Senate fraternity. One senior Republican noted sourly that one day Bobby made two trips to the grave of John F. Kennedy on the anniversary of his brother's inauguration. The senator observed in cutting tones that the second trip was necessary because photographers were not present on the first visit. "This is a pretty sophisticated and hard-boiled crowd," the GOP veteran said. "They notice stuff like that." Another senator brushed aside Bobby's climb up Mount Kennedy, a 14,000-foot Canadian peak named in his late brother's memory, as "unnecessary showing off . . . just for advertising." Another agreed, adding, "We all admired him from a physical standpoint, but the whole thing was a publicity gimmick." A third noted that "mountain climbing is fine when Congress is not in session, but New York's legislation is important and he should have been *here*."

The day Bobby drove Ted to the Senate for the swearing-in ceremonies, he turned to his brother and asked: "Which way do I drive, Eddie? You know this routine better than I do." The remark, delivered deadpan, turned out to be more prediction than joke, for Ted understood one basic fact of senatorial life far better than Bobby ever would. Or Jack, for that matter.

The two older brothers were far more interested in articulating their positions on major domestic and international problems than they were in performing the full, unglamorous chores required of a senator. While they spoke their minds well, clearly and forcefully, the fact is that power in the Senate is not won this way. Harry Truman once observed shortly after he was elected to the Senate: "I soon found out that, among my 95 colleagues, the real business of the Senate is carried on by unassuming and conscientious men, not by those who managed to get the most publicity."

Ed McCormack, who once scoffed at Ted's qualifications and remained to praise him, said of the three Kennedys in their senatorial roles: "Neither Bob nor Jack were willing to do the spadework essential to translate an idea into a law. Ted does it and, as a consequence, he is a better senator than his brothers were."

Robert's major concern in his Senate years was the war in Vietnam, which he had supported earlier, but came to regard as an exercise in futility that "promises only years and decades of further draining conflict." He struck hard and often, prompting President Johnson to remark: "If you keep talking like this, you won't have a political future in six months." Johnson's warning didn't stop him: Robert Kennedy called for the inclusion of the Viet Cong in the Saigon government, against which Vice President Humphrey argued that it would be like "putting a fox in a chicken coop." On vital domestic issues he was no less outspoken. At the University of Mississippi, he pleaded for a "society in which Negroes will be as free as other Americans." He pleaded for a curb on the interstate shipment of firearms. And he even tackled General Motors on the issue of auto safety, forcing its president, James M. Roche, to admit GM had spent less than one per cent of its 1964 profits on ways to make cars more accident-proof.

Ted was cautious. He continued to be a mostly behind-the-scenes senator, feeling his way carefully, rarely touching sensitive nerves. He spoke out on Vietnam, but never as boldly and sharply as Bobby. He spoke out on civil rights but not as a crusader. He felt as strongly as his older brother on the war, on the problems of the ghettos, on the minorities, but he believed that muscle tissue in the Senate must be built up layer by layer with hard, plodding, infinitely careful inside work.

Bobby was impatient. If Edward's start in the Senate was auspicious, Robert's earned him poor marks. Ted marked time for fourteen months before delivering his maiden speech; John held off for five, but Bobby waited scarcely four weeks. He offered an amendment to President Johnson's $1.1 million aid-to-Appalachia program, extending federal anti-poverty help to thirteen counties in New York state. He was in such a hurry that he failed to do his homework. Moreover, he was the only senator to ignore Majority Leader Mansfield's plea to stay off the gravy train, and he did not bother to discuss his ideas either with Gov. Nelson Rockefeller or his GOP colleague, Javits.

The Appalachia aid bill, which included 355 counties in eleven states, was a tempting barrel of pork. A number of senators, including Kennedy of Massachusetts, wanted to submit amendments putting some of their home counties into the measure, but Mansfield called them off, explaining that more programs affecting other regions would soon be forthcoming from the White House. All agreed except the freshman senator from New York. In his speech, he argued that Governor Rockefeller was "shortsighted" for not asking a share of federal money. Javits politely reminded him that, in his amendment, he had failed to name the counties he had in mind for aid. Bobby altered his amendment accordingly. Then Javits, again unfailingly polite, told Bobby that the measure specified that governors must approve any programs provided for their states. Bobby again revised his amendment to include gubernatorial approval. Kennedy's amendment passed as gravy train legislation such as this generally does — even though Rockefeller said later than twelve of the thirteen counties did not require federal aid.

Bobby had no patience, either, with the amenities. When he entered the chamber, he went straight to his seat, never stopping to chat or pass the time with the other senators. He was candid to the point of giving offense. "He rubbed many senators the wrong way," Tydings said. "He didn't take the trouble to polish his phraseology very often." Dick Schaap wrote: "He could not guide a bill neatly to passage. He could not often sway his colleagues' votes. He could not trade senatorial favors."

And Bob Kennedy knew it. Once, when Edward was delivering a flowery compliment to a fellow senator on the floor, Bobby scribbled a note and asked a page to deliver it to his brother: "How long do you have to go on with this to make them think you're a good senator?" Ted could dish it out, too. At a meeting of the Labor Committee, on which they both served, Bobby launched on a rambling explanation of an amendment he was sponsoring. Ted sent him a note reading: "Don't you wish you were in the club so you wouldn't have to do all this?"

Dun Gifford, who served as Bobby's campaign aide in 1968 and was a legislative assistant to Teddy, summed up the brothers thus in *American Journey:* "In the Senate committees, on the floor, you always had the feeling that Bobby was about to explode. He had this tremendous energy, and he was never very good at hiding it. There was so much to do, and he never saw any reason for just not going ahead and doing it. You could always see those explosions coming, and it made us all a little nervous sometimes. His brother Ted was different. Two completely different styles. Ted always wanted everyone to know what he's trying to do, to understand that he has studied and thought and talked the whole thing over, which he generally has. It's not caution, really, as much as it is knowing how the Senate really works."

Ted could carry the good-fellowship business further than most of his colleagues. In 1967, when Sen. Thomas J. Dodd of Connecticut was facing censure on charges of appropriating campaign funds for his own use, Ted was the only member of the body to visit him and say how sorry he was that he would have to vote for the resolution. One observer saw in this single action a revealing difference between the three brothers. Said he: "Jack Kennedy would have ignored the likes of Dodd. Bobby Kennedy would have threatened to punch him in the mouth. Ted Kennedy paid a social call on him."

Teddy, of course, enjoyed a considerably better relationship with the White House than did Bobby who was embroiled in a marathon feud with Lyndon Johnson. Asked how the President reacted to Ted in view of his running battle with Bobby, a White House aide said: "Well it's been different, the relationship. Not as tight. We've felt freer being frank with him [Ted], telling him what the problem was on something without worrying what he would do with it." Teddy himself insisted that his relationship with the White House was never strained despite the fact that the Johnson administration tended to regard Bobby as hostile.

Bobby was a loner, Ted a team player. Bobby was brusque with his elders and made enemies, Ted was respectful and made friends. Bobby was restless in a place where extreme patience ranks as one of man's highest virtues. Bobby was ambitious among men who can sniff out the trait like dogs after truffles. And Bobby had longer hair which, though it endeared him to the younger people in his audiences, caused a surprising amount of grumbling among his seniors in the cloakrooms.

The year before, when Bobby visited Ted in the hospital after the plane crash, a news photographer asked the older Kennedy: "Step back a little. You're casting a shadow on Ted." Edward grinned as he answered: "It'll be the same when we get down to Washington."

It didn't happen that way at all. As Ted Kennedy himself admits — while loyally insisting that his brother was a "good legislator": "He didn't get high marks for it."

At 10 a.m. on Saturday, March 16, Robert Kennedy stood in the Senate caucus room and announced his candidacy for the Democratic Presidential nomination. Months of pressure, counter-pressure and soul-searching had preceded the decision. He had been pushed toward the race by some of his closest advisers, Kennedy clansmen who wanted to recapture Camelot, and some members of his family, notably his wife Ethel. But other advisers and other family members, like Ted and Steve Smith, had counseled caution. Lyndon Johnson, they said, was an impregnable fortress. Bob should wait until the Johnson era ended in 1972. Ever since winter, Kennedy had been certain that Johnson's Southeast Asia policies were deeply wrong, and that they were having devastating impact on the nation. He yearned to act but, at the same time, political caution restrained him. As one wise observer said: "From the neck down he wanted to go; from the neck up it just didn't make sense to him."

Even as he vacillated, Eugene McCarthy of Minnesota, up in New Hampshire with thousands of eager young collegians working under his banner, stunned the nation by capturing forty-two per cent of the primary votes. Lyndon Johnson had been savagely clawed. The President was more vulnerable than anybody had thought.

Four frantic days followed. Bob Kennedy was pursued everywhere by newsmen who wanted to know: what now? He told them that it now appeared that there was a "deep division" in the Party, that he was now "reassessing" the possibility of running. Day and night, conferences were held in New York and Washington, at Steve Smith's Fifth Avenue apartment, at Hickory Hill, in Kennedy's offices. Some 2,000 telegrams arrived at his office, the phones were never silent, the mail sacks bulged with letters offering advice to run, to stay out.

By late evening on March 15, Kennedy had made up his mind. He told Jack Newfield that night: "My brother Ted still thinks I'm a little nutty for doing this, but he's an entirely different kind of person. You just have to march to the beat of your own drummer."

But with Bobby in, Ted was in too. In the next two and one-half months, Ted was to be on the road all but five nights. His first job was to organize the first of the primary campaigns, on May 7 in Indiana. Enlisting the help of Gerry Doherty and utilizing the same methods they had employed so successfully back home in Massachusetts, they published 2,500,000 copies of a tabloid newspaper detailing Bobby's career and explaining his views. Members of the Kennedy family, including its (by now) thoroughly experienced women's corps, went into every Indiana city and every community; they saturated radio and television with commercials. There were luncheons, breakfasts, dinners, motorcades, rallies. And, late on May 7, Bobby racked up forty-two per cent of the vote to Gene McCarthy's twenty-seven. Governor Roger Branigan, a stand-in for Hubert Humphrey, drew only thirty-one per cent.

Bobby won more than half the votes cast in Nebraska — 51.5 per cent to McCarthy's 31. There was a setback on May 28 in Oregon where, for the first time in his life, Kennedy was defeated in a campaign in which he was either a candidate or manager of one: he received 38.8 per cent of the total to McCarthy's 44.7.

But just one week ahead lay another primary, the really big test — the one in California.

XIII

Three Cities

1. San Francisco

At almost the same hour that Bobby Kennedy was murdered in a Los Angeles hotel pantry, his brother Ted was being shoved, tugged and screamed at by a crowd during the victory rally in a San Francisco auditorium. David Burke, his administrative assistant, said afterward: "We were lucky to get out of there."

In the tragedy that exploded with terrifying suddenness 500 miles south, the incident has gone unnoticed and unrecorded.

On Election night, Edward Kennedy, in a euphoric mood, made the rounds of the three network television stations in San Francisco, bantering with newscasters, predicting a large victory for his brother. Even as he went from one studio to another, it became increasingly clear that Bobby would defeat McCarthy and Ted's jubilation grew.

At 10:30, he arrived at a municipal auditorium for a victory rally, accompanied by the red-haired, stoop-shouldered Burke and several other aides. The paths of the brothers had criss-crossed during the past few days but, though they both had suites at the Fairmont Hotel atop Nob Hill — Bobby on the top floor, Ted on the fourth — they had met only briefly. Ted had arrived in California the week before for a campaign swing

166

through the areas north of the city, returning to San Francisco on Saturday, June 2.

Meanwhile, Robert was in the city for whistle-stop tours, receptions, and for the television debate with McCarthy at the studios of KGO-TV on Golden Gate Avenue. On Sunday, Bobby flew to Los Angeles for a strawberry festival in Garden Grove City Park. He took his children to Disneyland where delighted tourists manhandled him, then flew back to San Francisco for a final motorcade and a luncheon speech at Fisherman's Wharf. Talking to a group of Italian-Americans at DiMaggio's Restaurant, he said America's racial crisis "won't disappear automatically if we just say a prayer . . ." Glancing to his right, he saw a nun at a corner table. He continued: "With all deference to you, sister, I think we have to work to supplement what He is doing."

After the luncheon, Bobby, Ethel and the campaign staff flew to San Diego for one final rally where, on the verge of collapse from exhaustion, the candidate addressed crowds at the El Cortez Hotel. At one point, Bobby abruptly walked to one side of the stage and sat on the steps leading to the auditorium, his head buried in his hands. Bill Barry, his security man, and Rafer Johnson, the Olympic decathlon champion who was traveling with the senator, led him to a men's room. He recovered in a few minutes. Bobby and Ethel flew back to Los Angeles to spend the night at the Malibu Beach home of John Frankenheimer, the movie director.

The following day, Bobby slept late, played with his children on the beach and in the pool, and chatted with friends; it was the first day of total relaxation he had had in weeks. Shortly after six, with two more hours before the polls closed, he drove back to Los Angeles, deposited the children with a governess at the Beverly Hills Hotel, and went on to the Ambassador Hotel to await the returns.

By 9, things looked good; by 10 they looked better and a half-hour after that Bobby's victory seemed assured. He left his fifth floor suite at the Ambassador to be interviewed separately by Sander Vanocur for NBC and then by Roger Mudd for CBS. At the same time, Ted Kennedy, after talking to broadcasters in San Francisco, was entering the auditorium for the victory rally.

David Burke: "That was a rough affair, that rally. There were a lot of unfamiliar faces, a lot of people who were pushing and shoving, and it was difficult to reach the stage and to get off. A group in the balcony was chanting loudly: 'Free Huey! Free Huey!'* and it made me feel very uneasy. It was a push-shove kind of thing, with no decorum. There was an awful lot of physical shoving of the senator. There was no sense of control. And people kept yelling and screaming things that had nothing to do with Robert Kennedy's victory, and I felt frankly un-comfortable for Edward Kennedy. I told him we ought to get out of there, and we did as soon as possible.

"We drove back to the Fairmont and went to our suite up there on the fourth floor, and of course the first thing we did was turn on the television set in the living room to get the latest results and see what was happening down there in L.A. The instant the set lit up we heard someone say there's been a shoot-ing at the rally.

"I assumed, and I think Edward Kennedy assumed, that the rally they were talking about was the one we had just left. Nor was it especially farfetched to believe there could have been trouble there because it was a nasty kind of affair. I remember remarking to the senator we were lucky to get out of there safely, that I didn't like it at all, and that we would have to handle security a different way if we were going to be doing things like that.

"The senator nodded but didn't answer. He kept watching the television to find out just what had happened at that rally.

"As we were listening we saw Steve Smith on the screen asking people, over and over, to be calm and be quiet and leave the auditorium. We knew, of course, that he hadn't been at our rally. This was Los Angeles and there had been a shooting down there.

"And then there was the sudden, horrible dawning realization that Robert Kennedy had been shot.

"Ted Kennedy stood in the middle of the living room, staring at the screen. I stood beside him, unable to say anything. I heard him say: 'We have to get down there.' That was all. We just stood there, the two of us, staring at the screen, watching this thing unfold. I don't know how long we stood there; it may

*Huey P. Newton, co-founder of the Black Panther Party, was then under arrest, charged with the slaying of a policeman in Oakland, California. In the summer of 1971, his second trial ended in a hung jury. He was later freed.

have been thirty seconds or it could have been three to ten minutes. We were just frozen there, because we were learning things that were more horrible all the time.

"I bolted from the room and ran down the stairs into the lobby to find someone who would help me get transportation right away. I couldn't make the night manager, the girls at the desk or anyone understand what I was talking about. Not that I was incoherent, but the people in the lobby hadn't heard — it was absolutely that moment's news. The problem was I was trying to describe a situation most people would react to with disbelief. They looked at me blankly and then stared at each other.

"Finally I got them to realize what had happened. The phone girl got me American Airlines; from the assistant manager's desk I asked them for a plane, a charter, an executive jet — anything to get to L.A. They said they'd call back; I called other airlines and made the same request. In between calls, I raced up to the room three or four times and Edward Kennedy was always standing there, in front of the television set, his jacket off, just standing there watching and not saying a word.

"I kept checking my progress on the arrangements with him and I don't know why I kept running back and forth because I wasn't getting much response from him. Finally, we got the Hamilton Air Force Base in Marin County to provide a military jet. By this time, his cousin Bob Fitzgerald and John Seigenthaler [a former administrative assistant to Robert Kennedy] had come in. It was now past one a.m.

"In a few minutes, two California Highway Patrol cars and four motorcycle policemen were in front of the hotel. At 1:16, we left the Fairmont, got into the cars and raced across the Golden Gate Bridge to the base twenty-five miles away.

"At the airport, Pierre Salinger was on the phone from Los Angeles. Edward Kennedy took the call in the operations room, spoke about a minute, then walked out to the plane. On the way I asked him how things were down there. He said: 'It's going to be all right.' Later I learned that Pierre hadn't told him it was going to be all right at all. He saw I was distraught. It's the kind of thing he would say to reassure me, which he had no business doing.

"The four of us climbed into the plane and took off. He didn't speak during the entire flight. Nobody spoke."

2. Los Angeles

At Los Angeles Airport, a helicopter was waiting to take them to Good Samaritan Hospital, a square stone structure on Shatto Street near Wilshire Boulevard. Bobby, gunned down at the Ambassador Hotel after delivering a victory speech in the Embassy Ballroom, had been rushed for emergency treatment to Central Receiving Hospital two miles away, then taken to Good Samaritan. Ted arrived at the hospital while his brother was in surgery on the ninth floor, where a team headed by Dr. Henry Cuneo, a leading Los Angeles neurosurgeon, worked desperately, though without much hope, to repair Kennedy's bullet-shattered brain.

With Ethel, Steve and Jean Smith, Pat Lawford, Dave Hackett and a few other close friends, Ted waited in a room near the intensive care unit on the fifth floor until Bobby was brought down. He went into the room where his brother lay and stood looking at him. He remained for ten minutes, then left. From time to time, he would come back to stand by the bedside and look at the silent figure, the head swathed in bandages, electrodes taped to his body so that nurses monitoring outside could catch the minutest change in his vital signs. He was lying on a mattress filled with ice to cool the blood and slow its passage through the lacerated brain areas.

Early in the morning, Ted telephoned Boston and talked with Dr. James Poppen, the Lahey Clinic's chief of neurosurgery who had treated John Kennedy for his back problems, Joseph Kennedy for the after-effects of his stroke, and Ted himself for his cracked vertebrae after the plane crash. Dr. Poppen agreed to come. He reached Los Angeles later in the day aboard an Air Force jet provided by Vice President Hubert Humphrey.

After arranging for Dr. Poppen to come, Ted made the first of many calls that day and the next to Hyannis Port. Rose already knew: Ann Gargan, who had been watching television, had gone to Mrs. Kennedy's room to see if she was asleep. But Rose was awake. Soon, Ted called and explained what the doctors were saying, that Bobby was in critical condition.

Two rooms adjoining the one where Bobby lay had been set aside for the family. Ted went from one to another, talking quietly to Ethel and the others. In Bobby's room, he inspected the medical charts carefully and asked doctors innumerable questions about what they meant. Once he sat on a rolling stretcher in the corridor and leaned his head wearily against the wall. And once he went outside to pace the blacktop parking lot with a friend, as Robert had paced in the park four years before when Ted lay on a hospital bed with a broken back.

The day passed, and then the night. Dr. Poppen, who had examined Bobby, said nothing more could be done. In the early hours of Wednesday morning Edward Kennedy watched another brother die.

When the blue hearse bearing the body of Robert Kennedy arrived at the Los Angeles Airport, Ted Kennedy helped load the casket onto the Air Force 707 dispatched by President Johnson. With Bobby's closest friends, he helped carry the heavy African mahogany coffin onto the hydraulically-operated loading platform and into the front compartment, ordinarily used for communications equipment. After it had been placed in the narrow corridor next to the pilot's cabin, he stepped out again onto the cargo lift to pick up a wreath of flowers that had fallen off the casket.

3. New York

The day before the funeral at St. Patrick's Cathedral in New York City, the family and members of the Kennedy team met in Steve Smith's apartment at 1030 Fifth Ave. The enormous task of sending out invitations, selecting the gravesite at Arlington and obtaining official government approval, arranging for the transportation of people from the cathedral to Pennsylvania Station and the body to Washington by special train — all this had been accomplished by teams working in New York and Washington.

At the meeting, Edward Kennedy announced that he wanted to deliver a eulogy to his brother. Several of those present thought it was an excellent idea but Dave Burke, the peppery and brilliant tactician who was intensely loyal to — and protective of — his boss, was aghast.

Dave Burke: "I didn't think any human being could go through what Ted Kennedy underwent, and then stand up in that cathedral. I was firmly opposed because I didn't want to see him put himself through that terrible ordeal. I told him so but he answered that he wanted to do it. My opposition was so strong that I told him frankly I didn't want to participate in it."

Adam Walinsky, one of Bobby's speech writers, Milton Gwirtzman and Ted began developing a concept of the eulogy. Kennedy felt it should consist mainly of a reading of Robert's own words, the ideas that best summed up the man and his ideals.

Shortly after 10 a.m., after the clerical procession had moved up the center aisle of the great Gothic cathedral to the elaborately carved wooden seats in the white marble sanctuary, Monsignor Eugene V. Clarke, secretary to Archbishop Terence J. Cooke of New York, came forward. At the same time, Edward Kennedy rose from his seat in the front pew. Monsignor Clarke led the young senator to a lectern in front of the sanctuary. There was a slight stirring among the guests: this had not been expected.

Kennedy, in a dark suit and dark, narrow tie, put his hands on the sides of the wooden lectern. The flag-draped coffin was a few feet below his eyes, and beyond, in the front pew, sat the bereaved Kennedy family. He took a sheaf of white cards from an inside pocket, placed them on the lectern and began reading.

Almost at once, it appeared as though Dave Burke's prediction would prove correct, for Kennedy's voice faltered noticeably:

> We loved him as a brother and as a father and as a son. From his parents and from his older brothers and sisters, Joe and Kathleen and Jack, he received an inspiration which he passed on to all of us.
>
> He gave us strength in time of trouble, wisdom in time of uncertainty and sharing in time of happiness. He will always be by our side.

But he gripped the lectern sides and steadied himself. His voice rose as he talked about Bobby's capacity to love, his ability to relate with and understand others, a great and indispensable gift given to him in the household in which he was reared. And, along with love, had come the gift of a social conscience, the realization that those who are born into comfort have the responsibility to right wrongs and help those less fortunate.

A talk Bobby had given in 1966 to young people in South Africa summed up best his concern and compassion for mankind. Edward Kennedy quoted from this speech:

There is discrimination in this world and slavery and slaughter and starvation. Governments repress their people. Millions are trapped in poverty, while the nation grows rich and wealth is lavished on armaments everywhere.

These are different evils, but they are the common works of man. They reflect the imperfection of human justice, the inadequacy of human compassion, our lack of sensibility towards the suffering of our fellows.

But we can perhaps remember, even if only for a time, that those who live with us are our brothers, that they share with us the same short moment of life, that they seek as we do nothing but the chance to live out their lives in purpose and happiness, winning what satisfaction and fulfillment they can.

Surely this bond of common faith, this bond of common goals, can begin to teach us something. Surely we can learn at least to look at those around us as fellow men. And surely we can begin to work a little harder to bind up the wounds among us and to become in our own hearts brothers and countrymen once again.

The answer is to rely on youth, not a time of life but a state of mind, a temper of the will, a quality of imagination, a predominance of courage over timidity, of the appetite for adventure over the love of ease. The cruelties and obstacles of this swiftly changing planet will not yield to the obsolete dogmas and outworn slogans; they cannot be moved by those who cling to a present that is already dying, who prefer the illusion of security to the excitement and danger that come with even the most peaceful progress.

It is a revolutionary world which we live in, and this generation at home and around the world has had thrust upon it a greater burden of responsibility than any generation that has ever lived. Some believe there is nothing one man or one woman can do against the enormous array of the world's ills. Yet many of the world's great movements of thought and action have flowed from the work of a single man.

A young monk began the Protestant Reformation. A young general extended an empire from Macedonia to the borders of the earth. A young woman reclaimed the territory of France, and it was a young Italian explorer who discovered the New World, and the thirty-two-year-old Thomas Jefferson who explained that all men are created equal.

These men moved the world, and so can we all. Few will

have the greatness to bend history itself, but each of us can work to change a small portion of events, and in the total of all those acts will be written the history of this generation.

Each time a man stands for an ideal, or acts to improve the lot of others, or strikes out against injustice, he sends forth a tiny ripple of hope.

And crossing each other from a million different centers of energy and daring, those ripples build a current that can sweep down the mightiest walls of oppression and resistance. . .

Our future may lie beyond our vision, but it is not completely beyond our control. It is the shaping impulse of America that . . . the work of our own hands matched to reason and principle will determine our destiny."

Rose Kennedy, in the front row of pews directly behind the flag-draped casket, sat with head bowed and eyes closed as her son spoke. From time to time, she would raise her head and look at him, and then her lips would tighten as she fought to hold back tears, and she would shut her eyes and bow her head again. Ethel, her pale sad face covered by a sheer black veil, did not take her eyes from him. Mrs. John F. Kennedy, in a black lace mantilla, was composed now. The day before she had sobbed beside the coffin when, with Caroline and John, she had come to pray at the cathedral.

Edward's voice broke as he concluded the reading of the Africa speech and began his own peroration. He was plainly close to tears. Burke, watching him intently, wondered once again why a human being would put himself through an ordeal so emotionally searing. The moment of intense grief was watched with compassion by the dignitaries at the cathedral and millions of Americans over television.

Edward Kennedy paused, shifted his feet slightly and, his jaw muscles working, gained control. He continued in a thick, choked voice:

My brother need not be idealized or enlarged in death beyond what he was in life. He should be remembered simply as a good and decent man who saw wrong and tried to right it, saw suffering and tried to heal it, saw war and tried to stop it.

Those of us who loved him and who take him to his rest

today pray that what he was to us, and what he wished for others, will some day come to pass for all the world.

As he said many times, in many parts of this nation, to those he touched and who sought to touch him:

"Some men see things as they are and say, *why*. I dream things that never were and say, *why not*."

He returned to the front row pew beside Ethel and sat composed for the remainder of the one hour, forty-minute service.

Almost twelve hours later, after the long slow ride in the funeral train to Washington, after the last journey through the streets of Washington before crowds silent in the darkness, after a service by moonlight and floodlight, Edward Kennedy saw his brother Robert buried at Arlington, fifty feet down the slope from John.

XIV

Dark Summer

1. Kennedys Do Cry

The time of gravest personal crisis in the life of Edward Kennedy had come. The murder of Robert shocked him more than anything else in his entire life. With John's death, Ted had suffered a great sense of loss and was left with a deep sorrow. His own narrow escape had given him, for the first time, a sharp awareness of his own mortality. Until it happened, he had lived, in his word, a "limited" kind of life, bounded by college, law school and the heady excitement of politics. Vigorous, extroverted, life-loving, he had rarely turned his thoughts inward. The realization that his own life had very nearly been extinguished sobered him.

But the assassination of Bobby had a different, and more profound, impact.

Since boyhood, Ted had looked upon Bobby — again his own words — as a "second father." Joe and Jack were the heroes, but Bobby was the friendly protector, and we are closest to those who provide essential security when threatening situations arise. People tend to forget that the independent, aggressive, competitive Kennedys were, as children, prey to many of the same fears and insecurities in childhood as anyone else. For Ted, Bobby was a private little shelter within the larger harbor of his family. His father was away much of the time, not available to straighten out the minor problems. Rose tried to give attention to all her children and their troubles, but there were many of both and only so many hours in the day.

Once Ted described his early relationship with Bobby: "When I was about eleven years old," he said, "I was at the Fessenden School in West Newton, Massachusetts. My brothers and sisters were all away, and dad and mother were in New York; Dad had just resigned as ambassador to Great Britain. Bobby was only a few years older than I was, but he was the one who used to call me up to see how I was getting along. On the two or three weekends I was able to get off from school, if I couldn't get home, he'd spend the weekend with me. I'll never forget how we used to go to the big empty house at Cape Cod — just the two of us rattling around alone. But Bobby was in charge, taking care of me and always making sure I had something to do."

There was a rare intimacy between the two brothers that persisted through the years. They exchanged personal and family confidences constantly and, before every important decision, asked one another's advice. When they served in the Senate, they installed special private telephone lines so that one could reach the other quickly. William J. vanden Heuvel, who served with Robert in the Department of Justice and knew Ted well, once said: "Edward Kennedy depended on his brother, for advice, example and strength, more than on any other man. . . . They were totally devoted to each other's careers."

They called one another, not by the names used by the public or even by their wives — Ted or Teddy, Bob or Bobby — but "Robbie" and "Eddie." And, more than most people realized, they were inseparable.

"To one who has lost a loved person," Joshua Loth Liebman wrote, "the world is a dreary wasteland. Grief, loneliness, despair possess his soul." After the first numbness had worn off, Ted Kennedy's mood swung from cold anger to utter despondency. On board the plane which bore Bobby's body to New York he raged against the "faceless men" who had gunned down both his brothers and the civil rights leaders, Martin Luther King and Medgar Evers. Sandor Vanocur, the television newsman who is also a family friend, said after the flight: "He's mad. I might as well say it — he's mad. He's mad at what happens in this country. He does not know if this is the act of a single person or if this is the act of a conspiracy."

On the funeral train to Washington, campaign workers told one another: "Don't close headquarters yet — Teddy's fighting mad."

Ever since early childhood, when he sailed with his brothers at Cape Cod, Kennedy had drawn comfort from the sea. Now he went out upon the water nearly every day on his rented sixty-foot yawl, *Mira*, sometimes alone, sometimes with the children, often with his first cousin, Joseph F. Gargan, with whom he had grown up. Joe, the son of Rose's sister, Agnes, was thirty-nine, two years older than Ted. Later, Joe Gargan was to play an important role in still another tragic event. Instinctively, Ted turned to Gargan now for comfort, as he would turn to him the following summer.

Ted cut himself off from the press and political associates. All he wanted those first few weeks was family, a few close friends, and the lonely sea.

Early in July, he took his teen-age nephew Joe to Spain, returning alone after a few days; Joe remained on a ranch at Finca, near Madrid, to study Spanish and history. He kept in touch with his Washington staff by telephone, but his associates clearly detected a loss of any real interest in what was going on. He would respond laconically to the briefings on Senate activities they gave him. One day late in July, he journeyed to Washington to sign some important papers. He sat numbly in his car outside the Old Senate Office Building for several minutes, then shook his head and took off again for the seclusion of the Kennedy compound in Massachusetts. "I just couldn't go in and face them all," he said.

Once he sailed randomly in Nantucket Sound, stopping at harbors whenever food ran out, returning two weeks later looking like a grizzled seaman, with a growth of bright-orange beard. Disheveled and still unshaven, he walked into his parents' home. Joe Kennedy stared at him and pointed at his face. Ted went to the wheel chair where his father sat and bent over to kiss him. Mr. Kennedy, still staring at the beard, suddenly began to laugh. Rose Kennedy, laughing too, said she thought she'd get a razor and shave the beard off herself. Ted, rubbing his face, realizing how he must have looked to his startled parents, laughed too.

It was the first laughter after the tears.

Almost at the same moment, a new drama was shaping up and again a Kennedy would be at center stage.

2. Boom in Chicago

Democrats were getting ready to descend upon Chicago to name a Presidential candidate. Mayor Richard J. Daley had much on his mind. He had heard that 100,000 anti-war protesters would try to disrupt the nominating convention in August. He made plans to turn Chicago into a fortress: the city's 11,900 policemen would be placed on full alert, and 6,000 Illinois National Guardsmen and 7,500 regular army troops would be standing by. The route to the International Amphitheater, the convention hall, would be a barbed-wire, troop-encircled no-man's-land. Delegates would be transported there by special buses from their hotels, under the guns of armed troops.

Dick Daley was as powerful an Irish political boss as any the Kennedys had known in Boston and indeed among the last of his breed in the country. He had a man to head the ticket, a man who, as the convention time approached, was watching a sunset off Nantucket Island and asking questions no one could answer.

Daley wasn't alone. It came as little surprise that the minds of many Democrats were turning to Edward Kennedy as the logical contender for the Presidency, and they apparently did not give much thought to whether the bereaved brother wanted it or not. At thirty-six, the freshman senator from Massachusetts had become head of the most distinguished political family in America. And in the view of many, he had more charisma than either John or Bobby. With this, plus the Kennedy name, he seemed like a natural for the White House.

From the moment Bobby died, the American press and a great many U.S. politicians placed Ted foremost among potential candidates for the nomination. Members of the Kennedy political machine, one of the smoothest running the nation had ever seen, turned instinctively to Ted.

Kennedy, aware of the rising tide, gave no hint of his intentions when he went on television on June 15 from the lawn of his parents' home to thank the public for its expressions of sympathy over Bobby's death. "Each of us will have to decide in a private way," he said, choosing his words with obvious care, "in our own hearts, in our own consciences, what we will do in the course of this summer and future summers."

A flurry of speculation was touched off by word that before leaving for Spain, Ted had called a meeting of the Kennedy faithful, ostensibly to discuss "a living memorial" for Bob Kennedy. Among the key figures who attended the session were Robert McNamara, Ted Sorenson, John Siegenthaler, Adam Walinsky and Dave Burke. After the formal gathering, Sorenson, Burke, and Siegenthaler remained to talk over Ted's political future. They decided that Ted should make a speech removing himself from the national political scene for that year, but that he would also keep himself in the public eye by calling for a halt to the bombing over North Vietnam.

But the politicos were determined to see the name Kennedy on their state slates, and they set up a hue and cry for his entry in the lists. A Harris poll indicated that Kennedy would add five million votes to the Democratic ticket. Then, on July 14, former Gov. Michael DiSalle of Ohio let it be known that he would nominate Ted for the Presidency itself, even if he did not wish it. When Kennedy, deep in his bereavement, was informed in Hyannis Port, he could only respond with an unenthusiastic, "Isn't that something."

Statements of endorsement soon followed from Sen. Philip Hart of Michigan, Gov. Richard J. Hughes of New Jersey and Gov. Sam Shapiro of Illinois, the latter a political protégé of Chicago's Mayor Daley. Three days later, Daley himself publicly joined the swelling chorus, though privately he had had the idea all along. Asked by newsmen whether he had talked to Kennedy about the vice presidential nomination, Daley replied, "No, but I think the convention will draft him."

Daley telephoned Kennedy and confided that he was concerned over the expected nomination of Hubert Humphrey. Daley had come to the conclusion, he said, that the vice president was fated to lose and the Illinois slate would go down to defeat with him. "But you," Daley told Kennedy, "you are a winner. You can carry the convention, you can carry Illinois, you can carry the country."

Daley's approach was received with caution by the Kennedy clan. They expressed concern that Chicago's mayor might be trying to bring Ted out of seclusion to force him to run in the

No. 2 spot on Humphrey's ticket. Finally Ted telephoned Daley, thanked him for his kind words, but made it clear that he was not interested in running for vice president. Daley asked him to give the matter some more thought.

The situation became so acute that Kennedy issued a statement on July 26 expressing appreciation for the "honor" many prominent Democrats had paid him. "But for me," he went on, "this year, it is impossible. My reasons are purely personal . . . I have informed the Democratic candidates for the presidency and the chairman of the convention that I will not be able to accept the vice presidential nomination if offered, and that my decision is final, firm, and not subject to further consideration." It was noted that Teddy said not one word about the nomination for President. Only a week earlier, Humphrey had appealed to Eugene McCarthy, his fellow senator from Minnesota to run with him on the presidential ticket and had gotten a flat turndown. Humphrey, in desperation, had then turned to Teddy who told him, "I am not a candidate."

By that time, Kennedy had made another decision — to remain in Hyannis Port during the convention. He also requested his own staff to stay away from Chicago at that time, but experienced observers recalled that the Kennedys usually preferred to have members of the family handle the sensitive assignments.

Sure enough, on August 23, Stephen Smith, the tense, able brother-in-law who was also a member of the New York delegation, made a scouting mission to Chicago. He saw a number of people, including Mayor Daley who gave his solemn word: he was not baiting a trap to get Kennedy to admit that he might accept the presidential nomination so that he could not turn down the vice presidential one. But Daley countered with an urgent request that Ted give a firm answer before the Illinois caucus met the following Sunday afternoon. Ted remained silent and Daley backed off, postponing the caucus. Jesse Unruh did the same with the California delegation, and rumors began spreading that a move was in the works to draft Teddy. As followers of Humphrey, McGovern and McCarthy indicated a willingness to fall into line, Ted Sorenson did some quick figuring and concluded that Kennedy was within a hundred votes of the needed convention majority.

As the pressure mounted, Kennedy turned to friends for counsel. Sorenson advised him not to place himself in a position where the convention would offer him the nomination, for no man could reject a legitimate draft. Sorenson himself had many reservations: "Despite my own desire to resume the effort twice tragically interrupted, and despite the heady excitement over the Ted Kennedy boom, which was by then seizing many of my close friends among the delegates, I had several questions," he recounted in *The Kennedy Legacy*. Once the frenzy of convention week died down, how vulnerable would he be in a more conservative electorate to suspicions (and Nixon charges) about his experience and maturity, to the kindly-sounding suggestion (not without merit) that it would be better to let this family alone for this year, and to a feeling that he was seeking to capitalize on tragedy, on public emotion, and on a famous name?" If elected, would he have had time to gain sufficient standing with the Congress, with the disaffected groups in this country, and with other nations, to provide the kind of leadership he could provide at a later date? Should he, at this stage of his life, and in that year of years, be required to give up his remaining privacy, to expose himself in an emotion-charged atmosphere to every suggestible psychopath seized with the notion of shooting another Kennedy?

There were appeals from others still closer to Teddy. Friends of the family said that his wife pleaded with the senator not to run because the Kennedys had enough dead heroes. And Richard Cardinal Cushing, the spiritual advisor of old Joe Kennedy and the rest of the clan, also begged Ted not to risk another tragedy.

But in Chicago, a Kennedy bandwagon continued to build. Steve Smith found that members of almost every delegation he contacted were convinced that Humphrey could not be elected. The signs indicated that New York would go for Kennedy. So would California and Illinois. If Teddy let his name be placed in nomination it looked as though he could stop Humphrey on the first ballot.

Pierre Salinger later recalled the snowballing move for Kennedy: "I was on the floor of the convention. I saw more of the old Kennedy advance men there . . . than I had ever seen in my life. Everywhere I would turn there were guys that I knew. You could see their lips moving, and they were all saying 'Kennedy.' They were all there — Jerry Bruno, Don Dell, Gerry Doherty, Ken O'Donnell — primed and willing to go."

At this point Daley called Smith and told him, "I cannot make a move for Teddy, unless Teddy tells me he is a candidate." The harassed Smith called Hyannis Port to tell Kennedy of Daley's statement and of the mounting push for the senator.

By now rumors were flying in all directions and fights were flaring between followers of McCarthy and Smith's staff. Finally Salinger called Kennedy and told him it was high time to make a clear decision. "You must either fish or cut bait," he declared. Kennedy replied that his mind was made up and that he was going to call Humphrey. He told the vice-president, "I have been listening, but I am not a candidate." With that terse sentence, the Kennedy balloon was shot down.

Later, after Chicago's police went wild in the streets and parks, savagely assaulting demonstrators and even spectators with clubs and tear gas, the Democratic convention nominated Hubert H. Humphrey as its Presidential candidate.

Recalling that summer, Kennedy told me later: "Did I ever at any time think I would do that [accept the nomination]? The answer to that would be no. Did I think about it seriously? The answer is yes.

"On the one hand, I had seen that the issues that still were involved were the same ones my brother Robert had campaigned on, believed in deeply, in which I shared, in [pursuit of] which he lost his life. They mattered very deeply to me. It would have appeared that had I been successful in the nomination and the election, I would have been able to achieve the things that he and President Kennedy believed in very deeply and that I shared. For this reason, I did not want to dismiss it lightly.

"But on the other hand, it was just so overwhelming — the reasons not to — that I never really thought of it in terms of attempting to encourage it or pursue it.

"It was the wrong time and under the wrong circumstances."

3. Winning the Whip Job

When the 91st Congress convened as 1968 opened, Ted Kennedy came out fighting: he decided to try to wrest the post of Democratic whip or assistant majority leader from Sen. Russell B. Long of Louisiana.

Even among Kennedy's admirers, reaction was decidedly mixed. For one thing, there was confusion over the offhand manner of his eleventh hour announcement. Many senators learned of Ted's decision only four days before the actual vote was to take place on January 3, 1970. Kennedy apparently made his decision to enter the lists during a family skiing excursion to Sun Valley, where back trouble kept him off the slopes most of the time. Associates said later that the senator had telephoned Edmund Muskie after hearing word that the Maine Democrat was reconsidering his own refusal to challenge Long; Kennedy promised Muskie his support. To Ted's relief, Muskie said that his decision to stay out of the race was firm. He in turn urged Kennedy to throw his own hat into the ring. Next, Ted got the blessings of Hubert Humphrey and, his thirst for advancement whetted, he got on the phone in his room at the Sun Valley Lodge and called about fifty of his colleagues, serving notice that he might make a fight for the whip job.

Moreover, few legislators had expected the last surviving Kennedy to claim such a donkey-work job as whip, and told him so. Later, Ted would say many friends came to him, open-eyed in astonishment that he would want such an "insignificant" job, one that would restrict his traveling and take valuable time from his own senatorial duties. Others, however, advanced the argument that, as whip, he could do more about putting across his own notions, and Bobby's for that matter, than he ever could as a back bencher.

The pro-whip arguments prevailed, and Teddy made up his mind to plunge into his first major fight on the national stage. The decision made, he abruptly left Sun Valley and headed back to Washington.

Senator Long treated the Kennedy announcement with detached amusement. "Senator Kennedy has every right to run against me or anyone else in the leadership, and I welcome the challenge with good humor," he said. The Louisiana senator had known for some time that Teddy was viewing the whip post with more than academic interest and he staged a precautionary counter-offensive, getting lobbyists for oil, milk and other industries busy on the telephone. So confident was he of victory that he left Washington for New Orleans on New Year's Eve to attend the Sugar Bowl game.

But Long forgot the Kennedy family thoroughness and efficiency, once a battle was joined. From his home in McLean, Virginia, Kennedy began calling scores of colleagues seeking their support. Those in the doubtful column got telephoned pep talks from party officials in their home states and from campaign contributors. "My God, that Kennedy machine is really alive!" exclaimed one senator in open awe.

Came the day of the closed door caucus and Muskie himself nominated Kennedy. Albert Gore of Tennessee risked reprisals from Long by seconding it. Long's cause was advanced by Allen Ellender of Louisiana and Spessard Holland of Florida. Finally the secret ballots were cast and Teddy emerged the winner, 31 to 20, surprising everyone but himself.

Thus in an amazing one-week offensive, Teddy had propelled himself from the Senate's back bench to its front-rank leadership. With one swift stroke he had catapulted into a position of national leadership within the party. Even more notably, his blitz had drawn a sharp line between himself and two other potential party leaders, Muskie and McCarthy. He had thus taken a giant step toward his party's presidential nomination in 1972.

Long was plainly stunned by the result. "I had him outgunned in the United States Senate," he said, "but he had me outgunned in the United States." Senate Democratic Leader Mike Mansfield who looks favorably on the Kennedy family appeared elated by the result. He hailed the Kennedy election as "a link with the younger generation," a link that the 65-year-old Mansfield could profit from.

The outcome sent a tremor through the ranks of the Republican party which was still trying to adjust to its new position of authority. "No matter how good a President Nixon makes," said one Republican senator, "Ted will be a formidable opponent. I don't say he necessarily can beat Nixon — but Nixon will know he's been in a fight."

While he probably owed his victory as much to the enemies that Long had acquired over the years as to his own following, Kennedy quickly noted national significance in his selection. He obliquely recalled the challenge posed by both McCarthy and his late brother Robert in the 1968 presidential race. "The winds of change that were so evident in 1968 have expressed themselves in the Senate," he told newsmen. Kennedy described his victory as an expression of support for a "constructive, creative and positive" Democratic legislative program during Nixon's regime.

Kennedy's victory pointed up the difference in his tactics

from those his brother Jack had employed in winning the Presidency. Teddy had chosen the climb up the Senate political ladder. When he was senator, on the other hand, John F. Kennedy had gone hunting for convention votes out in the countryside and he wound up with the brass ring.

The chief irony, however, lay in the fact that Long had been growing weary of the whip's job; he had been ready to give it up until he received word that someone might challenge him.

XV

A Night on Chappaquiddick

1. The Cookout

Ever since 1939, some member of the Kennedy family has tried for a cup in the annual regatta of the Edgartown Yacht Club off Martha's Vineyard, a triangular island under the flexed arm of land that forms Cape Cod. But nobody had ever won anything. On July 18, a hazy Friday in 1969, two Kennedy entries tried again. One, somewhat embarrassingly named the *Victura*,* could do no better than ninth place among thirty-one contestants. Another, the *Resolute*, skippered by eighteen-year-old Joe, Bobby's boy, was twenty-sixth.

It wasn't much of a race, as Ted Kennedy, at the tiller of the *Victura*, had to admit. With only a whisper of a wind, it was unexciting going around the 18.8-mile course laid out in Nantucket Sound. His craft, a 27-foot Wianno Senior exactly his own age, could give a pretty good account of itself on occasion but, though well-tuned and aggressively sailed, it just wasn't her day. He docked the boat in the Edgartown harbor and went aboard

---

*"My father gave the boat to my brother John when he was at Choate," Kennedy says. "The name means 'about to conquer' and sometimes she does." The Kennedys have the cups to prove it.

the *Betawin*, which had won the race, to congratulate the skipper and crew.

But racing is only part of the activity at regatta time. In the tradition of the Kentucky Derby at Churchill Downs, a Harvard-Yale game or any other classic, the sporting phase of the afternoon at Edgartown is generally followed by a fun phase at night. There are parties aboard the sailing craft, in hotels and lodging houses. These are attended by crewmen and their guests which range from quiet affairs at which the races of the day are rerun and dissected by serious yachtsmen, to all-out bashes where the liquor flows freely and the sex is uninhibited.

Following custom, a party had been arranged for the crew of the *Victura* and a number of special guests who had come to watch it race. These people were all alumnae of Robert Kennedy's last campaign the year before, six dedicated young women whose task had been to keep a close watch on the delegates to the Democratic convention — who they are, where they travel, to whom they were swinging, why, and how they could be made to swing to Robert Kennedy. Delegate-tracking around convention time is a critical factor in anyone's political machine and the Kennedys do it better than most. The six had been humorously tagged "boiler room girls" because they would spend fourteen hours daily, including weekends, working the phones like stock salesmen pressuring customers to invest in gold or uranium mines.

It is part of Kennedy political planning to keep dedicated workers dedicated. Moreover, Kennedy organization leaders genuinely *liked* these young women for their loyalty, their incredibly hard work and their buoyant enthusiasm. And so they had been invited to a number of house parties, even after they had scattered to other jobs following the assassination of Robert. The year before, in the springtime while Bobby's campaign was in full cry, the same group had attended a party at the Maryland home of attorney David Hackett, Bobby's roommate at Milton and his oldest friend. "There was dancing and singing and the expected quota of in-group reminiscences," the *Washington Post* reported. "It was a merry, though completely decorous affair." That summer, after the assassination, the "alumnae" had been invited to the Kennedy compound for a sad reunion and a day of quiet sailing.

Now there was to be another reunion. The idea was first

broached by the "boiler-room" group themselves, one of them — Susan Tannenbaum — told Jane Whitmore, a correspondent for *Newsweek*. Miss Tannenbaum, who was working in the office of Allard Lowenstein, Democratic congressman from Long Island, said the young ladies had been asking the Kennedy men to "take us sailing again." And the Kennedy men made arrangements to put them up on Martha's Vineyard and end the day with a cookout. The site chosen for the barbecue was a sparsely populated blob of land, five by three miles, an island named Chappaquiddick which was known for absolutely nothing. (It is a source of a certain species of microscopic crustacean called the *Chappaquiddicka pulchella*, significant only to marine biologists, and not too many of them either.)

Chappaquiddick is linked to the eastern end of Martha's Vineyard by a privately-owned ferry, painted grey and white, whose hull proudly bears the name *On Time*. A small, barge-like affair with wooden seats along the sides for passengers, it has room for only two automobiles on its deck. It chugs across the 500-foot salt water channel in four minutes. There is a sign on a post at the ferry proclaiming the hours of operation: 7:30 a.m. to 12 p.m. The fare in 1968 was fifteen cents per passenger, seventy-five cents for an automobile.

There wasn't much on the island, neither stores nor churches nor even a motel or gas station; just a few dozen homes for its privacy-loving inhabitants, most of whom pack on Labor Day, leaving the place to the gulls and the dozen or so year-rounders. Those who remain, like the Foster Silvas, love the island. "It's just great in the winter," says Mrs. Silva, whose husband is a general contractor. "There's hardly any snow, and it's so lovely and quiet."

In mid-June, Joseph F. Gargan, Kennedy's first cousin, who had grown up around the Cape and knew it well, had rented the Lawrence cottage on the island through Stephen Gentle, an Edgartown real estate agent. Gargan, son of Rose Kennedy's sister Agnes, who planned to vacation there with his wife and another couple, paid $200 for eight days beginning Saturday, June 12. Joan Kennedy did not plan to come because she was two months pregnant and, since she had already suffered two miscarriages, was advised that the drive down might be too strenuous.

A few days before he was to leave, Joe Gargan's mother-in-law fell ill and was taken to a hospital. His wife, Betty, remained with her mother and Joe stayed too, coming down only on regatta day instead of earlier as he had planned. He, Paul Markham, formerly United States Attorney for Massachusetts, and a youth named Howie Hall, that morning sailed the *Victura* down from Hyannis Port. That same morning, Kennedy had flown to Martha's Vineyard from Cape Cod and had been met at the airport by sixty-three-year-old John B. Crimmins, a family aid and part-time chauffeur.

Crimmins had driven down from Boston two days earlier. Chores had to be done: he had to buy steaks, groceries, charcoal and other supplies and stock them in the freezer, refrigerator and cabinets at the cottage. With him, he had also brought down a quantity of liquor — three half-gallons of vodka, four fifths of scotch and two bottles of rum, bought in South Boston. In Edgartown, he had stopped at Mercier's market on Main Street to pick up two cases of canned beer. Since his arrival, Crimmins had been staying at the cottage.

The young ladies, who also came down on regatta day, had registered at the Katama Shores Motor Inn on Martha's Vineyard, three miles from Edgartown on South Beach. A fifty dollar deposit had been made by Crimmins the week before.

Soon after their arrival, the guests were driven to the rented cottage where they got into bathing suits for a pre-race dip. There was a beach a little more than a mile away on the other side of a crude wooden bridge. While they were cavorting in the water, they shouted a welcome to another arrival — Ted Kennedy. Upon reaching Edgartown, he had not gone directly to his motel, the Shiretown Inn, where Room No. 6 had been reserved for him. Instead, he had asked Crimmins to drive him to the Lawrence cottage where he donned swim trunks, and from there to the beach across the bridge.

Kennedy remained at the beach about an hour. Crimmins drove him back across the bridge to the ferry, where he crossed into Edgartown to board the *Victura* and get ready for the race. Meanwhile, the women and men returned to watch the regatta from a chartered fishing boat, the *Bonnie Lisa*, skippered by one Manuel DeFrates.

About 7 p.m., Kennedy went to his room at the Shiretown, which was only a block from the ferry slip, where he changed clothes while Crimmins waited. Then, with Crimmins at the wheel of his black 1967 Oldsmobile 88, he arrived at the cottage about 7:30.

After the races, the ladies returned to the motel to rest and freshen up. Shortly after eight, Raymond S. LaRosa, a frequent sailing companion of Ted Kennedy, picked them up, crossed the ferry and drove the three miles down Chappaquiddick Road to the cottage.

Twelve principals made up the party. The men were: Joe Gargan, Paul Markham, Ray LaRosa (who crewed for Skipper Kennedy during the race), Charles C. Tretter, an attorney who once worked for the Justice Department, Crimmins and the senator.

The six women were: Esther R. Newburgh, then with the Urban Institute in Washington; Rosemary Keough, with the Children's Foundation in Washington, whom friends called "Cricket;" Susan Tannenbaum; Nance Lyons of Senator Kennedy's Massachusetts staff; her sister, Maryellen, who worked for State Senator Beryl Cohen of Massachusetts; and a blond, wholesomely pretty business major graduate of a New Jersey Catholic college, Mary Jo Kopechne.

2. Mary Jo

She was short, barely five feet two inches tall, and so slender her friends sometimes called her "Twiggy." She loved dancing, rock music, chocolate ice cream, swimming, tennis and the Kennedys. A boy friend once waited hours for her to return home from a special assignment. "She'll never marry me," he told her mother sadly. "She's married to the Kennedys."

Mary Jo was devout — a "Novena Catholic," she once described herself — the only child of Joseph and Gwendolyn Kopechne. She was born July 26, 1941 in Plymouth, a tiny community just outside Wilkes-Barre, Pennsylvania, which calls itself the anthracite capital of the world. Joseph Kopechne sold insurance and made a modest living for his family. After attending local schools, she enrolled at the Caldwell College for Women near Newark, New Jersey, a liberal arts institution run by a Catholic order, the Sisters of St. Dominic.

After graduation, she decided to "give a year to God," before embarking on a life work, a commitment the church suggests to all young women fresh from school, though only the most devout and socially dedicated accept. At first she intended to teach on an Indian reservation in Oklahoma, but changed her mind when she discovered she would not be able to return home during the entire twelve-month period. Instead, she chose the Mission of St. Jude in Montgomery, Alabama, where she was paid $50 a month to teach black children.

Early during her year in Alabama, she thought she would devote her life to teaching the underprivileged, but as time passed she felt that her emotional temperament clashed with the requirements of the work. "She became so emotionally involved in the children's problems," her mother later explained. "She felt she wasn't quite mature enough to know how to reserve a part of herself for her own life."

And so, when the year ended, she went to Washington, where the Camelot years had begun. Swept up in the excitement of the New Frontier, Mary Jo sought a job in the Administration and landed one in the office of Sen. George Smathers, the Florida Democrat who knew President Kennedy well.

Mary Jo became an incurable Kennedy buff. She had pictures of President Kennedy (one autographed by him and presented to her after she met him) and Robert Kennedy all over her desk. After Bobby's election to the Senate, she worked for him during a short leave from Smathers. Not long after she returned to her job, Kennedy and her boss walked into her office, her mother recalls. Apparently Bobby had asked for her because Smathers said, as Mary Jo grinned happily: "Well, you might as well take her. There are no pictures of *me* around. Just you and the President."

Everyone who worked for Bobby Kennedy was touched to some degree with hero-worship. Mary Jo was positively overcome. She came early and stayed late; she worked hard, far above and beyond the call of ordinary secretarial duty. She would trot over to Hickory Hill and help Ethel with her correspondence. In February, 1966, she stayed up all night to type a statement Bobby issued on Vietnam, calling for a negotiated settlement. Only Washington secretaries know how tough a chore this could be; with many minds working on a speech or statement, the deletions and additions and rewrites could drive anyone up a wall. Mrs. Kopechne: "If the senator had asked her to, Mary Jo would have tackled Joe Namath."

During Bobby's final campaign, while she worked in the "boiler room" on the sixth floor of a top-secret location in Washington, Mary Jo lived with three other Washington career girls in a small house in the Georgetown section. Her assignment was to track delegates in Indiana, Pennsylvania, Kentucky and the District of Columbia. Above her desk were huge maps of these areas; she could tell at a glance which sections were pro-Bobby, which against. While some stories have reported that her lengthy workday precluded a social life, her mother has said that Mary Jo did manage to "squeeze" one in, though it was hardly hectic. A boyfriend once insisted that she choose between him and the Kennedys. She chose the Kennedys.

When Bobby died, Mary Jo was one of many friends and aides who helped Ethel answer the many thousands of letters and acknowledge the gifts that poured into Hickory Hill. Later, she worked briefly with a political action group registering blacks to vote in Florida elections. In September 1968, she took a job with a private organization, Matt Reese Associates, which sets up campaign headquarters for Democratic candidates.

She kept in close touch with her old friends in the "boiler room" and, the following July, came the invitation to the regatta and cookout at Martha's Vineyard.

3. The Car in Poucha Pond

Dusk comes late on Chappaquiddick Island in mid-summer. It was still daylight when Crimmins pulled the black Olds into the parking area in front of the cottage Joe Gargan had rented. Owned by Sidney K. Lawrence, a Scarsdale, New York, attorney, it was a weathered Cape Codder with two bedrooms and a combination living room and kitchen. And it was hardly a hideaway: the house sat fifty feet from the island's main road, Chappaquiddick Avenue. Diagonally across, 200 feet away, was a home occupied by Mr. and Mrs. James Sullivan, who were renting for the summer. On the same side of the road, 125 yards off, was the year-round residence where Mr. and Mrs. Foster Silva, their daughter and son-in-law and five dogs lived.

Joe Gargan bustled around as host. He arrived at the cottage about 8:30 and commenced preparations: he put the grill some twenty-five feet outside the house, placing it in front of the window so that he could see it from the kitchen. He lit the charcoal, then turned on the oven to heat a tray of frozen hors d'oeuvres: cheese bits, "pigs in blankets," canapés. In twelve minutes they were ready and he began to pass them around to the company.

The first thing Kennedy did on arriving at the cottage was soak in the bathtub for twenty minutes to relax and ease his back. When he emerged, John Crimmins mixed him a rum and Coca-Cola and he mingled with the guests while Gargan was bustling in and out of the kitchen, attending to his hors d'oeuvres and steaks, and a couple of the other men mixed the salad. At first, Ted Kennedy was the self-appointed bartender, but after a little while, everyone helped themselves. Later, Esther Newburgh recalled: "Nobody had more than one or two. We were all tired after the regatta."

Someone turned on a small Bell and Howell transistor radio for dancing but it sounded tinny and was hardly loud enough, so Charles Tretter said he'd go back to the Shiretown Inn to borrow a larger one. Rosemary Keough volunteered to accompany him and they took off in the black Olds. About forty-five minutes later, they returned with the radio. When Rosemary hopped from the car, she left her purse in the back seat.

Later, much would be made of the fact that Miss Keough's purse had been found in the automobile. Wasn't she along on the fateful trip too? Did she play some key role never brought to light?

To Mrs. Silva, who was at home, it was "a normal party with a bunch of happy people." To Mrs. Sullivan across the road, it was like "people in for the evening." Both women heard talking and laughing and singing but no "raucous noises"; in fact, Mrs. Sullivan would hardly even call it a party. And Miss Newburgh, slim, pretty and outspokenly indignant at innuendos that were to be made, was to snap: "It was a steak cookout, not a Roman orgy."

As the steaks cooked, a few of the guests danced, others sang. Senator Kennedy asked for another rum and Coca-Cola and sipped it slowly as he chatted with the guests. Twenty-eight-year-old Mary Jo, Esther Newburgh remembered, had only one drink and appeared completely sober.

When the steaks were ready, the company trooped into the

combination living room-kitchen to eat them. Afterward, there was more music, talk and dancing.

Time passed quickly. A few minutes after eleven, Kennedy was to say later in sworn testimony, he glanced at his watch while he was chatting with Mary Jo. He said it was getting late and that he wanted to return to town. Mary Jo said she too wanted to leave to catch the last run of the ferry before it tied up for the night at twelve.

Usually Crimmins drives Kennedy wherever he wants to go. This time, Ted said, the chauffeur was "enjoying the fellowship" and "it didn't appear to me to be necessary to require him to bring me back to Edgartown." He asked Crimmins for the keys to the Olds, telling him he was tired and wanted to retire and that he would drop Mary Jo off at her motel.

Mary Jo did not tell anyone she was leaving but Esther Newburgh, glancing at the door, saw her depart with the senator. At the same time, she looked at her watch — "a large watch that I wear all the time" — it was 11:30 p.m. Esther remembered thinking: Maybe she's going into the front yard. Later, she had another thought — "that it was a long day watching the race; she was exhausted, and the senator was probably driving her back to the motel so that she could get some rest."

Kennedy slipped behind the wheel and Mary Jo sat beside him. He wheeled the black sedan onto the road, turned right and drove a half-mile to a T-intersection. Here the hard-surfaced, 20-foot-wide Chappaquiddick Road upon which he was traveling turned sharply left at almost a 90-degree angle toward the ferry slip two and a half miles away.

About 500 feet from the intersection, on the right side of Chappaquiddick Road, was a metal sign with a reflecting arrow pointing left toward the ferry landing. At the T and continuing to the right was a road of dirt and sand, 17 to 19 feet wide.

Instead of bearing left on the sharp curve, Kennedy turned right. Some time within the next few moments — he could not recall precisely when — he realized the car was not traveling along a paved roadway, but he did not stop.

Seven-tenths of a mile further down the unsurfaced road was Dyke Bridge, ten feet wide, a wooden hump on piles across a salt water tidal basin called Poucha Pond. The 81-foot-long span veered leftward 27 degrees from the road at the crucial point where the road and bridge met. To cross safely, a motorist must turn his wheel to the left as he enters upon the bridge. Following the straightaway direction of the road will send him over the unrailed sides into the water.

Dyke Bridge loomed in front of the headlights. The front wheels of the car, moving in the direction of the road, rumbled onto the wooden flooring. Kennedy saw blackness ahead. His foot went to the brake pedal, but the right wheel was over the edge before he could press down. The car toppled from the bridge, landing on its roof as it sank ten feet to the bottom of the pond.

Ted Kennedy (testifying at the inquest into the death of Mary Jo, held at Edgartown from January 5 to January 8, 1969): "I remember the vehicle itself going off Dyke Bridge, and the next thing I recall is the movement of Mary Jo next to me, the struggling, perhaps hitting or kicking me, and I, at this time, opened my eyes and realized I was upside down, that water was crashing in on me, that it was pitch-black. I knew that, and I was able to get half a gulp, I would say, of air before I became completely immersed in the water. I realized that Mary Jo and I had to get out of the car.

"I can remember reaching down to try and get the door knob of the car and lifting the door handle and pressing against the door and it not moving. I can remember reaching what I thought was down, which was really up, to where I thought the window was, and feeling along the side to see if the window was open and the window was closed, and I can remember the last sensation of being completely out of air and inhaling what must have been half a lungful of water and assuming that I was going to drown and the full realization that no one was going to be looking for us that night until the next morning and that I wasn't going to get out of that car alive. And then somehow I can remember coming up to the last energy of just pushing, pressing and coming up to the surface. . . .

"There was complete blackness. Water seemed to rush in from every point, from the windshield, from underneath me, above me. It almost seemed like you couldn't hold the water back even with your hands. What I was conscious of was the rushing of the water, the blackness, the fact that it was impossible even to hold it back. . . . I was sure that I was going to drown."

As the current, unusually strong at the point where Poucha

Pond narrows at the bridge, swept Kennedy toward the bank, he called out: "Mary Jo!" a number of times. He waded back into the water to his waist and swam back to the spot. The headlights were still on, enabling him to make out the front of the car. Then, "gasping and belching and coughing," he dived into the water in an effort to rescue the girl.

Ted Kennedy: "And then I dove repeatedly from this side [of the bank] until, I would say, the end, and then I will be swept away the first couple of times, again back over to this side. I would come back again and again . . . until at the very end when I couldn't hold my breath any longer. I was breathing so heavily it was down to just a matter of seconds. I would hold my breath and I could barely get underneath the water. I was just able to hold on to the metal undercarriage here, and the water itself came right out to where I was breathing and I could hold on, I knew that I just could not get under water any more.

"I was fully aware that I was trying to get the girl out of that car, and I was fully aware that I was doing everything that I possibly could to get her out of that car, and I was fully aware at that time that my head was throbbing and my neck was aching and I was breathless, and at that time, the last, hopelessly exhausted."

Kennedy made seven or eight dives until, his strength gone, he was unable to remain submerged more than a few seconds. When, at last, he couldn't even come close to the window or door of the automobile, he came to the surface and let the tide carry him to shore. He crawled upon the bank and lay spent on the grass.

Ted Kennedy: "After I was able to regain my breath I went back to the road, and I started down the road and it was extremely dark, and I could make out no forms or shapes or figures. And the only way that I could even see the path of the road was looking down the silhouettes of the trees on the two sides. . . . And I started going down the road walking, trotting, jogging, stumbling as fast as I possibly could."

His destination was the Lawrence cottage. During the journey back, a distance of over a mile, he did not notice any houses or lights. It took fifteen minutes to reach the cottage.

The lights still blazed and voices floated out into the night. Outside, Kennedy saw his friend Ray LaRosa.

He called to him: "Get me Joe Gargan." LaRosa, surprised,

quickly entered the cottage and emerged with Gargan. Kennedy said, "You had better get Paul, too." Kennedy had climbed into the back seat of a rented white Valiant which had been used for transportation between the cottage and the motels.

"There's been a terrible accident," Kennedy told them. "We've got to go. . . ."

Markham and Gargan entered the car and, Joe at the wheel, drove to Dyke Bridge, arriving at 12:20. Both men took off their clothes and, as Kennedy had done, dived repeatedly into the water to reach Mary Jo in the submerged car. Once Gargan was able to get halfway into the car, bruising and scraping an arm to the elbow, but was unable to reach the girl.

For forty-five minutes, Gargan and Markham dived into the water until they too were exhausted by the struggles. They returned to the car and drove back along Dyke Road, past the intersection and onto Chappaquiddick Road toward the ferry slip.

Ted Kennedy: "They said to me, Mr. Markham and Mr. Gargan, at different times as we drove down the road towards the ferry, that it was necessary to report this accident.

"A lot of different thoughts came into my mind at that time about how I was going to really be able to call Mrs. Kopechne at some time in the middle of the night to tell her that her daughter was drowned, to be able to call my own mother and father, relate to them, my wife. And I even — even though I knew that Mary Jo Kopechne was dead and believed firmly that she was in the back of that car — I willed that she remained alive.

"As we drove down that road I was almost looking out the front window and windows trying to see her walking down that road. I related this to Gargan and Markham and they said they understood this feeling, but it was necessary to report it. And about this time we got to the ferry crossing, and I got out of the car and we talked there just a few minutes.

"I just wondered how all this could possibly have happened. I also had a sort of thought and the wish and desire and the hope that suddenly this whole accident would disappear. And they reiterated that this has to be reported and I understood at the time that I left that ferry boat, left the slip where the ferry boat was, that it had to be reported and I had full intention of reporting it. And I mentioned to Gargan and Markham something like, 'You take care of the girls, I will take care of the accident.' That is what I said and I dove into the water.

"Now, I started to swim out into that tide and the tide suddenly became, felt an extraordinary shove and almost pulling me down again, the water pulling me down and suddenly I realized at that time even as I failed to realize before I dove into the water that I was in a weakened condition. Although as I had looked over that distance between the ferry slip and the other side, it seemed to me an inconsequential swim. But the water got colder, the tide began to draw me out and for the second time that evening I knew I was going to drown and the strength continued to leave me. By this time I was probably fifty yards off the shore and I remembered being swept down toward the direction of the Edgartown Light and well out into the darkness, and I continued to attempt to swim, tried to swim at a slower pace to be able to regain whatever kind of strength that was left in me.

"And some time after, I think it was about the middle of the channel, a little further than that, the tide was much calmer, gentler, and I began to get my — make some progress, and finally was able to reach the other shore and all the nightmares all the tragedy and all the loss of Mary Jo's death was right before me again. And when I was able to gain this shore, this Edgartown side, I pulled myself on the beach and then attempted to gain some strength.

"After that I walked up one of the streets in the direction of the Shiretown Inn.

"By walking up one of the streets I walked into a parking lot that was adjacent to the Inn and I can remember almost having no further strength to continue, and leaning against a tree for a length of time, walking through the parking lot, trying to really gather some kind of idea as to what happened and feeling that I just had to go to my room at that time, which I did by walking through the front entrance of the Shiretown Inn up the stairs."

The Inn is only a block from the harbor. Kennedy got to his room, he said, a little before 2 a.m., shivering with chill. Removing all his clothes, he collapsed on the bed.

Ted Kennedy: "I could hear noise that was taking place. It seemed around me, on top of me, almost in the room, and after a period of time I wasn't sure whether it was morning or afternoon or nighttime."

According to the senator's account, he rose, dressed and opened the door of his room. "I saw what I believed to be a tourist or someone standing under the light off the balcony and asked what time it was. He mentioned to me it was, I think, 2:30, and went back into the room." Kennedy had talked to Russell G. Peachey, a co-owner of the inn, who said the senator complained of noise from a post-regatta party at the nearby Colonial Inn. Peachey telephoned the inn and, in a few minutes, the noise subsided. Kennedy said he reentered his room and tried to sleep.

It was a macabre night. Sleep was impossible. He turned and tossed; he rose and paced the floor. Once more, he "willed that Mary Jo still lived." As the night wore on, he allowed himself the desperate hope that, when the sun came up and a new morning came that "what had happened the night before would not have happened." Nor could he summon the moral strength to call Mary Jo's mother that middle of the night and tell her that her daughter was dead.

In the morning, Gargan and Markham arrived at the Shiretown Inn. Kennedy, already dressed, was waiting for them. The three men returned to Chappaquiddick. As soon as the ferry pulled into the island slip, Kennedy went to a pay telephone in a shack and put in a call for Burke Marshall, an attorney who once headed the civil rights division of the Justice Department, later named associate dean of the Yale Law School. But Marshall could not be found.

Then, accompanied by Gargan and Markham, he returned once again to Edgartown by ferry and walked to the police station, to report the accident.

He arrived a little after 10 a.m., more than ten hours after his automobile fell from Dyke Bridge.

At 2 a.m., after watching Kennedy plunge into the water, Gargan and Markham returned to the cottage. To Esther Newburgh, Kennedy's cousin looked "red in the face and exhausted," but she and the other girls were too sleepy to ask questions. Having missed the last ferry, the group was scattered throughout the cottage, some curled up on the floor for lack of sleeping accommodations. That night, Gargan and Markham, following Kennedy's instructions not to alarm the girls, said nothing about the accident at the bridge.

Next morning, the party returned to Edgartown. "We were fully expecting to find Miss Kopechne there," Nance Lyons said, "but she wasn't and we waited."

While they were waiting, Senator Kennedy was at the Edgartown police station in an office building a few miles away. But the police chief wasn't there. Dominic J. Arena, the six-foot four-inch former State Trooper who heads the force had gone out to investigate some trouble out at Dyke Bridge. Two young fishermen had seen the wheel of a submerged car sticking out of Poucha Pond.

When he reached the scene, the police chief at once radioed a call to the Edgartown Fire Department to send a scuba diver. Then, figuring that maybe, just maybe, a few minutes' time could help, he decided to go down himself. From the home of Mrs. Pierre Malm, a summer resident whose cottage is only 100 feet from the bridge, he borrowed a pair of swimming trunks. The chief dived into the water, cold in the early morning, and tried several times to reach the car, but was swept away by the strong currents. Breathing heavily, he waited on the bank for the diver, 33-year-old John Farrar, captain of the Edgartown Fire Department Scuba Search and Rescue Division, who donned his gear and, handing Arena one end of a stout rope, lowered himself into the water.

Farrar, who made his living as manager of the Turf and Tackle shop in Edgartown, looked into the automobile. Mary Jo Kopechne was in the rear seat, dressed in a white long-sleeved blouse, dark slacks and sandals, her head on the floor, her sandaled feet visible through the rear window. He tied the rope to her waist and, aided by Arena, pulled her body to the surface and placed it on the grassy bank.

While he waited, Arena had sent in a call to the Communications section to check the ownership of the car — License No. L78207, State of Massachusetts — with the State's Registry of Motor Vehicles. Thanks to the memory banks of computers, the answer came within minutes. The car was registered in the name of Edward M. Kennedy.

Arena, who assumed that the senator was unaware of the accident, called headquarters and asked that a radio call be put out to locate Kennedy. Just as the police chief was calling, Kennedy himself walked into the station house.

Kennedy told the chief he had to talk to him. Without waiting to change from his swim trunks, Arena drove rapidly to his headquarters, where Kennedy, aided by Markham, drafted a statement which the police chief typed himself:

"On July 18, 1969, at approximately 11:15 p.m. in Chappaquiddick, Martha's Vineyard, Massachusetts, I was driving my car on Main Street on my way to get the ferry back to Edgartown. I was unfamiliar with the road and turned right onto Dyke Road, instead of bearing hard left on Main Street. After proceeding for approximately one-half mile on Dyke Road I descended a hill and came upon a narrow bridge (arrow on map). The car went off the side of the bridge. There was one passenger with me, one Miss Mary [here the police chief paused, indicated that Kennedy was not sure of the spelling of the dead girl's last name, and offered a rough phonetic approximation], a former secretary of my brother Sen. Robert Kennedy. The car turned over and sank into the water and landed with the roof resting on the bottom. I attempted to open the door and the window of the car but have no recollection of how I got out of the car. I came to the surface and then repeatedly dove down to the car in an attempt to see if the passenger was still in the car. I was unsuccessful in the attempt. I was exhausted and in a state of shock. I recall walking back to where my friends were eating. There was a car parked in front of the cottage and I climbed into the back seat. I then asked for someone to bring me back to Edgartown. I remember walking around for a period of time and then going back to my hotel room. When I fully realized what had happened this morning, I immediately contacted the police."

When the statement was finished, Gargan returned to the Katama Shores motel and, for the first time, told the girls Mary Jo was dead. He told them how the senator had dived repeatedly into the pond to save Mary Jo. "I want you all to know that I believe it," he told them as they sat, wide-eyed, staring at him, "and I want you all to know that every single effort possible was made to save her."

At the police station, Kennedy had another duty to perform — informing Mary Jo's parents. At 10:30, he picked up the phone.

In her home at Berkeley Heights, New Jersey, Mrs. Kopechne

answered the ring. "Mary Jo's been in an accident," Ted Kennedy said in a low voice.

Gwendolyn Kopechne's words came out in a rush: "Was she killed?"

Ted Kennedy replied: "Yes."

Mrs. Kopechne, alone in her small house, screamed out her anguish. She screamed again and again, terrifying sounds that brought her neighbor's daughter to her door. She cannot recall now what she did but, even in her hysteria, she must have unlatched the door to admit her. Over and over, she screamed, "Mary Jo! Mary Jo's been killed!" as the girl slapped her face to snap the panic. Other neighbors found Joseph Kopechne who rushed home and together they wept.

Later, Ted Kennedy called his mother, who was just leaving to attend a book sale for the benefit of St. Francis Xavier church, where she would autograph books about her dead sons. Briefly, he told her what had happened. Rose cancelled her appearance at the book sale.

Mary Jo's body had been taken to the Martha's Vineyard Funeral Home after Dr. Donald R. Mills, an associate medical examiner, had determined that the cause of death was drowning. Dr. Mills, who had been summoned to Dyke Bridge by Jim Arena, had examined Mary Jo at the water's edge and turned the body over to undertaker Eugene Frieh 'who removed it to his mortuary. The clothing and a sample of blood were turned over to the State Police for analysis. An autopsy was not performed: Neither Dr. Mills nor Chief Arena thought one necessary because all medical signs pointed to immersion as the cause of death and no wounds or bruises or other evidence of foul play were found on the body. Dr. Mills took the precaution of asking the District Attorney's office if, in anyone's opinion there, an autopsy was indicated. In the absence of District Attorney Edmund A. Dinis, Lieut. George Killen of the State Police, Dinis's associate, said if the doctor was satisfied there had been no foul play, as far as he was concerned there was no need for an autopsy to be done.

John J. McHugh, the State Police chemist, put Mary Jo's blood sample through the routine tests: Was there carbon monoxide in significant amounts, indicating she had been asphyxiated prior to drowning? No. Was there evidence of barbiturate poisoning? No. Had she taken amphetamines? No. Only in the test for ethyl alcohol was there a positive reading. The level of ethyl alcohol was 0.09 per cent. Chemist McHugh testified at the inquest that, in an individual weighing about 110 pounds, this amount "would be consistent with about 3.75 to 5 ounces, 80- to 90-proof liquor, within one hour prior to death. Or", he said, "since alcohol diminishes in the blood with the passage of time, such a level could indicate consumption of larger amounts of liquor over a longer period of time."

That day, the principals involved in the celebration and the subsequent tragedy left the island. The women packed and returned to their homes, the men to their families. Kennedy left for Hyannis Port. Later, Mary Jo's body was transported from the mortuary to her birthplace in Plymouth for burial in a hillside cemetery outside town.

A brief lull followed. Except in Massachusetts, the newest Kennedy tragedy did not receive the biggest headlines and little wonder: the story broke in the nation's newspapers the same Sunday morning that man first set foot on the moon.

Americans were digesting the sparse facts about the accident at the bridge and beginning to wonder about the details. Soon a tidal wave of shock would rise and engulf the country.

XVI

. . . Who Fights the Bull

1. Conclave at the Compound

Clearly, Kennedy was in the gravest political crisis of his career.

Even his strongest admirers saw gaping holes in the story he told. Doubts, suspicions and ugly rumors quickly arose. Moreover, there was the clear possibility that Ted Kennedy might wind up in prison. Chief Arena had filed a citation charging him with leaving the scene of an accident. Conviction could draw a jail term ranging from two months to two years. For a potential candidate for the Democratic Presidential nomination in 1972, the prospect was shattering. Could he remain a United States senator? Could he remain *anything* anymore in public life? What about the immediate future of the Democratic Party, which had hitched its wagon upon his rising star?

Kennedy's explanation left four main questions unanswered:

1. What kind of a relationship did he have with Mary Jo? Was he really taking her to the ferry, as he claimed? He said that instead of turning *left*, where Edgartown lay, he made a mistake and turned *right*. But the road to the ferry, which he had traveled before, was paved. And the road to the bridge, *upon which he had also driven* — recall he went swimming at the ocean beach beyond Dyke Bridge on his arrival at Martha's Vineyard — was dirt and sand. How could he have made the mistake? Assuming he did make a wrong turn, his lights should certainly have shown

the difference between a macadam and a dirt road, not to mention the roughness of the driving.

2. Why didn't he summon help at once instead of walking more than a mile to the cottage? Newsmen and investigators who swarmed onto the island pointed out these facts: Just one hundred feet from the bridge was the Malm house and the lights were shining. On the way back to the Lawrence cottage Kennedy had to pass four more houses, each of which was visible from the road, each of which had telephones. On Chappaquiddick Road, a few hundred feet before he reached the cottage, was the volunteer fire station, a square building of cement blocks, with a red light glowing. It was unlocked; inside was an alarm that could be pulled to summon help.

3. Why did he wait ten full hours before reporting the accident? Assuming he was in a state of shock, there may be a reasonable explanation to questions two and three, but then:

4. Why didn't Gargan and Markham report the accident as soon as they heard about it instead of returning to the site with Kennedy to attempt their own rescue? Why didn't they make a report after these fruitless efforts? Wasn't it all too clear that the men involved were desperately stalling for time until they could find a way out for Kennedy?

Small wonder, then, that the topmost layer of New Frontiersmen and political brain trusters dropped their work and cut short their vacations that July to catch the next planes for Hyannis Port.

Some arrived that Saturday night. By Sunday morning, fifteen had gathered, overflowing the senator's ten-room home on Squaw Island and spilling onto the celebrated compound a thousand yards away where they bunked anywhere they could find a space. This wasn't easy because all the Kennedy women and their families were summering in the weathered cottages behind the six-foot cedar fence at the bottom of Scudder Avenue.

Among those at the conclave were former Secretary of Defense Robert S. McNamara, Ted Sorensen, Burke Marshall, Steve Smith, Dave Burke, Paul Markham, Joe Gargan, Milt Gwirtzman, Richard Goodwin. Robert Clark Jr. and his son, Robert Clark III, considered to be the foremost motor vehicle accident attorneys in Massachusetts, were summoned. Former Presidential adviser Arthur M. Schlesinger, Jr., the history professor, reached New York on Thursday from a conference in Rumania and flew up to the Cape. Former Ambassador to India John

Kenneth Galbraith, the Harvard economist, unable to come because of illness, contributed advice by telephone from his Vermont home.

As the brain trust deliberated, America had a field day with gossip. *Newsweek* magazine fanned the flame of speculation when it published its now-famous sentence: "The senator's closest associates were known to have been powerfully concerned over his indulgent drinking habits, his dare-devil driving, and his ever-ready eye for a pretty face." The Washington *Post* reported that elaborations on that theme "became an obsessive conversational topic all over the country."

Rumor turned Mary Jo into a "chic and pretty blonde." New Yorkers told each other the "real" story — that she was actually found nude when the car was brought to the surface. In Houston and Chicago, newspapers were flooded with calls from readers who had heard Mary Jo had been pregnant.

Chappaquiddick quickly became a tourist mecca. Visitors poured onto Martha's Vineyard, asking to see Room 6 at the Shiretown Inn where Kennedy had stayed, crossing on the ferry, driving to Dyke Bridge and staring into Poucha Pond, driving back along the road where Kennedy walked to gawk at the Lawrence cottage. Jerry Grant, the ferryman of the *On Time*, observed sardonically: "Finally Edgartown is on the map."

In Waltham, Dave Powers, who always had a smile and a quip for John Kennedy and who loved the entire family as his own, was so distraught he gave up reading about the accident after the third day. He sent Ted a note, reminding him that after the Bay of Pigs episode, President Kennedy had received a four-line poem from a friend which he kept with him constantly and would quote often:

> "Bullfight critics, row on row,
> Crowd the enormous plaza full;
> But there's only one man there who knows,
> And he's the man who fights the bull."

2. Man Alone

Kennedy was plainly in anguish. His face bore a look of utter sadness and, as the days passed, grew haggard from lack of sleep. He ate almost nothing. He seemed perpetually on the verge of tears.

One close friend and associate, one of the first arrivals, won't ever forget how he looked:

"He was confused, still obviously in a condition of shock. His eyes would mist over and you could almost feel his pain."

As the braintrusters arrived, Kennedy would greet them. Then, as they talked, he would wander away to sit on his terrace and stare out across the waters of Nantucket Sound. After a while he would rise and pace the square, blue-carpeted living room, take a book from one of the shelves, riffle its pages, put it back.

On Sunday, in a chill, driving rain, he left the house and walked for two hours along the deserted beach that stretched in front of his house, turning over and over in his mind the events of that terrible night, trying to understand his actions, wondering if the time had now come when he should leave public life for good. On Monday, another wet, raw day, he and Joan walked for an hour on the beach.

At the compound, the other Kennedys were following the family tradition that life goes on, whatever may happen. Ethel, after visiting Ted at his home, was organizing touch football games as usual, tennis games as usual, swimming parties as usual. And, as usual, a Kennedy limb was broken during a game, this time a leg belonging to Ethel's son, David, then fourteen.

Ted Kennedy, however, could not bring himself to join in the games. To Ted Sorensen, President Kennedy's special assistant who watched him closely, he was grief-stricken — "unable to comprehend his own actions that nightmarish night." To another associate, he was plainly a man in a daze: "It was hard to talk to him. Few of us even tried."

As the days passed, the shock wore off, and Kennedy was able to focus his mind on the problems he faced. He joined in the talks and planning, offering his own suggestions.

On Tuesday, while the conferences continued, Kennedy, accompanied by Joan, Ethel, and Joe Gargan, flew to Mary Jo's funeral in northern Pennsylvania, his neck in a surgical collar. On Friday, minus the brace, he arrived shortly after 8 a.m. at the Dukes County Court House in Edgartown to answer a complaint filed against him by Chief Arena, charging him with leaving the scene of an accident after "knowingly causing injury" to Miss Kopechne. He pleaded guilty before District Court Judge James A. Boyle and received a two-month suspended sentence. Because of the guilty plea, he was not required to undergo any cross-examination. That evening, he appeared on network television from his father's home to explain what happened seven days before on Chappaquiddick Island.

He denied rumors about Mary Jo and himself:

"There is no truth, no truth whatsoever, to the widely circulated suspicions of immoral conduct that have been leveled at my behavior and hers regarding that evening. There has never been a private relationship between us of any kind.

"I know of nothing in Mary Jo's conduct on that or any other occasion — the same is true of the other girls at that party — that would lend substance to such ugly speculation about their characters. Nor was I driving under the influence of liquor."

He described the plunge from the bridge, his efforts to save Mary Jo and his conduct during the next few hours which, he admitted, made "no sense to me at all." He told of his confused thoughts which "were reflected in the various inexplicable, inconsistent and inconclusive things I said and did, including such questions as whether the girl might still be alive somewhere out of that immediate area, whether some awful curse did actually hang over all the Kennedys, whether there was some justifiable reason for me to doubt what had happened, and to delay my report, whether somehow the awful weight of this incredible incident might in some way pass from my shoulders."

He was overcome by "a jumble of emotions, grief, fear, doubt, exhaustion, panic, confusion and shock." Even so, he said:

"I do not seek to escape responsibility for my actions by placing the blame either on the physical, emotional trauma brought on by the accident, or on anyone else. I regard as indefensible the fact that I did not report the accident to the police immediately."

Finally, he confessed that he doubted whether he ought to remain in the Senate: "I understand full well why some might think it right for me to resign." He submitted the question of his resignation to the people of Massachusetts.

It was a remarkable gesture; nobody in living memory had done anything quite like it before. But, given Kennedy's enormous popularity in Massachusetts and the proven ability of the Kennedy machine to get out the vote, it was hardly a risky one.

By 8 a.m. the next morning, 7,500 telegrams were piled on the floor, sofas and tables of his living room and den. Another 7,500 were stacked in the small local Western Union office which had doubled its staff from three to six to handle the flow. "They're calling by the millions," an editor of the Boston *Globe* told a *Time* magazine correspondent. Radio station WCAS in Cambridge reported that its switchboard "looks like Times Square, the way it's lit up." On Monday, six sacks of letters and postcards were deposited at the compound. On Tuesday, there were nine. Within a week, more than 100,000 letters, cards, calls and telegrams were counted, the overwhelming majority asking Kennedy to retain his seat.

The Massachusetts response was favorable indeed, but Massachusetts was not the nation and the criticisms were hardly laid to rest by Kennedy's explanation. *The New York Times* thought the referendum he requested and the swift answer from the people "suggest a carefully worked-out plan to reestablish his political position in the eyes of the voters of his state."

Ted Lewis, political columnist of the New York *Daily News*, reported that loyal Kennedy precinct workers in key cities helped spur the favorable missives and calls. Doubtless this helped; but the magic of the Kennedy name in Massachusetts helped more. Ted replied to the outpouring of sentiment by announcing he would indeed remain, but, recognizing the blow to his national future, he removed himself from all consideration from the ticket in 1972.

3. Joan

Six weeks after the accident, Joan Kennedy, home only a few days from the hospital, was idly watching a television program in the upstairs sitting room at Squaw Island when a news broadcast began. Before long, a commentator was discussing the latest development in the accident at Chappaquiddick.

On the other side of the room, Nurse Luella Hennessey's lips tightened. Why, she thought, must Joan have to listen, again and again, to these same stories, especially now when she hadn't quite recovered her strength? Luella had an urge to snap off the newsman's account but she refrained; Joan must not get the idea that she was being shielded from realities. Instead, she asked:

"Shall I turn it off?"

Joan, still watching the screen, replied: "No, don't bother."

"They're just rehashing it over and over," Luella said. "Just over and over."

"I know," Joan answered, turning away from the television set.

Joan had just returned home from Cape Cod Hospital in Hyannis. On August 29, signs had appeared that she might lose the baby she was expecting in February. Accompanied by Ethel and Jean Smith, Joan was driven to the hospital. Soon after her arrival, she suffered a miscarriage, her third in six years. Minor surgery, routine in such cases, was performed. Word reached Ted Kennedy at Nantucket Island, where he had gone on a camping trip. He returned at once and, a few days later, took Joan back to Squaw Island.

Luella Hennessey: "It happened so often, the news suddenly coming over the radio and television, but Joan never became agitated. Nor did she listen avidly. She would watch or listen for a while, then go on with whatever business she was doing.

"She talked a great deal about getting Kara and Teddy junior ready for the opening of school, about family matters, of poor Mr. Joseph Kennedy, who was so sick, but never about the accident. She felt, as all the Kennedys do, that unless you can do something about a problem, all you do is talk and talk and get no place. Best to do something else."

In their most intimate moments, the Kennedys do not dwell on the facts of their tragedies. While John and Robert are alive in their thoughts, the details of their assassinations are never mentioned. So too with Chappaquiddick.

Miss Hennessey: "The subject was never brought up. There were no 'Isn't it terrible?' and 'What do you think?' and all that. They go on, trying to live as normal lives as they can."

Nonetheless, the shock to the family was profound.

Publicly, Rose took her familiar stiff-upper-lip, carry-on attitude, telling newsmen: "I'm sure Ted will rise above all this. How you cope is the important thing, not the events. Teddy has been so magnificent under a tremendous strain. He has been overly conscientious about his father, about me and about Ethel, in addition to his own obligations."

Privately, she was a mother all but shattered by still another calamity in her family. "She was upset, terribly upset," says Mrs. Vincent Greene, her oldest friend. "Rose never shows emotion. She is the most controlled person I have ever known, but now I knew she was upset. I just knew."

To Marie Greene, Rose revealed more of the feelings than she had to the press: "Teddy has had to bear so much, so much. After all those other tragedies, to have this terrible thing happen to him." Her compassion went out to the Kopechnes. "It's so terrible and so tragic for that lovely girl and her parents," she said. Rose wrote a personal note to the parents, expressing her sorrow.

It was an especially trying time for Joan, who was spending most of her time at home. (After the accident her children, Kara, Edward junior and Patrick, were taken to Ethel's house.) Although many persons reported that the marriage had suffered an acute strain, the fact is that Joan never doubted her husband. Though heartsick for Mary Jo whom she knew well, Joan remained by his side, devoting herself to his recovery from the emotional tailspin into which he was plunged.

Ted Kennedy continued to suffer. He tried to force down food but couldn't. Once he was unable to finish even a small bowl of soup. His face became sickly-yellow and the bones stuck out. His handshake, usually so firm it made people wince, became limp and damp, his perspiring palms revealed an inner turbulence. Within two months, he had lost twenty pounds, inspiring a sick joke on Capitol Hill: "There must be an easier way to lose weight."

It was difficult for friends to talk to him. "He would listen to you," an aide recalls, "and then begin an answer. Pretty soon you would see his eyes move from you to a corner of the room or a faraway point if we were outside, and his words would just fade away. You knew what he was thinking and it was hurting like hell and there wasn't a damn thing either he or you could do about it."

The hate mail, vicious gossip and sick jokes were extraordinarily heavy. Friends tried to shield him from these but Kennedy knew they were there. Once he remarked to an aide: "We Kennedys sure bring out the best in some people, don't we?"

Thousands of handbills were circulated, pretending to be reproductions of an Irish newspaper. It read:

DUBLIN DISPATCH

The Voice of the Irish Free World

GOD SAVES SENATOR KENNEDY AS GIRL DROWNS

DEVOUT PAIR BELIEVED TO BE ON WAY TO MIDNIGHT MASS

Ted Prays for Almost Nine Hours Before Leaving Accident Scene

IRISH GOVERNMENT BLAMES ITALIAN CONTRACTOR FOR FAULTY BRIDGE

Gossipers had a field day, the tales becoming increasingly lurid and venomous as days passed: Because Mary Jo was really pregnant, they said, Kennedy had paid off everyone not to perform an autopsy. The cookout was actually an orgy, with everyone "playing switch." Kennedy had bribed the girls to stay silent about this. Incredibly, a high official in the Johnson administration passed this one along to writer Liz Smith, when she interviewed him for a newspaper series on Ted Kennedy: "It is untrue that Gargan and Markham tried to rescue Mary Jo. One of them doesn't even swim." (Both are excellent swimmers.) The same official said: "Washington's bitterest cynics don't even believe Joan Kennedy was pregnant nor that she miscarried. They are saying that the Kennedys would not be beyond using such a story to gain sympathy."

One of the sick jokes that made the rounds had a Democrat pointing to Richard Nixon's picture and asking: "Would you buy a used car from this man?" His Republican companion answered: "Yes, but I sure as hell wouldn't let that fellow Teddy drive it."

Theories were plentiful, and fanciful: Kennedy was dead drunk and his two friends really were walking him around for ten hours to sober him up before they allowed him to face the police. Kennedy was so drunk Mary Jo tried to drive him home, lost her way and fell off the bridge. An entire book (*The Bridge at Chappaquiddick* by Jack Olsen) was written about the incident, elaborately "proving" that Kennedy had left the car to avoid being seen in an embarrassing situation by Deputy Sheriff Look, that he instructed Mary Jo to drive around and pick him up later and that she had driven off the bridge in the dark.

One wild story had Joe Kennedy III, who had raced in the regatta, at the wheel of the car; Ted was actually "covering up for the kid." In his syndicated column, Jack Anderson claimed that Ted, desperately trying to get off the hook, asked Joe Gargan to "confess" he was driving the car and that Gargan agreed, but Kennedy later changed his mind. Kennedy, who had ignored all the other wild tales, was furious at this one; he issued a swift denial.

A book called *Teddy Bare*, which reveals more about the sources of anti-Kennedy fulminations than it does about the accident, was written by "Zad Rust"* and published by Western Islands of Belmont, Massachusetts. It begins with a prologue which asserts that Ted, along with his brothers, is "one of the prominent operators chosen by the Hidden Forces that are hurling the countries of Western Civilization toward the Animal Farm world willed by Lenin and his successors. . . ." The opening chapter offers this: "Beware of the Camelot people! They are the framework of the Establishment and the chief operators of the Conspiracy. . . . In the White House, in the legislatures, in the courts, on the campuses, or in the streets, they represent all that is necessary to bring about the social, spiritual, and military downfall of the last non-Communist big power. . . . They are diametrically opposed to all that other men — men like Douglas MacArthur, George Patton, Robert Taft, James Forrestal, Pat McCarran, and Joe McCarthy — have dreamed and sought for the greatness and glory of their country." After this, one can hardly be blamed for harboring some doubts that the rest of the book contains, as the jacket proclaims, a "careful and honest presentation" of the case.

*"Zad Rust" is an anagram of the surname of Prince Michel Sturdza, an 80 year old Romanian nobleman and former diplomat who headed the Romanian legation to the United States in the late 1920s. The Western Islands is owned by Robert Welch, Inc. Welch is founder and president of The John Birch Society.

4. Boyle's Report

In January the following year, all the principals once again gathered in Edgartown for the long-delayed inquest into the death of Mary Jo. Originally scheduled for September, a post-ponement had been requested by Kennedy's lawyers, who also asked that the January proceedings be held in private. The re-quest was granted by the Supreme Judicial Court of Massachu-setts, which ordered the records impounded until the case was finally closed. A total of twenty-eight witnesses were heard during four-day hearings; their testimony filled five thick volumes totaling 763 pages and 33 exhibits.

Four more months were to pass before the huge transcript was at last released for publication. The story told by the group which had attended the cookout, by the investigators and other witnesses, has been described. The one thing nobody expected was Judge Boyle's own twelve-page summation which shocked the Kennedys to their back teeth.

Judge Boyle reached two conclusions: that Kennedy was not telling the truth when he said he was taking Mary Jo to Edgar-town; and that Kennedy's "negligent" driving "appears to have contributed to the death of Mary Jo Kopechne."

Mary Jo, the judge reported, did not ask Esther Newburgh for the key to her motel room when she left with Kennedy, informed nobody she was going and left her pocketbook at the cottage. And Kennedy, who "rarely drives himself," asked his chauffeur for the keys to the Oldsmobile. He, too, told nobody but Crim-mins that he was leaving. Wrote the judge: "I infer a reasonable and probable explanation . . . is that Kennedy and Kopechne did *not* intend to return to Edgartown at that time; that Ken-nedy did *not* intend to drive to the ferry slip, and his turn onto Dyke Road was intentional. The question then arises as to whether there was anything criminal in his operation of the motor vehicle," the judge said.

Kennedy, he said, had driven over Dyke Bridge twice on the afternoon of that fateful day; thus the judge believed it "prob-able" he knew of the hazard that lay ahead of him on Dyke Road — "but that, for some reason not apparent from the testimony, he failed to exercise due care as he approached the bridge." The judge pointed out that Kennedy testified he was traveling at a speed of twenty miles per hour which, considering the weight of the car and the hazardous crossing, "would at least be negligent and, possibly, reckless."

"I, therefor, find there is probable cause to believe that Edward M. Kennedy operated his motor vehicle negligently in a way or in a place to which the public have a right of access and that such operation appears to have contributed to the death of Mary Jo Kopechne."

Despite this finding, Judge Boyle did not order the senator's arrest and trial, which he was empowered to do under the Massachusetts inquest law. This statute, which dates back to 1877, states that a judge *may* issue a warrant for the arrest of an individual "whose unlawful act or negligence appears to have contributed" to the fatality under inquest. But it does not say *shall*, and the judge did not. He retired next day from the bench and never explained why.

Judge Boyle's report angered Kennedy supporters who pointed out that he had implied a violation of the law but was not prepared to put it to a test by trial. As one friend said: "The judge should have put up or shut up, either stood behind his finding and ordered a prosecution or said nothing. The way he did it, the senator was not given a chance to clear himself in open court." A leading Boston Democrat, quoted by *Newsweek* magazine, exploded: "What the hell do you expect from a renegade Irish Republican who wears sneakers to court?" *The New York Times* observed: "Because of the extraordinary features of the Massachusetts inquest law, the cloud left over Senator Kennedy may never be completely dispelled."

Kennedy himself, replying to the court's findings, asserted they "are not justified and I reject them." He added: "The facts of this incident are now fully public, and eventual judgment and understanding rests where it belongs. For myself, I plan no further statement on this tragic matter. Both our families have suffered enough from public utterances and speculations."

So far as the courts were concerned, the case was closed the day the transcript was released. Perhaps the most significant comment came from Robert H. Quinn, the Massachusetts Attorney General:

"The legal aspects are over. But politically it remains to be seen."

5. Fall and Rise

In the black summer and fall of 1969, Kennedy was written off as a major political force and certainly as a Presidential candidate in 1972 or ever.

"Teddy's finished," *Time* magazine quoted a leading Indiana Democrat. A pro-Kennedy Democratic senator said: "I think we have finally come to the end of Camelot." Gail Cameron, Rose's biographer, wrote: "It seemed sure that Teddy . . . had committed political suicide." A Louis Harris poll found that forty-seven per cent of Americans believed Kennedy displayed qualities that disqualify him for high public trust. One of Lyndon Johnson's former aides said bluntly: "He is even through as a potential leader in the Senate. He can't even make those light-hearted speeches and tell the Irish tales he was so good at. That won't sit well. He can't lead a crusade either. He can never moralize again. He is finished." This same official added: "Congressman (John) Tunney is already not going to be the senator from California because of his association with the Kennedys." Prominent Massachusetts Republicans said his chances for reelection to the Senate in 1970 were ruined and many gloomy Democrats were secretly fearful they could be right.

And yet it didn't turn out that way at all, even though Kennedy himself, in those first weeks, had grave doubts about his future effectiveness. However, having made his decision to run after exhaustive discussions with his family and close advisers, he did not dwell overlong on what *may* lie ahead. Recalling a bitter observation made by his brother Bobby, he told Dave Powers: "In our family, it doesn't pay to plan too far ahead."

When he returned to the Senate three weeks after the accident, his colleagues were astonished at his appearance. Despite Mike Mansfield's hearty welcome — "Come in, Ted, you're right back where you belong now!" — despite all the handshakes and well-wishing, he looked and acted like a beaten man. The bounce and verve were gone; in their place was a hang-dog look, a slow, eyes-cast-down walk, and still the limp handshake.

The snap-back did not come until the middle of September and was signaled by a swift and sharp denunciation of President Nixon's Vietnam policy at a cancer society dinner in Boston. A clear-eyed, vigorous Ted Kennedy, having obviously prepared carefully for the "comeback," delivered a speech in which he charged that the administration's escalation tactics would "lead down the road to war, and war, and more war." The American involvement in Southeast Asia, he said, his voice so loud it caused a hum in the public-address system, was "not worthy of our lives and efforts." It was a conflict, he told the assembled doctors, "that has made us ill as a people, as surely as any disease that attacks the body." The path we have taken, he said, "will continue to erode the health, the economy, and the moral and spiritual strength of the United States of America."

The reaction to the speech was a tonic to Kennedy who, returning to Washington, plunged zestfully into work. His job as Senate Democratic whip left little time to brood: hardly a sinecure, it required him to keep constant track of all legislation and, more importantly, the legislators and how they were voting. He ate and slept better. Angelique Voutselas, his loyal secretary, found it was no longer necessary to order tempting dishes from the Senate restaurant to place before him; he asked for lunch long before it was time.

The strange alchemy which the Kennedys can work on people began to operate once again. Far from being shunned, Ted Kennedy attracted more public attention than ever. When he walked on the street, heads snapped in his direction and he was besieged by picture-takers and autograph seekers. When he appeared in public, people rushed to see and hear him, pushing and straining to get close to him.

All this was reflected in votes and the popularity polls. In 1970, ten months after the release of the inquest testimony and Judge Boyle's harsh judgment of his conduct, Kennedy was reelected to the Senate from Massachusetts, defeating Josiah A. Spaulding by a margin of 469,434. He received sixty-three per cent of the total vote, although his staff had predicted fifty-eight per cent. The victory prompted Matthew Storin to state in the *Boston Globe:* "A year after one of the greatest setbacks in American political history, it must be said that Kennedy has salvaged much of his political potential. . . ." (Confounding the prediction of the L.B.J. aide that Kennedy would drag his friend Tunney to defeat with him, the Californian drew fifty-four per cent of the vote for a stronger victory than Gov. Ronald Reagan, who got fifty-three per cent.)

Just as his star was rising again, came another sharp setback.

6. Losing the Whip

If the election of Ted Kennedy as whip in 1968 surprised many, his abrupt ouster from that post two years later in favor of a virtually unknown legislative technician named Robert Carlyle Byrd of West Virginia hit the Senate like a thunderclap.

The coup was staged as the Democratic-controlled 92nd Congress convened just ten years and one day after John F. Kennedy was inaugurated President. In a move that shook the Senate leadership, Byrd who had been doing the duller chores as No. 3 man in the legislature, toppled Kennedy by a vote of 31-24 in secret balloting by the Senate Democratic caucus.

Kennedy was plainly stunned, as were his liberal allies in the Senate. But actually he had been hearing rumbles for several days that he was losing ground in his effort to retain the whip job. He was also well aware that the post was coveted by Byrd who had made a career out of doing favors for his colleagues. But Kennedy had gone into the caucus confident that he had twenty-eight commitments to retain the job he had wrested from Long.

Byrd, who was not an admirer of the Kennedy clan, had taken potshots at all three brothers along the way. In 1960, when Jack Kennedy was testing out the religious issue in the West Virginia primary, he ran into sharp opposition from Byrd. Byrd had insisted that he was not anti-Catholic, but he did not convince many of his colleagues. They remembered only too well that Byrd had served as a Kleagle organizer of the Ku Klux Klan during World War II and that in 1946, he had written the imperial grand wizard of the organization calling for a rebirth of the hooded night riders "in every state of the union."

Byrd later revealed to newsmen that he would have avoided the contest if Sen. Richard B. Russell of Georgia had died before the party caucus started in mid-morning, instead of four and one-half hours later. "I am a conservative counter," Byrd said, and he did not decide to make the bid until he was certain he had twenty-eight votes. The twenty-eighth vote, he said, had been a proxy from Russell lying on his death bed at Walter Reed Army Hospital.

Mystery surrounded the outcome which showed faulty calculation on the part of both Kennedy and Byrd. It meant that Kennedy had lost four men who had presumably pledged him their support. It also meant that Byrd had gained three votes that he had not counted on. Four men viewed as candidates for the Presidency — Muskie, McGovern, Hughes and Bayh — quickly insisted that they had supported Teddy. But Washington's Henry Jackson, also considered a White House possibility, and Warren G. Magnuson, his colleague from the same state, refused to reveal their preference. Several other senators, who would have suffered from an open association with a former Klan member, were similarly silent.

Why did Kennedy, the golden boy of the Democratic party, lose to such an unlikely figure? Many reasons were advanced by pundits and senators themselves. The widely held view — that Teddy was not adequately carrying out his duties as whip — had substance. He wasn't around enough to carry out his chores. The tragedy at Chappaquiddick had kept him away from the Senate for long intervals and put a damper on his customary desire to make speeches and take a leading role in making Senate policy. Also, he had spent much time campaigning for reelection in Massachusetts in 1970. As a result, resentment had been building up. A staff member of a prominent senator recalled: "One day toward the end of the session, when all the filibusters and pressures were building up, I ran into one of Mansfield's men in the back [of the Senate Chamber]. We talked briefly about some matter, and then he said that Mansfield was so goddamn busy and where the hell was Kennedy."

On the other hand, Byrd, in his post as secretary of the Democratic Conference, had showed a real liking and talent for the hard, dull work that went with the job. He had spent long days on the floor when his colleagues were fence-mending or disporting themselves elsewhere. Byrd, a Washington observer recalled, kept close watch on senators' pet bills, notifying them when they were wanted on the floor and handling many dull housekeeping chores for them. The majority leader himself, Mike Mansfield, said after the upset vote that Byrd's hard work on the floor "must have been a tremendous factor."

Senators have long memories. If Senators Jackson and Magnuson did vote against Kennedy for whip, *The New York Times'* R. W. Apple Jr. speculated, they might well have done so to punish him for voting against appropriations for the supersonic transport, a Seattle project.

But the pundits tended to over-react when Teddy was defeated. Just as many had hailed his election as whip as a giant step toward the White House, now these same criers were declaring that his defeat doomed any chances he might have had for the Presidency. Both claims were unrealistic. At most, his defeat could have indicated a feeling among fellow senators that Ted Kennedy had lost favor with the public.

Many may have felt that Teddy deserved to lose the whip job because he had seriously neglected his duties. But there was a parallel sentiment that his successor should not have been a man with so few visible convictions, a man who had boasted that his hard-line attitudes were not determined by his constituency, but were his personal views.

Adam Yarmolinsky, a Kennedy man, reasoned that Byrd was able to garner votes partly because nobody saw him as a rival for top leadership in the party. But Yarmolinsky warned that the leadership should give some thought to the value that it had bargained away. With the race for the Presidency looming over the horizon, the election of Robert Byrd to the number two Senate spot was certain to embarrass the party and make it particularly awkward for the so-called liberals from the North and West who voted for him.

Kennedy himself managed to take a philosophical view; shaking hands with the victor, he said: "I learned a long time ago that as long as you don't know how to lose — you don't deserve to win."

7. Assessment

In May, 1971, less than two years after the accident, and only months after losing the whip, the Gallup Poll asked registered Democrats whom they preferred to head the Presidential ticket the following year. Kennedy topped the list, eight percentage points ahead of Edmund Muskie, the acknowledged front-runner, and far in front of all the rest. A few days after the poll was published, R. W. Apple Jr. of *The New York Times* asked Kennedy if he thought he could win the nomination — if he tried. "I suppose I could," Kennedy answered, though he said he would not try.

Politicians have lived down scandals of one kind or another before. Jim Curley had been sent to Congress and then reelected Mayor of Boston even after he had been convicted on charges of fraud. Grover Cleveland was elected President amid charges of immorality.* Richard Nixon came back after his personal integrity was seriously challenged in the "slush fund" incident during the 1952 Presidential campaign when he was Dwight Eisenhower's running mate.

Daniel Webster had had a similar fund, and most people knew it, yet he was returned to the Senate from Massachusetts many times. David Lloyd George, whose son called him "probably the greatest natural Don Juan in the history of British politics," remained Prime Minister even though his affairs were common knowledge. If the late Rep. L. Mendel Rivers of South Carolina drank too much, he was reelected time and again and continued to be chairman of the powerful House Armed Services Committee.

Harold E. Hughes of Iowa was elected Governor and Senator, having lived down his reputation as an alcoholic. And, for that matter, Robert F. Kennedy was once a supporter and staff aide of the arch Red-hunter, Joseph McCarthy, but he managed to live that down without damaging his political career.

Only time will tell if Kennedy can live down the accident at Chappaquiddick. The point is not whether Americans *should* forget but *will* they? Astute politicians say that the electorate's memory is notoriously short — for the good things a man may do or the bad. The forgiving stance adopted by the parents of the dead girl could be a strong factor in allowing the memory to fade. In July, 1971, Gwen and Joe Kopechne read a magazine article in which Kennedy was quoted as saying that the accident loomed large in his decision not to seek the 1972 nomination. Promptly, they spoke up: it was time to forget. "The American public," Gwen said, "should vote for the man, not the mistake. If people feel the man has the qualities to do the job, then they should put Chappaquiddick aside." And Joe Kopechne added: "If we're not bitter about it, why should anyone else feel bitter?"

Surely one of the least edifying aspects of the entire incident

*Cleveland admitted being intimate with a young widow named Maria Halpin in Buffalo but denied her claim that he fathered her child, a denial few believed. During his first term as President, Cleveland wrote a friend that, even though he did not know whether he actually was responsible, he did agree to provide for the child, a boy named Oscar Folsom Cleveland. In the campaign of 1884, Republicans played the issue for all it was worth: they distributed cartoons of a baby captioned: "One more vote for Cleveland." Paraders wound through the streets chanting: "Ma, Ma, where's my pa? Gone to the White House, ha, ha, ha."

was the mass dash of old Kennedy hands to Hyannis Port for conferences on what the senator should do next, though newspaper reports exaggerated the scene there. With secrecy clamped on activities at the compound, nobody really knew what was happening inside. Dispatches made it seem as though some kind of week-long convention was underway, with main meetings, subcommittee meetings, liaison people and all the rest. Actually, only Dave Burke and Burke Marshall remained all week; McNamara, Goodwin and Gwirtzman remained only overnight. Ted Sorensen stayed two nights. Ken O'Donnell, who was reported to be there, wasn't. While the television speech that ultimately evolved was the most important item on the agenda, there was far less disagreement on its subject matter than there was over the question of whether Kennedy should speak out at once instead of waiting. The political men urged him to go before the public immediately, but the legal men said no. The political men warned that every hour's delay would increase suspicion that something was wrong and a way out was being desperately sought. The legal men couldn't care less about image. They argued that Kennedy had been charged with a crime and that it would be improper, and perhaps harmful, to state any facts in advance of a court hearing. As usual, the legal men won out.

The question of whether Ted Kennedy was taking Mary Jo to the ferry or to the beach has received considerable attention, even though it should properly be of no concern to anyone but Mrs. Kennedy and Miss Kopechne's parents. Of greater significance is Judge Boyle's report that he was driving too fast, even at 20 miles an hour, to negotiate the hazard safely. (Kennedy's driving reputation through the years is none too good. In 1958, during his second year at law school, he was found guilty of speeding 65 miles an hour in a 55-mile zone in Charlotesville, and fined $15 and court costs. Once in Indiana he became impatient when a young man who was driving him lost his way and Ted took the wheel. When they arrived finally at their destination, the young man sighed to a Kennedy aide: "Last night, when they told me I was going to drive Senator Kennedy, I prayed that nothing should happen to him in my car. When he started driving, I prayed nothing should happen to me.")

The conduct of Gargan and Markham remains incomprehensible. Perhaps the best commentary on their actions has come from the Kopechnes, the next best from a journalist. Said Gwen

Kopechne: "Gargan and Markham are my puzzle. Why wasn't help called for my daughter by Gargan and Markham? I can understand shock, but I don't see where they went into shock." And Jack Newfield wrote that "the behavior of the two was so bad that Ted would have done better going for help to the nearest Legal Aid."

So far as Kennedy and the Presidency are concerned, the one truly significant question concerns the man and his behavior in a crisis. Why didn't he tell all, and at once? Did he act with a panic unseemly in a man who aspires to lead the country? Was he primarily motivated by consideration of self?

Had Kennedy acted forthrightly and told the press and public the full story, and damn the consequences, the consequences would doubtless have been far less serious. He might have been criticized for imprudence but frankness immediately afterward would not have allowed the damaging doubts about his fitness to govern to arise and grow.

Kennedy's behavior that night was deplorable, even stupid. His failure to report the accident immediately was, in his word, "indefensible."

And yet one is nagged, just a little, by a doubt. For out of the welter of rumors and fact arising from the tragedy, too little attention has been paid to the testimony of two doctors who gave Kennedy exhaustive physical examinations on July 19 and 22.

Let us look closely at their findings. Does a measure of explanation lie there?

Dr. Robert D. Watt of Hyannis, associate chief of trauma at Cape Cod Hospital and a diplomate of the National Boards, who has been in practice in Hyannis for twenty-one years, was summoned to see Kennedy the day after the accident. Kennedy's chief complaints, he said, were headache, neck pain, generalized stiffness and soreness. In an affidavit offered as evidence at the inquest, Dr. Watt stated:

"Physical examination revealed his vital signs and neurological examination to be within normal limits. Positive findings included a one-half inch abrasion and hematoma over the right mastoid, a contusion of the vertex, spasm of the posterior cervical musculature with tenderness over the fifth and sixth cervical vertebrae [the area just above the nape of the neck], motion of his head was limited and was accomplished with difficulty, tenderness and soreness of the lumbar area without radiation.

"Diagnosis: Concussion, contusions and abrasions of the scalp, acute cervical strain. The contusion of the vertex was demonstrated by tenderness and a spongy swelling at the top of his head. The abrasion over the right mastoid was obvious. The acute cervical strain was substantiated by X-ray studies which showed a loss of the normal cervical lordosis, which was due to spasm of the cervical musculature. The diagnosis of concussion was predicated upon the foregoing objective evidence of injury and the history of the temporary loss of consciousness and retrograde amnesia. *Impairment of judgment, and confused behavior are symptoms consistent with an injury of the character sustained by the patient* (author's italics).

Dr. Watt prescribed bed rest and a muscle relaxant. On July 21, Dr. Watt saw his patient again and found his condition unchanged. He recommended X-rays of his skull and cervical spine, which were taken the following day at Cape Cod Hospital. After reviewing the X-rays where Dr. Watt found "obvious evidence of an acute cervical strain," the doctor fitted him with a cervical collar. Because of his findings, Dr. Watt felt that neurosurgical consultation was indicated. He called Dr. Milton F. Brougham, chief of neurosurgery at the Faulkner Hospital, the Carney Hospital, the Jordan Hospital and the Cape Cod Hospital, who gave Kennedy a neurological examination.

As a result of his tests, Dr. Brougham found that further studies were called for. On July 23, he and a technician went to Kennedy's home and did an electroencephalogram, a measurement by electronic means of brain waves which can determine whether brain injury has been suffered. Dr. Watt did not see Kennedy after July 23, but was in contact by telephone and found that the neck stiffness continued for more than a month.

The X-ray and brain studies proved negative. Dr. Brougham in his neurological work-up found Kennedy alert and fully oriented, his speech normal. He found a zone of tenderness on the scalp approximately three centimeters in diameter and a swelling and discoloration behind the right mastoid. Kennedy could only extend his neck half the normal range and there was a "moderate" limitation of side-to-side rotation. Dr. Brougham's diagnosis was: "Cerebral concussion. Contusions and abrasions of Scalp. Acute Cervical Strain." His comments:

"This patient gives a history of loss of consciousness and retrograde amnesia sustained at the time of his accident, and the occurrence of the head injury is corroborated by the contusions of the scalp over the vertex and in the right mastoid area. There is also still evidence on examination of an acute cervical strain."

How much of Kennedy's conduct could be blamed on shock? There can, of course, never be an accurate measurement but, as we weigh his behavior that night on Chappaquiddick, the physical and emotional factor must be placed on the scales.

XVII

EMK—The Man

1. "His Heart Isn't in It Any More"

The fun has gone out of politics for Edward Moore Kennedy.

Gerry Doherty, his campaign manager who has barnstormed through every hamlet and every neighborhood of every Massachusetts city with "the boss" since he launched his career, sees it clearly. His old Harvard buddies, the Winthrop House jocks with whom he has maintained close ties through the years, are certain of it. Dave Powers, the political lieutenant of President Kennedy who has been a family intimate for a quarter of a century, *knows* it's true.

And Ted Kennedy himself agrees.

He will still flash his dazzling white-toothed smile from a podium, wave to cheers as he strides in a parade behind an oom-pah band, stand on barroom tables to bellow old songs, dash across a street to pump hands until his own huge ones are red and sore. He will still stand easily before an audience, warming them, teasing them, knowing precisely where to drop a punch line to win the explosive laugh. He will pose for pictures for any-one who asks and, following political tradition, heroically risk stomach distress, not to mention an expanded waistline, by wolfing down hot dogs, fried clams and barbecued chicken at picnics, ice cream at resorts and homemade cake with molasses topping at church bazaars. When a campaign heats up, he will do all of these things from the first light of dawn until the stars are high.

The performance is there, and it is great. He gives the people what they want to see and hear, a gracious, warm, exciting Kennedy with the same kinetic charm of the other Kennedys they remember. But most of the time, as he goes politicking in between and during campaigns, he is an actor playing a role he knows well and carries off with professional polish.

Dave Powers: "His heart just isn't in it any longer. He used to enjoy it so, the marching in the street, the crowds, the big picnics. He'd have that smile from ear to ear. He just loved it all and he was so good at it."

He still is, whenever he chooses to be, but now it's make-believe. As part of the profound change his personality has undergone, he finds it increasingly difficult to derive joy from anything. Dick Clasby, the Harvard football star who married his cousin, Mary Jo Gargan, and knows him as intimately as anyone, says Ted "was one of the greatest people to laugh I had ever known. There was a joy in the guy that came from deep within." Grown up, he was still Luella Hennessey's happy little boy with the sweet, unflappable disposition. "Now he has to reach for the enjoyment," Clasby says. "It's not spontaneous any more — the fun he gets out of things — and it never lasts very long."

Kennedy himself knows he is a different man now. "There is a challenge in politics," he has said. "You say to yourself, 'I wonder if I can do it,' and then, later, you might say, 'I think I can do it,' and you try and you succeed and it's a wonderful thing.

"I used to like the people, the rough-and-tumble of politics, but all that changed after. . . after. . . after 1963."

And all those other people who saw him and worked with him daily — office aides, intimate friends, household staff, senatorial colleagues — have become sharply aware that the man once described by William V. Shannon as "the most extroverted, relaxed and genial of all the brothers" was no longer, as one buddy put it, "the same old Ted."

Rita Dallas, a sprightly, no-nonsense registered nurse who cared for Joe Kennedy for eight years until his death, has vivid recollections of Ted "before and after." In her Alexandria apartment, filled with photos of the Kennedys, she says:

"Ted doesn't have anyone to turn to now, only his sisters, but they're not the same for him. He misses his brothers very, very much. He seems so alone now. The family doesn't allow any sadness to creep into its daily life and so the fun is all there when the gang gets together. The homes are filled with guests and it all looks the same; and Ted mixes in and talks and smiles.

"But then, and this happened so often, the next thing I know he would be walking alone on the lawn and along the dunes. Watching him, you get the feeling that he's now so terribly alone."

Except for Joan whom he needs now more than ever. "We are closer than ever before in our marriage," Joan says.

2. Talk at Squaw Island

The famous Kennedy summer retreat on the ocean bluffs at Hyannis Port is hardly impressive from the two-lane macadam road that winds from the souvenir shops of tourist-swollen Hyannis two miles back. The homes lie behind a six-foot cedar fence, built after John Kennedy was elected President, and there's nothing much to see from the road. Only the presence of a youthful policeman, stationed there to hurry sightseeing motorists along, suggests the place may be something special.

Squaw Island, where the Ted Kennedys have their vacation home, is a mile away, across the causeway, through two great stone pillars, up a hill. "Private road," a sign says here, "residents only." No name marks the entrance to the eleven-room cottage, Early American like its neighbors and, like them, hidden behind the tall trees and bushes that line the narrow road. Its shingles haven't weathered yet: they are still silvery-grey though in time they will darken in the salt air. In front of the house is a small paved area. A bicycle lies on its side just inside the two-car garage. An unwashed white Pontiac GTO stands before the white door where Kennedy had parked it the night before.

I rang the bell and, a moment later, a barefoot Ted Kennedy came to the door in deep purple knit slacks and a black open-throat shirt, exposing a mat of grey chest hair. He had returned the evening before from a five-day sailing and camping trip with his children and some other Kennedys. ("We sailed along the coast and just put in for the night at any likely spot we found and made camp.") The August sun had burned his nose and fore-head, which were bright red and peeling; the mosquitoes had not been kind; but it had all been great. "Old Ethel got all bitten," he chuckled, "but she loved it and so did the kids. Teddy is especially crazy about camping and he's awfully good at it. Knows what to do, makes the fire, cooks. He wants to do it all the time."

While we talked in the large square living room, young Teddy came down, his blond hair shoulder length, his slender body in a sports shirt and tie-dyed shorts, and barefoot like his father. His features, pre-adolescent delicate, bear a striking resemblance to his mother. He shook hands gravely and disappeared outside.

Like all rooms in which the Kennedys live and work, this one is filled with family memorabilia. Pictures are everywhere. On the piano are cups of all sizes for yachting races won by the boys. "My mother was cleaning out the attic," Ted said, "and she wanted to throw these out! Look at them!" They were inscribed to Joe junior, John and Ted.

In front of a window is a five-foot long, hand-crafted model of an old sailing ship, perfect in every detail. "My brother Bobby," Ted said, "gave it to us as a wedding present. He saw it in Altman's one day and knew right away we'd love it. It couldn't be stripped down nor wrapped, so he just said he'd take it the way it was, and he did. He carried it down the elevator, out the door and all the way down Park Avenue and, somehow, got it to us."

Kennedy led the way across the room to the railed-in terrace, beyond which was a small patch of lawn, with a lazily-turning sprinkler, before the slope to the beach. Originally there had been a wall here but Joan had replaced it with sliding glass doors for a view of the Sound. André brought a tray with coffee. Kennedy popped a saccharin tablet in his cup.

He grabbed cushions from a stack and put them on the metal sun chairs. Looking over the rail of the terrace, he pointed out the sights. "Over there," he said, "at the foot of the breakwater, is Dad's house. There's a fine stretch of beach down there." He grinned. "It was down there that I asked Joan to marry me."

"Ahead" — pointing — "just at the horizon is Martha's Vineyard. You can just barely make out the outlines of the shore. It's about twenty-five miles, a nice sail."

Close, his face was unlined, the bluish-green eyes set deep and

narrowing when he smiles. The teeth were white, strong, straight,
the nose prominent and slightly curved, the chin jutting. His hair
was long in the current fashion, reaching his collar in the back,
damp now with perspiration. Strands of grey were sprinkled
liberally among the brown, a fact that may come as a jolt to
those who still look upon him as the "kid brother," but this is
another fact: on February 22, 1972, Ted Kennedy reached his
fortieth birthday.

Kennedy's words come rapidly and they are delivered in complete sentences. The famous Boston "accent," the unmistakable
Kennedy intonation, is there but the listener is surprised to discover that it is considerably less apparent when he speaks in a
conversational tone.

He does not hesitate over a thought but says it straight out.
Nor does he set any ground rules, customary in interviews with
highranking political figures — that "quotes" be cleared before
publication, that certain statements be considered "off the
record" or "for background only."

Young people interest him enormously and he wanted to talk
about them. He spoke compassionately of their anger, bewilder-
ment and frustrations. He is convinced they can help ease
this country's tensions and heal its ominous divisiveness. He is
convinced that eventually they will "turn this nation around."

"Young people are way out in front already," he said. "They
see things with greater clarity than the old-line politicians presently in charge. They cut through the old slogans and meaning-
less rhetoric down to the bone, and they see much that is wrong,
unfair, intolerable.

"Look at the two most important issues of our times for the
past ten years — the war in Southeast Asia and civil rights. In
both of these, the kids have been out in front. Back in 1962, the
young people were talking about the war, and they didn't like it
even then, although in 1963 we had lost only 137 Americans there
and the year before hardly 50. And still the kids were cutting to
the bone and telling us we were wrong to be there.

"In the 1960s, the kids, both white and black, were in the fore-
front of the battle for civil rights. On a Monday afternoon,
February 1, 1960, four freshmen from the all-black North
Carolina Agricultural and Technical College in Greensboro
asked for service at a Woolworth's lunch counter, were refused
— and they stayed.

"The incident was headlined in the newspapers. In my own student days, I suppose my college generation would have shrugged its shoulders and gone on to the sports pages. But this time it was different. Students throughout the north identified with the young idealists sitting in at the Woolworth lunch counter. Before long, many thousands were demonstrating in sympathy in some way.

"From that point on, student involvement in the cause of civil rights grew and grew. They came from the north to demonstrate, to teach black children. They were our national conscience, telling us loudly that something was terribly wrong, and eventually they helped awaken the whole country.

"They were way ahead of the politicians on these issues, just as they're ahead of them in other ways. This is more than a generation in protest; this is a generation in action, and there's a vast difference.

"In a book I wrote a few years back (*Decisions for a Decade*, 1968) I said that youth today wants, more genuinely and thoroughly than any other generation, to help change the world. In the 1960s, they won the right to be heeded and to be taken seriously through such successes as the Peace Corps, VISTA, tutorial programs and community action projects.

"Last spring, the overwhelming majority of law school graduates at Harvard went into some area of public service. Only five entered law firms! In medical schools, it's the same thing — many young doctors are by-passing private practice for some form of public health service. Increasing numbers of business school graduates are moving into the development of minority enterprises."

He warned of a danger: that young people, passionately seeking change, may be discouraged when change does not come rapidly enough. It won't, because each of our vast problems has grown like some virulent organism and has spread its poison throughout our system.

"There are no easy answers, no panacea ," he said. "No one candidate will come searing out of the sky and, after one campaign, suddenly make all things right. There's a long pull ahead and young people must not sink into apathy."

A few weeks later, in an address before the Harvard Law School Forum, Kennedy was to warn students about a creeping apathy that was more reminiscent of the 1950s silent generation than the activism of the 1960s. He urged the college generation: to register to vote; work to prevent infringement of voting rights by local officials; use the "leverage of the campus" to organize young people, and especially young people in the ghettos.

And a few weeks before, on what would have been President Kennedy's 53rd birthday, he had said in a television interview that he would urge all the Kennedy children to join in this great drive and devote their lives to public service.

"Their talents should be devoted toward not their own personal kinds of satisfaction but toward helping others," he said. "That's really what Robert Kennedy would have wanted of his children and President Kennedy would have wanted of his."

Chappaquiddick is never far from his mind. Since it was the most important tragedy in terms of his political career and personal impact, I asked if we might talk about it.

As to the facts, they have been given under oath and the testimony is now a matter of court record. Legally, the case is closed and Kennedy won't discuss the details. He would talk about the tragedy in terms of its effect upon him and his family.

"Obviously it has had a deep personal impact in terms of my own personal existence. It's with me, and will always be with me." The surf swished gently a few dozen yards down the slope. His voice was dropping and I leaned close to catch his words.

"I'll never forget that," he said. He was silent for a long moment and then repeated, this time almost in a whisper: "I'll never forget that."

In January of 1971, shortly after the inquest, he was having dinner with Joan at a hotel on one of the Caribbean islands. He pecked morosely at his food throughout the meal, saying little. Joan did most of the talking. Finally, toward the close of the meal, Joan leaned over the table and grasped his hand. "But Ted," she said, loudly enough to be overheard. "You've got to forget about that. You can't live with it forever."

He is acutely aware of the damage the tragedy has done to his family. Even though all the Kennedys have grown more or less hardened to scandal, the gossip that swept the world about this incident hurt more than almost anything else said about any of them. A few days before, a close friend had told me: "It depresses him that people would consider him so abysmally brainless as to mastermind a sex binge so close to his own home, with so many people, in the presence of an employee and in a place right on a main road with other people and other houses around. People who want to think the worst don't stop to consider the utter brainlessness of such a thing, and in the meantime the story is spread and all the Kennedys get tarred."

"Do you think," I now asked, "that the accident will have a continuing impact so far as your political career is concerned?"

"I suppose it will," he replied. Nevertheless, he told me, he will not allow the issue and the possible reaction to it to affect his political plans: "For me, whether the accident is fading or not as an issue is not the criterion for being in public office or staying out of it."

"On January 21 of 1971, you were deposed as Senate Democratic whip, though most experts counted you a sure winner. Do you believe this stunning reversal may have been due, at least in part, to what happened on Chappaquiddick?"

"No, I don't think so."

He looked out over the calm blue-grey water, then leaned over to toy with his coffee cup, which he had emptied in a single gulp.

"You talk about the tragedy on the island and that's something I cannot forget. But can one assign priorities to tragedies, distinguish one from the other? There have been a lot in my life, and I'm not going to forget them either."

I recalled that a Marine Corps sergeant in Washington had told me something about Kennedy few people know. Two or three evenings each week, between 10 and 11 o'clock, he drives alone to his brothers' graves in Arlington National Cemetery and stands for twenty minutes to a half-hour in silent prayer and thought. Then he walks down the gentle slope of his waiting car and drives home.

How does a man endure so much without being destroyed inside? The reply comes in a low voice, the eyes, narrowing in the sunlight, fixed out across the waters of the Sound.

"I was fortunate," he said, "to have had a father who was such a forceful personality, and a mother who was not only strong but believed in some basic but pretty sensible virtues that work. My parents had a rather simple philosophy, actually. We were loved but we were never pampered. My parents believed in instilling into their children a love of God, the need to be self-reliant and a deep respect for America and its institutions. They believed that if you were lucky to have made a good life in this country, you must be grateful enough to give a great deal back in the form of public service.

"I was also fortunate to have had the guidance and example of my brothers and sisters. It wasn't always the easiest thing to be the youngest in the family, but it was a good spot from which to learn.

"You come out of such a crucible," he said, "able to face life, able to face its harsh realities, able to go on meeting the challenges. You have a faith in God and a confidence in yourself, and this lets you go on."

He fell silent. I groped for another question, stumbled and was grateful for an interruption. Flame-haired Patrick, a month past his fourth birthday, appeared to claim his father's attention.

"Hi-i-i-i, Patrick!" the senator called, his mood changing swiftly. He picked up his youngest child and swung him high above his head, then lowered him to his face, kissed him and whispered: "Will you take me swimming today, huh? Will you take me swimming?" Patrick nodded vigorously.

On his feet, the little boy thrust upward a yellow and purple toy: "I've got my ho-ho daddy," he said.

Kennedy said: "Oh, your yo-yo. Say, what a lucky boy you are! You're really lucky to have that! Can you show me how it works?"

Patrick tried but the string wouldn't take hold. "Let me try," Ted suggested. To me, he whispered: "I never knew how to work these things." He wound it up, and had it spinning, somewhat to his own surprise.

"Hey," he said, "look at that going. Look at it. Here, Patrick, give me your hand . . ." He put the string in the boy's hand and pumped it up and down with him. "Look," he said, "you're doing this too. You're making it work!" Patrick giggled in glee.

3. Scandal-Prone

Gossip has plagued all the Kennedy males and buzzes thickest around the handome youngest son.

The Kennedys, it must be said, did little to stem the flow of gossip and much to speed it along. Max Lerner once wrote:

"The historian will note that the Kennedy males, like many of their contemporaries, expressed a lusty vigor that is very much of the present era." And the one just past as well, for three of the four brothers — Bobby is not included though his name was mentioned prominently in at least one case — had acquired an incredible reputation through the years for girl-chasing.

Joe junior, as his friend Tex McCrary, the publicist, once put it, was "the best swordsman in the E.T.O." during World War II. Stories of John Kennedy's roving eye, even while he was President, made fascinating cocktail party chit-chat and still do. He was linked to several well-known actresses. Indeed, his activities from Harvard days forward were so impressive, some members of the press corps irreverently called him Jack the Zipper. The writer Dick Schaap once asked a high newspaper official in Washington: "There's a strong rumor that Bobby is sleeping with Marilyn Monroe. Do you know anything about it?" The executive replied: "If he's not, he's not Jack Kennedy's brother." *

Grandfather Honey Fitz had his problems too with story-spreaders. He was linked with a blond young cigarette girl who went by the name of "Toodles" Ryan, about whom some raunchy limericks were passed along in the saloons during Honey Fitz's heyday. Miss Ryan was even injected into the 1917 mayoralty campaign by Fitzgerald's great enemy and opponent for the office, Jim Curley. The incumbent Curley had given his approval for speeches and a parade at Boston Common by a socialist organization strongly opposed to America's entry into the war. Honey Fitz seized upon Curley's actions to denounce him for sanctioning the march and the speech. Curley's response was a classic.

He wrote a statement charging that Fitzgerald was seeking to stifle free speech "as a measure of personal protection from the truth, which in its nakedness is sometimes hideous though necessary." And so therefore:

"I am preparing three addresses which, if necessary, I shall deliver in the fall, and which, if a certain individual had the right to restrict free speech, I would not be permitted to deliver.

"One of these addresses is entitled: 'Graft Ancient and

---

*Robert Kennedy's friendship with Miss Monroe is discussed in this author's biography, *Ethel: The Story of Mrs. Robert F. Kennedy*. According to stories, none of them documented, Bobby had a special relationship with the late film star during the last summer of her life, 1961, while he was attorney general.

Modern,' another, 'Great Lovers: From Cleopatra to Toodles,' and last but not least interesting, 'Libertines: From Henry VIII to the Present Day.' "

It is a matter of record that Honey Fitz withdrew his candidacy, making it unnecessary for Curley to offer further enlightenment on Toodles Ryan and her dalliances.

Joseph Kennedy Sr. was partners with Gloria Swanson in a number of film ventures, leading to rumors that there was a personal relationship as well. Writes Richard Whalen in *The Founding Father:* "Kennedy won entry to her circle, becoming banker, adviser, and close friend. They were seen together frequently at parties and dinners in New York and California, their mutual admiration apparent to everyone."

Rose Kennedy's biographer, Gail Cameron, says there were other rumors — "of girls in Palm Beach and one woman whom F.D.R. eventually had to advise Joe against seeing further." Miss Cameron quotes a close friend of the Kennedys: "I don't know whether Joe ever went to bed with Gloria or not, but I don't think Rose thought so. If she had, I think she would have locked her door."

In 1971 a reporter for *The New York Times* finally asked Miss Swanson to comment on the rumor, almost a half-century old, that her son Joseph, then forty-eight, was Joseph Kennedy's illegitimate son. "You know, you're the first one who's ever come right out and asked me about that," Miss Swanson told Judy Klemesrud. "They called him Kennedy's child, they called him Mr. [Cecil B.] DeMille's child. Well, he was born in 1922, and I never laid eyes on Joseph Kennedy until 1928. The Joseph he is named after is my father. After my daughter, Gloria, was born, I never thought I'd get married again, and I wanted twelve children. So I went to an orphanage, because illegitimacy wasn't as fashionable in those days as it is now. Besides, I was making four pictures a year then, with only six weeks in between, and I could hardly have had a baby." Joseph lives in Palo Alto, California, where he is an electronics engineer.

Teddy-gossip, almost a parlor game in political circles, is passed around like stock tips. "Have you heard the latest about *him?* No? Well, listen . . ." *Whisper, whisper.*

Where do they come from, these whispers? Some originate with newsmen who cover the senator and claim to be eyewitnesses, and newswomen who claim to have been bedmates. Some are passed along by the other women allegedly involved and by Washington officials who are not friendly to the Kennedys. (The former member of the Lyndon Johnson White House staff quoted in an earlier chapter, says: "The amazing thing about all of the Kennedy men to me is how they found the time and energy to both work and play as they did. It was incredible. . . . The Kennedy boys were all the same way, except for Bobby who was puritanical save when it suited him. Women were a relaxation, a preoccupation between serious tasks, something to fill up the gaps in a man's life. . . . Somebody is going to tie the women-chasing Kennedy men all together and do a book or something on them that is going to shake everybody up.")

How much truth is there in all this? Much, little, none? Who can tell? We should recall that some of the nastier tales spread after Chappaquiddick — the stories that Mary Jo was nude when pulled from the water, that her hands were bloody and the nails gone — were false.

Nor is it inconceivable that a young woman who has received a measure of personal attention from so celebrated a personage as Edward Kennedy might be tempted to embroider the tale as she relates it to friends back home. A smile becomes an invitation, a few pleasant words a pass, a flirtation becomes whatever fantasy wishes.

More to the point is the question: Why is Ted Kennedy so scandal-prone? Why does he, more than his brothers, more than almost any other person in political life today, stimulate such attention from gossipers? Why, for example, was an ordinary evening in November, 1970, enlarged into something approaching an international incident? Stories circulated that he "danced till dawn" in a Paris night club with an Italian princess on the eve of Charles de Gaulle's funeral.

Kennedy had attended a small dinner party at La Chaumière restaurant arranged by Mr. and Mrs. Hugo Gautier, who were old friends, then went to Il Club Privato on the Champs-Elysées for after-dinner drinks. Maria Pia, thirty-five-year-old daughter of former King Humbert of Italy, was in the party. There was no dancing till dawn, or anything else. Kennedy was but one of many hundreds of dignitaries who dined that evening in Parisian restaurants, and later went to late night spots for drinks, yet his "adventure" made headlines.

Perhaps part of the answer may be rooted deep in the human psyche, in the part called envy.

Dr. Joyce Brothers, the psychologist: "Throughout history, attractive men with money and position have attracted gossip. Kings, queens, high courtiers have always been talked about by the populace whose lives were dull and uninteresting and who could thereby savor a few delightful moments, vicariously. We should note that others in political life who do not possess Senator Kennedy's attributes would not be gossiped about. Hubert Humphrey, for example, may be a fine man but he is not young and handsome, hence not associated with love and sex, and not rich, hence not associated with the glamorous world of beautiful people."

The gossip would diminish markedly, Dr. Brothers believes, were Kennedy more circumspect in his behavior. "The political personality who offers nothing for gossipers to chew upon is rarely a target," she says. "Some in public life will not allow themselves to be photographed with a drink in their hands nor go anywhere even slightly questionable."

Ted Kennedy is not at all circumspect. He is, on occasion, an outrageous flirt, turning on the full candle-power of his great charm before an attractive woman. For a Kennedy, this in itself amounts to an indiscretion.

Following his election to the Senate in 1962, Kennedy curbed his natural exuberance, eliminating visits to night clubs and other places of public entertainment where he could be seen and gossiped about. Night clubs are still taboo but the exuberance sometimes bursts out and then something happens that can make headlines. On a fact-finding tour of Alaska in 1969, for example, he took a few draughts from a flask he carried in his briefcase and some hi-jinks followed. He tossed some airline pillows around and led the officials and newsmen in chanting: "Eskimo power! Esss-ki-mo-o-o-o Power!!" That Kennedy may have been entitled to a bracer after a 3,600-mile flight across the tundra was understandable. That he should have been so indiscreet as to take it in full view of the press corps, and then cavort like a Harvard junior on a big football weekend, was lamentable.

Ted Kennedy's youth and sexual magnetism often generates more than gossip: it seems to bother some political critics as well. So it was too, with John and Bobby, whose electric effect upon women was also treated as though it were some kind of baleful influence. One unremitting opponent stated that girls "tugged at their bikinis" when Bobby appeared at a beach resort. Another writer, observing Ted Kennedy's effect upon girls at a Massachusetts community college, said: "Reaction was setting in already, I saw: the coeds were moving around inside the scoops of their auditorium folding chairs, crossing thighs, wriggling, rotating sneaker tips. . . ." Later: "There is much recrossing of mini-skirted legs" as Kennedy concluded his address. The suggestion that Kennedy's appearance arouses young girls may be interesting but it is hardly relevant political analysis. However, these and similar observations continue to be made, with the implication that there is not much else Kennedy has to offer besides sex appeal. Moreover, such reporting may say less about Ted Kennedy than it does about the reporters, who might have been better advised to observe Kennedy more and the thighs and bikinis less.

"Tip" O'Neill, the Massachusetts congressman who has known all the Kennedys well, analyzes Ted's unique talent for attracting gossip this way:

"Ted's personality has always been a great deal more outgoing than Jack's and certainly more than Bobby's, which could lead people to assume a great deal more about him than is actually the case. Let me illustrate what I mean:

"When Jack Kennedy gave a cocktail party, the invitations would set a time limit: 'From six to eight p.m.' And he meant it. Promptly at eight, the guests would be expected to pick themselves up and go, and the party would be over.

"After his election to the Senate, Ted gave a cocktail party at his Georgetown home and the invitations, as usual, read the same as Jack's — six to eight. When the guests rose to leave, Ted asked in astonishment: 'Where you fellows going?' He was told what the invitation said and that his brother had expected his guests to stick to it.

" 'Well,' he answered, 'I'm not my brother! Take off your coats. Besides, we've got all that food.' And so we all stayed there, swapping stories until 3 a.m.

"This kind of convivial nature can easily be translated into playboyishness. Just that one party, for instance, could have been blown out of all proportion by gossipers: 'Hey, did you hear about the blast at Ted's house the other night? Boy, I heard a half-dozen congressmen got plastered and Ted himself was lit up like a Christmas tree and . . .' You can fill it all in yourself.

"This is an in-bred, gossipy kind of town. We love to swap tidbits even more than other towns because the important people are here. The stories that used to go around about Estes Kefauver, God rest his soul, would curl your hair."

I discussed this subject of gossip with Ted Kennedy one warm May afternoon in Washington as we sat on a stone bench a few hundred yards from the Capitol building. In a few minutes he was due on the Senate floor for a roll call vote on raising military pay by $2.7 billion a year. Two school girls approached for an autograph, holding out the inside of a candy wrapper, the only paper they had. Grinning, he borrowed my pencil and a sheet from my notebook and signed his name for them.

Why do people gossip so much about him?

"I suppose there's a lot of interest in terms of the family, in terms of my brothers. And I suppose it all makes interesting reading for some people."

"But why so much about you?"

"Because I'm the last one left. I imagine that's the only answer. Stories such as these have always risen about people in public life. It's the price people must pay for being there, and when you add to that the fact that the Kennedys have always been controversial, the gossip flow enlarges.

"But I wouldn't want to dignify the stories with answers. All that garbage that's being spread — I don't think it's worth commenting about. There will always be sensation-seekers, those who will talk and print stories for their own reasons."

4. Himself

His reading ranges widely. Often he would discover an author or subject and chase down everything he could find about them. On his journey to India in the summer of 1971, he became entranced with the mystical philosophy of the great Indian poet Rabindranath Tagore and read him far into many nights. He was deeply impressed by Jawaharlal Nehru's *Glimpses of World History* and *Letters from a Father to a Daughter*. Back home, on his desk, are three works by Henry David Thoreau whom he greatly admires: *Cape Cod, A Week on the Concord and Merrimack Rivers* and *The Maine Woods.* History, politics, biographies, rank high and often he reads several at once: Thomas Fleming's biography of Thomas Jefferson, *The Man from Monti-*

cello and Clinton Rossiter's works covering the founding of the nation; Barbara Tuchman's *Stilwell and the American Experience in China* and Frederick Dutton's *Changing Sources of Power;* Edwin O. Guthman's *We Band of Brothers* (about Robert F. Kennedy and his circle), and Albert Speer's *Inside the Third Reich*.

As a former Harvard jock who knew a Radcliffe girl or two in his time, he was curious about *Love Story*, the sentimental novel by Erich Segal that drowned America in its own tears in 1970. "I was really touched," he says. Nevertheless, he felt the hero was not typical of Harvard athletes, at least not any he ever knew, and his judgment of the tragic heroine whose language abounds with scatalogical references sheds some light on his taste in women. "I thought she could have been somewhat softer," he says.

His musical preferences are unlike those of his father who, as a young man, developed a love for classical music. In moments of relaxation and his times of grief, Joe Kennedy would sit alone listening to his large collection of symphonic recordings. Ted's taste runs to the lighter classics — Puccini's *Madama Butterfly* is a special favorite. During his long months in the hospital after recovering from his broken back Ted played it constantly. He likes Andy Williams, Engelbert Humperdinck, the Supremes, Dionne Warwick and folk rock. In movies, he prefers Westerns and action films.

As mentioned earlier, he loves food, and can gulp Andrée's chocolate chip cookies by the dozen. But he prudently restrains himself, or tries to. Rose Kennedy once remarked: "Teddy spends a great deal of time worrying about his weight, usually while he's eating ice cream. He doesn't exactly have the Lincolnesque look which he'd like."

His sense of humor on the platform is mischievous, more robust than John Kennedy's, but sometimes as deft and understated. Often, like John, he would make references to the family.

At a campaign dinner in Washington, he said: "My mother called to say she had read that our new President (Nixon) wasn't going to use the Oval Room in the White House. She said she thought someone ought to use it." He paused as a small ripple of laughter swept the audience, then sprung the punch line: "We're looking into that."

Bobby would rib him gleefully but he'd give as good as he received. Talking to a refugee organization in 1968, after his brother had announced his candidacy for the White House job, he explained he had a great personal interest in the plight of refugees anywhere. "Bobby," he explained, "left Massachusetts three years ago and is still looking for a place to settle."

Some of his jokes are hand-me-downs. When he himself was fifteen and chubby, John would point to him on the platform and tell an audience: "You all know what Ted needs. . . ." Five years ago, Bob Kennedy would run his fingers through his own hair and say: "You all know what I need — a haircut. Well, I just got one yesterday." Now Ted Kennedy introduces his nephew Joe, nearly nineteen, whose hair is shoulder length, with the observation: "You all know what Joe needs . . . but he just had one last week."

He often kids himself, sometimes sharply. After he had been defeated for the job of Senate whip by Robert Byrd of West Virginia, he told the Gridiron Club: "I want to assure you that I have nothing against the man who beat me in that fight, Bob Byrd, but you have to admit he wouldn't even have been elected to the Senate if he hadn't run for office on the strength of a famous name."

Addressing the Consumer Federation of America, he took note of the fact that the press release announcing his appearance, issued just before the balloting, was still calling him the Senate whip. "Under the provisions of the Truth in Packaging Act," he told the consumer group, "I am obliged to tell you that I am indeed Edward Kennedy, but I am not the assistant majority leader of the Senate."

He can kid himself, too, while at the same time giving the needle to others. Thus, in an address before the Harvard Law School Forum, he said he had been told that the officials had hoped to get "a young, articulate, prominent Democrat who had serious national aspirations. But John V. Lindsay [New York's mayor who had just turned Democrat and was sounding more and more like a candidate] wasn't available. So they had to settle for me."

He can get off a letter that can skewer a critic, even one as formidable as William F. Buckley, Jr. Once Buckley, the arch-conservative, wrote in his magazine, *National Review:* "If anyone can find me one vote by Senator Kennedy in favor of one measure designed to reduce government spending, I will retire to the DMZ." Promptly, Kennedy replied that he did indeed vote in favor of an amendment to reduce by $21 million the Independent Office Appropriations Bill for fiscal year 1968, concluding:

"So I did want to point out that you haven't given me proper credit for keeping my eye on the federal budget. And I can assure you that the DMZ is not such a bad place since we reduced the bombing. Best regards, Ted."

Although he is a rugged man with limitless physical courage who still plays hard at sports and competes fiercely, the bumptiousness and recklessness of his younger years are gone. Still, now and again, he is not above some rough horseplay and practical joking.

Dick Clasby: "I had never been on skis in my life. Ted took me to Stowe, up in Vermont, where I rented a pair of skis and boots. I figured he'd take it a little easy with me at the beginning, but we got into one lift after another and pretty soon we were way up on top of the mountain, literally in the clouds. Then, when we got off the last chair, we had to hike up to a place called the Nosedive, which was so high the clouds were swirling around us. All the time I'm looking at Ted and he has this straight face, as though this was the kind of thing every beginner does.

"Ted skiis down from Nosedive a couple of hundred yards, then turns and yells, 'Come on'! I stood there, looking at the steep slide and looking at Ted. He must have had a grin a mile wide but I couldn't see it. I said to myself, 'Oh well, here goes,' and went down. I literally went over the treetops and fell.

"I wasn't hurt but I did bust a ski and had to go down the slope on Ted's back because the snow was so deep. But I got even with him for the trick. Everytime we fell, I pushed his face into the snow to make up for the dirty deal he had given me. He thought we were falling because of my weight, but each time we got to a soft spot I would force him to fall and then push his face right into the snow."

Once Kennedy, Dick Drayne and Jim King, another aide, were flying in a small plane from Boston to the western part of Massachusetts for a speaking engagement. Kennedy, looking out the window, began muttering, as though to himself:

"You know," he said, "this is exactly the same type of plane we were flying in that night we had the accident." As Drayne and King squirmed unhappily, Kennedy kept on, in the same laconic tone: "It was the same kind of heavy weather, too, I remember. Couldn't see a thing outside, just like this. And we're flying just about in the same part of the state . . . "

By the time the plane landed, Drayne and King were frankly terrified. "I never was so happy to be on the ground," Drayne says.

He works harder and longer now than he did when he first arrived in the Senate in 1962. Dick Drayne shakes his head wonderingly and says: "Most men are grateful for a twenty-minute break in their day; the boss will look around for something to do." People who note his ebullience and relaxed, friendly manner on the platform are surprised and somewhat chagrined when he appears all business privately. A stewardess on an Indiana-bound jet from New York, excited when he boarded, pronounced him a "surly fellow"; he had buried himself in his briefcase and had never looked up during the entire journey.

Though he swims, skis, plays tennis and touch football, his favorite pastime is sailing, which he takes with the utmost seriousness. Those who crew with him find him all business after castoff. His orders are crisp and he expects them to be obeyed. Woe to the seaman who is slow to loosen a jib or reef a mainsail. Like all the Kennedys, he hates to lose a race. Once he and Bobby were disqualified in a regatta at the Cape. William vanden Heuvel recalls they went straight to the protest committee where, using model boats, they defended their position "with all the force they might have put into an argument before the Supreme Court." They lost.

If Kennedy finds relaxation on the water, he also seeks it *in* the water, a fact that has given his staff no end of problems. He soaks in a bathtub daily in late afternoon or before dinner. The water warms his skin, eases his tensed muscles and he emerges refreshed. This involves no trouble when he is at home but campaigning can be another story.

Gerry Doherty: "It gets tough when we're out in the boondocks someplace. Once he was speaking at a country fair at Gilbertville, which is between Springfield and Worcester. It got to be around that time of day and he had that look on his face; he wanted to soak in a tub.

"I went around knocking on doors, asking people if it would be all right if Edward Kennedy came in to take a bath in their bathtubs. People looked at me like I was nuts. Finally I found some guy who seemed to think it was okay. It's not so easy in the cities, either. Lots of times you go around and people in small apartments would gladly offer their showers but that wasn't the idea. We had to apologize and say it wasn't anything Ted Kennedy had against your apartment, he just wanted a bathtub."

He is absolutely fantastic with children, his own or anyone else's. He has an entire repertoire of stories which enthrall them, mostly because he does voice impersonations of animals and birds — crocodiles and rabbits, bears and lions, eagles and robins. He tells them nightly to his children, in person when he is home, over the telephone when he is not. One of the more remarkable things in Washington must surely be the sight — and sound — of a United States Senator talking like a crocodile into the mouthpiece of a phone as a small boy chortles at the other end.

He spends as much time as he can with the fatherless Kennedy children. He remembers all their birthdays with gifts and phone calls and personal visits. He is a frequent visitor at Hickory Hill and, in the warm months at their Hyannis Port homes, he plans special events for them, such as camping trips, boat rides and picnics.

One spring, he and John Tunney packed food, equipment and a crowd of kids into a mobile camper and took them to Douthat State Park near Clifton Forge, Virginia, where they swam, fished, hiked and rode horses. And when the fathers swam out past the buoys marking the swimming areas, a teenage lifeguard, unimpressed by their stature, motioned them to come back. They did.

He has been especially close with Bobby's oldest boy, Joe, who worked hard for Uncle Ted in the 1970 campaign — and who does not want him to run for President. Ted brought Joe along to private high-level political conferences, letting him see how things are run from the inside. In 1968, after Bobby's murder, he took Joe to Spain to test baby bulls, and was shaken when photos of the boy, blood flowing from a deep scratch, were published in the newspapers. "That's all Ethel needs now," he said.

He was distressed in the summer of 1970 when Bobby junior was taken to court on a charge of possessing marijuana; he dropped everything to rush to Hyannis Port, where he had a long talk with the boy. He takes John junior, son of the late President, sailing as often as he takes young Teddy. One day, the senator visited the temporary Kennedy library in Walpole, Massachusetts, which houses all the Presidential memorabilia that some day will be part of the museum section. Ted picked up the coconut shell upon which Lt. John Kennedy had scribbled a message for help after his PT-109 had been wrecked by a Japanese destroyer. "Some day," Ted told Dave Powers, the acting curator in charge of memorabilia, "I'd like to take young John out there to the Solomon Islands and let him see what his father did in World War II."

Ted takes seriously a child's worries, insignificant though they may appear to an adult, and he can interrupt important business to help solve a problem. In June, 1970, his town house in Charles River Square, Boston, was filled with newsmen and television equipment to hear his announcement that he will run for re-election to the Senate. He had just concluded his statement and opened the floor to questions when Patrick, then three, came up to him. "Daddy," he said, "the meow is here again." A stray cat had been hanging around the yard and Patrick was worried it might be hungry. "Okay," Kennedy said to his son, "let's go look." The reporters waited until the senator could help his son find and feed the cat.

While he endorses the family credo that winning is important, he applies the doctrine less rigidly to his children than his father did. To Joe senior, being first in any competition was all that mattered. Ted teaches his children to be good at games and he wants them to win, but he does not exhort with the same intensity as his father once did. When Teddy junior got a first and a fourth at a school field day, Ted did not demand to know why the fourth wasn't a first. "He did the best he could," he said.

Ted Kennedy has no special formula for rearing the best possible children. "I don't think one has ever been devised," he told me, "nor will it ever be." He understands them, though, perhaps more than most over-thirties.

A Lebanese poet and artist named Kahlil Gibran has been "discovered" in recent years by teenagers who relate strongly to his views of love, marriage, giving, unselfishness and the "larger self." Gibran's best work, *The Prophet*, which contains his philosophy of life he developed over twelve years, is widely read by young people, although few older ones even know of its existence. Kennedy has read it and from it extracted these words about children which he included in his own book, *Decisions for a Decade*, an analysis of national problems:

> You may give them your love but not your thoughts, for they have their own thoughts.

> You may house their bodies but not their souls, for their souls dwell in the house of tomorrow, which you cannot visit, not even in your dreams.

> You may strive to be like them, but seek not to make them like you.

> For life goes not backward nor tarries with yesterday.

> You are the bows from which your children as living arrows are sent forth.

5. Growth and Change

Edward Kennedy can look back upon no single event in his life that reshaped his personality, altered his outlook and sharpened his intellectual awareness. These things happened after his thirtieth year but for him there was no "turning point" as some Teddy-watchers have insisted, no climactic moment that could make him say: Before it happened, I was *this* kind of person, afterward I was *that* kind.

Once he observed: "I'll always remember Tennyson who said you are a product of the events and people you meet in life." The growth in the man and the changes in him (which were significant and even remarkable) can be traced to the influence of events and men — to the accumulation of happenings that unfolded during the entire decade of the 1960s and to the people with whom he came into close contact, especially his brothers. The events — the four great tragedies in the space of just seven years — deepened his compassion, humbled him and channeled his energies into reading, studying and enlarging his horizons. And the man strengthened his liberal thinking and put him unalterably upon the course he was to follow.

Up to the time he was elected to the Senate, Ted Kennedy had been a relatively uncomplex human being. He enjoyed the game of politics thoroughly, was exhilarated by athletics, liked good times, loved his family and had a sunny outlook on the life that could provide these things. If he had any of the self-doubts that racked Bobby, they were not evident. If he speculated in private moments about his identity and purpose, he told nobody.

He was not a brooder like Bobby nor did he possess his brother's bulldog aggressiveness. He was not as emotional as Bobby, nor driven by inner urgings as he was. Though he competed hard, he did not flog himself to increasingly better performance as Bobby did. He was not essentially a thinking man, like John, nor did he possess his unquenchable thirst for knowledge. He was not yet sobered by tragedy, as John had been: John had been old enough to be affected by the loss of his older brother Joe, whom he admired enormously, and his sister Kathleen.

Up to the opening of the sixties, Ted was essentially a big, happy, laugh-it-up Irish kid, essentially unspoiled by his family's millions, who skimmed along the surface of life, a swashbuckler often to the point of rashness and sometimes beyond.

His youthful exploits, which continued all through his twenties, were impressive:

Ted Carey, a Harvard roommate: "A bunch of us would go to the Cape and play a game of King of the Raft. We'd tie a raft to his father's cruiser. The captain would get her up to 20 knots, pretty fast going which made the raft hydroplane. On board the raft, we'd try to push each other into the water. At that clip, this was pretty rough play. The one who was left would be king of the raft and I can tell you that Teddy won pretty frequently. Afterward, the cruiser would turn around and pick up the fallen."

One summer, soon after his graduation from Harvard, he and Dave Hackett, Bobby's Milton roommate and a dear family friend ever since, engaged in a bit of derring-do that might have come out of a Humphrey Bogart movie. On a cruise from the Cape along the Maine coast with Ethel and Bobby and a few other friends, the two, clad only in swim trunks, took a dinghy to shore to pick up some supplies. They rowed past a sleek yacht where several couples were enjoying pre-dinner cocktails on deck. A man, glass in hand, leaned over the rail as Ted, straining at the oars, rowed past. "Faster, faster! Row faster," he called, joshing him. "Mind your own business," Ted snapped back, whereupon the man on the deck called to him: "Come back here and say that again."

Ted did. He reversed oars, rowed to the yacht's side and

clambered aboard. He was Errol Flynn avenging an insult. He was Tom Mix charging the cattle rustlers. He was Douglas Fairbanks as Robin Hood against the Sheriff of Nottingham's men. He grabbed the man who had offended him and threw him into the waters of Northeast Harbor. The women on deck, screaming, ran below; their men followed to see they were locked safely away from this apparently mad youth, then began returning to the deck.

By this time, Hackett had come aboard. The two husky young men stood on either side of the narrow hatchway, waiting for the men to come back. "As each guy appears," Hackett later told Paul B. (Red) Fay, who was to serve as Under Secretary of the Navy in the Kennedy Administration, "I grab him and spin him around and throw him to Teddy, and Teddy throws him overboard. In no time all of the men — there were about eight of them — were in the water. I never saw anything like it."

In Europe, he entered a one-man bobsled race and, though he had never been in one before, hurtled around the dangerous curves at a speed of well over 80 miles an hour to come in first. While climbing the 14,688-foot Matterhorn in the Pennine Alps, he slipped and dangled for heart-stopping moments over a sheer precipice. In this state of suspension, he coolly peeled and ate an orange, then climbed back and went on to the top.

Campaigning for his brother in 1960, he (1) got aboard a bucking bronco at a Montana rodeo and stayed put five seconds before being spilled into the dust, (2) made the first ski jump of his life — 180 feet — at a contest in Wisconsin, (3) barnstormed throughout the west in a plane he piloted himself, (4) took the controls of the *Caroline*, the Kennedy family campaign plane, and landed it at Las Vegas Airport with surprising smoothness. The only thing he wouldn't do was let a marksman shoot a cigarette from his lips.

His election to the Senate in 1962 did not, of course, instantly erase this reckless part of his nature but there was a marked diminution of the adventurous spirit. As we noted earlier, he stayed out of night clubs and swimming pools while fully dressed. He immersed himself instead in Senate work. His main concern was to become an effective senator, a concern that has remained and deepened. Throughout my conversations with him he constantly referred to his responsibilities to the Senate and his constituents and to his "effectiveness." This preoccupation left little time for daredeviltry.

Then came 1963.

To William Evans, his administrative assistant at the time, the change in Ted was clearly visible. "There was a void left in what his brother had launched," Evans says. "He felt, 'now I have more of a part.'" The realization that a responsibility had now been placed on his shoulders accelerated the transition from lighthearted youth to sober maturity.

This first of the four major tragedies of the decade for Ted Kennedy prepared him for the education he undertook during his convalescence from his injuries two years later. Had John Kennedy been alive, there might have been the same urgency to know more and study harder. With his brother gone, shocked into the awareness he had a larger role to fill, he focused his considerable energies to learn and study. As a result, he achieved a remarkable intellectual growth spurt during those eight months in the orthopedic frame.

Old classmate George Anderson feels the air crash was responsible for "the first real change in Ted." He says: "Instead of being an average student, easily diverted, he developed an intellectual curiosity that impelled him to dig deeply into all manner of subjects." John Galbraith saw him blossom, pronouncing him "first-rate as a quick study, almost as good as John F. Kennedy was."

Fundamental and puzzling questions about his own existence, the meaning of life itself, the influence of fate upon humanity and the individual human being, rarely troubled Ted Kennedy prior to 1965. There were, of course, the usual stirrings of curiosity in adolescence and in college days, but they were quickly dismissed as more immediate concerns, such as football and girls, arose. During those long months in the hospital, he turned his mind to intensive speculation on these and other basics for the first time. Not that he solved anything — few people do — but the important thing was that a reflective process which was to take him into deeper labyrinths, seeking elusive answers to more and more troubling questions, had begun. Never again would he be the same extroverted young man. People would soon begin to see in him a seriousness, a compassion, an understanding, a reaching out to other humans, they had never observed before.

Rita Dallas, his father's nurse in the final years, noticed this interesting change:

"After his own illness, he came to a deeper understanding of what sickness was and how sick people feel, something one doesn't truly know unless one has been there. Before his crash, Ted would come into the house singing, making jokes and trying to liven things up for his father who he felt wanted that kind of cheering. Afterward, he understood a sick man doesn't really want to be entertained all the time, that what he really wants is the presence of a loved one. So Ted would just sit there after he recovered, sit there quietly with his father. The feeling was there in the room, of two people extending out towards one another silently, and it was beautiful."

Nonetheless, Kennedy himself knows the crash was not the only episode responsible for the growth and the changes. "It had a significant impact," he told me, "but there were other changes, too, in different ways, all through that period."

After Bobby's death, Ted developed a strong streak of fatalism. Few hints of this had appeared before, but after Los Angeles there was no doubting that the attitude was there nor from whence it had come.

During his last years, Robert frequently gave voice to fatalistic thoughts. Once, during his Senate term, someone cautioned him against a move that might prove damaging to his political prospects later on. He replied: "I can't be sitting around here calculating whether something I do is going to hurt my political situation in 1972. Who knows whether I'm going to be alive in 1972?" One day in 1964, while he was pondering the decision whether or not to run for the Senate, he said despairingly: "I don't know that it makes any difference what I do. Maybe we're all doomed anyway." "Man is not made for safe havens," he said another time. "If it's going to happen, it's going to happen."

Ted's remarks in the last years of the 1960s are almost echoes. "Whatever is going to occur in life, will occur," he told Dave Burke. "What will be, will be," he told Gerry Doherty. "What God will ordain will happen." Paralleling Bobby's cry of despair, "maybe we're all doomed," was Ted's moment of hopelessness when he wondered if "some awful curse" hung over the family.

During the ten weeks of solitary mourning on Cape Cod, Ted Kennedy made the two major decisions of his life:

He would remain in public service. He saw much that was

wrong in the world: "So many people suffering needlessly," he said, "and if I think I can help, it seems to me I must try."

And he would carry on Bobby's unfinished work of helping the poor and disadvantaged. A number of times during our conversations he talked about "the voiceless and the powerless." He said: "I'd like to be their voice, their senator."

At the start of this chapter we noted that the fun had gone out of politics for Ted Kennedy, and now we see what has happened. The mature man has channeled his drive, his main focus of interest from the *game* of politics to the *changes* a man in politics can cause to happen. For him, the excitement, the satisfactions, the passion will henceforth lie not in the contest but the goals that can be attained.

He has become increasingly involved in the causes. He has visited refugee camps, nursing homes, hospitals, impoverished areas and come home with an ever deeper conviction that the poor, the hungry, the oppressed need a voice. And he will act on impulse in their behalf without thinking about, or caring about political or any other consequences.

In the spring of 1969, he told his incredulous aides that he would fly to Calexico on the California-Mexico border to demonstrate his support of Cesar Chavez and the strike he and his United Farm Workers Organizing Committee has been conducting against grape growers for four years. He had wanted to go for a long time but his staff had warned him off — Chavez had many enemies and he would be exposed to, who knows, some crazy people who might be angry enough to fire shots. He had already expressed his support; why anger other elements opposed to the strike by a personal appearance? He had listened. But one Saturday, following a touch football game at Hickory Hill, he went home, packed and took off for Dulles airport without informing any of his aides but Dave Burke, whom he called from the air field. Only three persons accompanied him on the flight: Burke; Sylvia Wright, a LIFE reporter; and John Loengaard, a LIFE photographer. Next day he addressed the strikers from a flat-bed truck: *"Viva la huelga!* [Long live the strike!] Cesar is my brother!" He admitted his aides had all the right reasons for not going. But he had wanted to show the strikers personally how he felt about them, and he did.

In late May, soon after his return, he was driving to his Senate office one morning when a news story on his car radio riveted his attention. For ten days, American forces had fought a bloody battle to capture Ap Bia Mountain in northwestern South Vietnam. Finally, on May 20, the hill was won at a cost of 84 dead and 480 wounded. Hill 937, the Army called it. U.S. troops had been so decimated by enemy rocket grenades, automatic weapons and mines that the GIs gave it their own name: Hamburger Hill.

Kennedy's indignation boiled over. Less than two hours later, and once more against the advice of his aides, he was standing on the Senate floor denouncing the army's actions as "senseless and irresponsible." Why, at this stage of the war, was the army still continuing to send young men to their deaths to capture hills and positions that have no relation to this conflict, he demanded. (Soon after the hill had been captured by the 101st Airborne Division, the army issued orders to abandon it!)

XVIII

EMK—The Issues

1. Domestic Program

The keystone of Senator Kennedy's domestic program is S.3 — the Health Security Act, his bill for national health insurance, co-sponsored principally by Senators John Sherman Cooper of Kentucky and William Saxbe of Ohio. "America," says Kennedy, "is a prisoner of a health care system designed for a bygone era. Doctors, hospitals and patients alike are trapped in a system they cannot change alone."

The Health Security Act would provide universal, mandatory health insurance for all workers, like Social Security. Deductions would be made, like Social Security, from pay checks and income. Employees would pay only one per cent of the total costs of the program, employers 3.5 per cent, while the remainder would come from general Federal revenues. (For the average working man, earning $7,000, the cost would run to $70.)

The Federal Government would set the standards and provide the coverage, thus putting private insurance companies out of the health coverage business. Kennedy says: "In our subcommittee hearings we have strong evidence that the insurance industry has neither the ability nor the will to control costs or promote efficiency in the health system."

The Kennedy plan would pay an individual's total medical bill

— all physician and institutional services, whether as an in- or out-patient, including psychiatric care, drugs, medical appliances and equipment. Basic dental care would be limited at first to children under fifteen. There would be no maximum limit, no waiting period before benefits commence, no deductibles. There would be some limitations on nursing home and long-term custodial care.

His concern extends also to the quality of the nation's health care. Increased appropriations are needed, he says, for health services, research, and manpower. His subcommittee has extended and expanded the Allied Health Manpower Act, allowing more funds to train large numbers of skilled personnel. He has called for more neighborhood health centers, better medical training programs for poverty areas, comprehensive new child and maternal care programs, training of new types of professionals such as family health workers, increased mobility of health professions through reform of licensing procedures and development of programs to attract more health workers to the ghetto.

Senator Kennedy is appalled at the trend toward repression in government. "Many of the signs are small," he says, "but they are ominous. Taken separately, some may not seem unbearable or worth fighting about. But taken together they suggest a trend and pattern which could lead to an even faster circle of repression and reaction with no conceivable end. They are gnawing at the precious foundations of our freedom, chipping away piece by piece the barriers against tyranny and oppression which the framers of the constitution erected." These are some of the symptoms he has listed, calling them "shocking and terrifying":

— more wiretapping in a widening variety of cases, and the assertion of the absolute power to "bug" dissenters without court orders;

— pressure for no-knock searches and for detention without bail;

— the use of scare tactics to discourage attendance at protest gatherings, and the obsessive focus on the few lawbreakers in peaceful crowds of tens of thousands;

— growing use of domestic spies — in schools, in political groups, at public meetings, of informants who sometimes help to foment the very acts they are supposed to be investigating;

— verbal harassment of dissenters by political leaders, not on the merits of the issues involved, but through guilt by association and exaggerated codewords;

— the new application form for Washington demonstration permits with blanks for everything from philosophy to arrest records;

— serious consideration being given to a proposal to remove five and six year old children from their homes into correctional camps on the basis of tests of their potential for later criminality;

— federal stockpiling of huge amounts of teargas, and equipping federal marshals with shotguns they do not need or want;

— sharp curtailment of the availability of federal parole, the best incentive known to give prisoners hope and a goal as they are rehabilitated.

Kennedy believes that the availability of firearms on an unrestricted basis is "the tragedy of a nation unable to keep the instruments of death out of the hands of its children, its criminals, its mental incompetents." At the annual meeting of the National Rifle Association in 1967, Kennedy cited the following statistics: In 1965, 5,600 murders, 34,700 assaults and most of the 68,400 armed robberies were committed with guns. He seeks the registration of all firearms, an inconvenience he regards as no more serious than car registration. The gun lobby's opposition to this minor regulation he regards as "a scandal which deprives the many of a measure of protection to satisfy the whims and emotions of a very few."

Despite his opposition to the Southeast Asian conflict, he does not favor the abolition of all military conscription. He has, however, long been opposed to what he calls the "gross inequities" which have been a part of the selective service system for years. He called the system, as it had been set up, "an outmoded patchwork of laws designed for other times . . ." and ". . . an obsolete, irrational and wholly unfair institution."

Kennedy was one of the early supporters of the lottery system of induction. On February 25, 1969, he introduced legislation to reform the draft system. Among those reforms which have become law are: random selection (the lottery), drafting of young men first, elimination of student and occupational deferments, prohibition of the use of the draft as punishment for protest activities and prohibition of discrimination on draft boards.

His primary concern with the draft is the question of equity. He questions a system which allows a Harvard student to avoid military conscription when a local mechanic cannot. He sees such a system as discriminating against the poor, many of whom cannot afford to attend college. Only a system in which all young men are equally subject to induction can be considered fair.

His anti-discrimination credentials are impeccable. As a member of the Judiciary Committee and its subcommittee on constitutional rights he has supported every major civil rights bill since 1962. He backs the Philadelphia Plan of joint business-government goal-setting as an effective means to increase the number of blacks on federally funded jobs. He opposed the Supreme Court nominations of G. Harrold Carswell and Clement Haynsworth partially on the grounds of their civil rights records.

In 1967, he introduced a bill establishing bilingual education programs for Mexican Americans. He supported the grape boycott and strike by Cesar Chavez. He supported voting rights legislation to end literacy requirements for English-speaking and non-English-speaking citizens. He asked the Civil Rights Commission to investigate discrimination against Puerto Ricans in New England.

While most members of Congress were debating whether or not a constitutional amendment lowering the voting age to eighteen could ever be ratified by the necessary three-fourths of the states' legislatures, Kennedy was investigating whether or not it would be possible to lower the voting age immediately by statute.

When he found it could — by the simple method of amending the voting rights bill — he circulated a memorandum among his colleagues urging their support. Overwhelmingly (by a 64-17 vote) the Senate accepted the idea and the lowered voting age was a reality. Its constitutionality has since been upheld. The Court struck down, however, the provision allowing eighteen-year-olds to vote in state and local elections. Kennedy introduced an amendment, quickly approved, to allow voting in all elections.

Encapsulated herewith are other elements of Kennedy's domestic program:

Pollution. He was a major supporter and a co-sponsor of the Water Quality Act. He has sponsored legislation to create extensive national recreation areas along the Connecticut River. In 1967 and 1969, he introduced bills calling for environmental controls of electric and other power facilities. He has offered a variety of suggestions to combat pollution — among them: a tax on industrial polluters; the construction of mass transit systems to reduce reliance on the internal combustion engine, a major source of pollution; development of federal manpower programs to train new types of workers in the service of environmental protection.

Tax reform: He seeks a minimum income tax so that no one would be able to use loopholes to escape paying taxes altogether; major tax relief for lower and middle income groups; reduction of tax preferences to the petroleum industry; modification of the capital gains tax; tighter controls on the deductions allowed for farm losses; tax credits for political contributions, to encourage political parties to broaden their base by soliciting contributions from small donors.

The Aged: Kennedy introduced an amendment, which passed, to require the licensing of all nursing homes. It is now in effect. He introduced the Older American Community Service Employment Act which would authorize the Secretary of Labor to establish and administer a community senior-service program for persons fifty-five and over who lack opportunities for other suitably paid employment. He seeks an increase in Social Security benefits, automatic increases tied to cost-of-living raises, protections assuring that a rise in benefits will not be balanced by cuts in old age insurance and other programs; an increase in widows' pensions; an increase in the costs paid by Medicare, and an increase in the kinds of medical services covered by Medicare; an increase in the amount of outside earnings that Social Security recipients can make before benefits are cut off.

Veterans: In a statement on the Senate floor on June 1, 1970, he decried the poor medical care Vietnam veterans have been receiving at Veterans Administration hospitals. He charged that the whole medical budget proposed by the Administration for fiscal 1971 is less than the cost of one month's fighting in Vietnam.

On June 24, 1970, Kennedy introduced a bill providing educational benefits for veterans, including remedial and other special services for veterans who require counseling or tutorial or remedial assistance. It also seeks to encourage colleges to admit veterans and develop special programs for them. He co-sponsored (with Sen. Ralph Yarborough of Texas) a bill which would increase veteran's educational allowance from $130 per month to $170 per month.

Drugs: He feels that the current drug situation should be approached also as a medical-psychological and social problem and that while enforcement, especially against illegal importers, manufacturers and pushers of drugs, is vital, a balanced anti-drug program must place equal stress on rehabilitation, education and research. He has co-sponsored legislation to increase federal support for those areas. The bill would provide $420 million in grants spread over three years to community-based facilities and programs.

Crime: Senator Kennedy has urged that any effort to curb crime in America should deal effectively and forcefully with its symptoms while at the same time attacking its root causes — poverty, discrimination, poor education, unemployment, illness and hopelessness. He has called for the modernization of our court system and the reform of our penal institutions. He also feels that we should provide police officers with adequate equipment and training. Such seemingly basic measures as improved street lighting can help deter crime, he feels.

Oil: Kennedy has urged President Nixon to abolish oil quotas on the petroleum products entering the U.S. He has charged that such limits on imports have had the effect of raising the costs the average American must pay for gasoline and heating.

Indians: As chairman of the Indian Education Subcommittee, Senator Kennedy called for the following reforms: (1) formulation of a national policy for Indians developed *by* Indians. He suggested a White House Conference on the subject; (2) formation of a select Committee on Human Needs of American Indians in the U.S. Senate; (3) reorganization of the Bureau of Indian Affairs to assure the proper measure of innovativeness, sensitivity and accountability, all of which it has lacked; (4) relocation of the Bureau of Indian Affairs from the Interior Department to the Executive Office of the President, in the hope of increasing its effectiveness; (5) formation of an Indian Development Corporation, modeled after the concept of the Bedford-Stuyvesant Corporation, initiated by Robert F. Kennedy.

In addition, he introduced a major Indian Education Act which would transform the Federal Indian Education structure into an exemplary system under Indian control.

2. Foreign Policy

By 1966, Ted Kennedy was calling for a negotiated settlement to the war in Vietnam and, if this could not be achieved, at least a "significant" moderation of America's military involvement "to levels more commensurate with the limited aims we have there." That year, he introduced an amendment to the Foreign Assistance Act to add $10 million for the aid of war refugees in Southeast Asia.

Two years later, he questioned whether the maintenance of the government of South Vietnam was worth the cost in American lives. He said: "The government we are supporting does not have its heart in the cause of the people and offers no indication that it can win their lasting confidence. . . . We should make it clear [to the leaders in Saigon] that we cannot continue year after year picking up the pieces of their own failures." In August, 1968, he sponsored a resolution to put the Southeast Asia conflict before the Security Council of the United Nations, outlining the following plan for peace: (1) an unconditional end to all bombing of the north; (2) negotiation with Hanoi for mutual withdrawal of forces; (3) help for South Vietnam to build a viable political, economic and legal structure; and (4) a demonstration of our sincerity by decreasing our military personnel and activities at once.

He opposed the invasion of Cambodia in May, 1970, saying, "We cannot be responsible for the internal machinations of different Southeast Asian countries. We should have learned that lesson in Vietnam. We moved, in the Cambodian war, from advisors to combat troops in a matter of days. This took us, in Vietnam, a matter of years. I think we should have learned from our involvement in Vietnam that we're not going to be able to resolve the situation by military means. This is basically and fundamentally a political problem."

Kennedy supported the court-martial of Lt. William Calley. He said: "We had scores of children lined up in a ditch and shot at point-blank range. I think individuals have to be held accountable for this." But, "I think what is perhaps of greater significance is what this is doing in terms of our own thinking about the war in Vietnam. Perhaps for the first time, Americans are really questioning what others have questioned for some time, and that is the whole question of the morality of our involvement in Southeast Asia."

Kennedy views the Middle East situation as "ominous" and contends that "the prospects for peace and the long-term security of Israel are being steadily swept away — in a tide of daily events which seem of little concern to our national leadership at a time when this concern is so critically needed." The President should make a major diplomatic initiative for peace in the area. Every effort should be made to reduce the violence there, if not end it completely. The Senator suggests that such a diplomatic initiative include the Secretary-General of the U.N. who, in close cooperation with Israel and the Arabs, should make necessary arrangements to reduce the flow of arms into the area and to declare the Mid-East a nuclear-free zone.

Long before the Nixon administration startled the world by moving toward a reconciliation with China, Kennedy was insisting that any foreign policy formulated by this country must "come to grips" with that vast country. He has never shared the fears expressed by many. "If we only look at China's rhetoric, the danger is apparent," he once said, "but if we look at what China has done, rather than what she has said, the portrait of a force hell-bent for trouble fades." Since Korea, he said, the only overt act of conquest by China has been Tibet, which had long been considered a part of China anyway. No Chinese soldiers, he pointed out, have been sent to Vietnam, and China has not even tried to recapture the offshore islands of Quemoy and Matsu. Her army, although formidable, is one primarily of defense.

In a major speech on March 20, 1969, he urged the following steps in pursuit of a new Chinese policy: (1) a proclamation by the U.S. of our willingness to adopt a new China policy; (2) an attempt to reconvene the Warsaw talks; (3) we should unilaterally do away with restrictions on travel and non-strategic trade; (4) we should announce our willingness to reestablish the consular offices we maintained in China during the earliest period of Communist rule, and we should welcome Chinese consular offices in the U.S.; (5) we should strive to include the Chinese in serious arms control talks; (6) we should negotiate the complex question of diplomatic recognition of China; (7) we should withdraw our opposition to Peking's entry into the U.N. (Over U.S. opposition, China was voted into the world body in October, 1971.)

In the nuclear arms race, Kennedy opposes the Sentinel antiballistics missile system (ABM) and the Safeguard system, claiming both are unnecessary, and probably won't work. Fearing that the MIRV proposals (multiple independently guided reentry vehicles) threaten a new and more dangerous round of nuclear arms one-upmanship, he has advocated a freeze on the deployment of both the ABM and MIRV systems.

As chairman of the Senate Refugee Subcommittee, Kennedy's efforts have extended from Cuba to Vietnam, from Biafra to Pakistan. In Cuba, he has supported Cuban Refugee Asylum, which allows the free movement of certain refugees from Cuba to the United States. He has worked to reunite refugee families and gain the release of political prisoners. He introduced an amendment, which passed, to eliminate the requirement that refugees had to leave the U.S. and reenter in order to obtain permanent residency and eventual citizenship.

After his return from Vietnam in October, 1965, he called for representatives from non-governmental charitable organizations throughout the world to join in a great international effort to help the people of South Vietnam in the areas of medical aid, sanitation and other aid programs.

In June, 1968, the Refugee Subcommittee issued a report which urged: (1) that the U.S. assume a far greater role in medical programs for civilian casualties; (2) that an immediate program be undertaken to improve provincial hospitals; (3) that the U.S. take over all medical supply logistics from the time of arrival to the time of use; and (4) that massive inoculation and immunization programs be initiated.

Kennedy persuaded President Johnson to sell eight C-97 cargo planes to the relief agencies helping the Biafrans. He called for the creation of a United Nations relief force which would aid the millions of people caught up in the conflict between Biafra and Nigeria.

In Pakistan, Kennedy called the situation there "the most appalling tide of human misery in modern times." During his trip there he saw "infants with their skins hanging loosely from their tiny bones — lacking the strength even to lift their heads."

He charged the Nixon administration with adding to the misery or refugees by continuing its arms shipments to Pakistan. "We must end immediately all further U.S. arms shipments to West Pakistan," he declared. By assisting the military government of President Mohammad Yahya Khan of West Pakistan in its suppression of the East Bengalis, the U.S. has contributed to a "monumental slaughter."

"Unfortunately," the Senator stated, "the face of America in South Asia today is not much different from its image over the past years in Southeast Asia. It is an image of an America that supports military repression and fuels military violence . . . comfortably consorting with an authoritarian regime."

XIX

EMK—The Presidency

1. Teddy Coming Along?

One day, after John Kennedy had been installed in the White House, Ted was lunching in Cambridge with old Harvard teammate Bill Frate at the Pi Eta club when another classmate, Dick Koch, stopped at their table. Dick had gone into the Navy after graduation and remained to become a career officer. Ted greeted him merrily: "When I'm in Washington, I'll look you up and get you assigned as my military aide!"

In 1968, on the stump in behalf of Bobby's bid for the nomination, he told a throng at a picnic in Iowa: "Eight years ago, I was introduced as the brother of a President. Today I'm infroduced as the brother of a presidential candidate. If about eight years from now you see me coming back to this picnic, well. . . ." His voice trailed off and a small smile appeared. The crowd erupted into cheers.

To students at Harvard, he said: "I know you look forward to starting the academic year under your dynamic new president, Derek Bok. I know when Dr. Bok was first proposed for the presidency, some said he was too young. But as for myself, I've always felt that the country needs more young presidents, so I was with him all the way." At Massachusetts Institute of Technology, he said of his good friend, Dr. Jerome B. Wiesner, its recently elected president: "I always knew one of us would be elected president some day. . . ."

John and Bobby would joke about it, too. In his 1968 drive for the nomination, Bobby got big laughs when he told throngs he had assigned Ted to get tens of thousands of campaign buttons manufactured. "When they arrived," he said, "they all had Teddy's name on them."

Jests? Of course, but the assumption was always there that Ted Kennedy some day would make the run for the White House. For all his affability he was, as his mother observed, "very ambitious, and naturally he wants to do what the other boys did." If there were a family gonfalon, inscribed thereupon would be the credo all accepted, John F. Kennedy's oft-quoted remark: "I came into politics in my brother Joe's place. If anything happens to me, Bobby will take my place, and if Bobby goes, we have Teddy coming along."

In mid-summer of 1971, as others began entering the lists for the Democratic nomination, Kennedy insisted he would not be a candidate. On a late afternoon in Washington, he told me what he had been saying to newsmen for months; "My sole ambition is to be a good senator." In the Senate, he said, he can help make a significant contribution toward the reduction of world and domestic tensions. He added that he hoped to have some influence on the direction the Democratic Party will take in the months ahead but would not actively seek the nomination in July of 1972. He needed time, he said, time to gain more experience, time to take care of all the children, time to assess the public mood.

All through that year he repeated the disclaimer: "I'm not a candidate." "It feels wrong in my gut." "I want to establish more of a record in the Senate." When the polls showed him well ahead of the entire pack he was still insisting: "I haven't changed my mind."

Meanwhile, there was considerable action among the Democratic hopefuls.

McGovern announced his candidacy and, feeling in his bones that he could lead the nation "in a more hopeful and joyful direction," pursued the quest with a quiet intensity. He added some lustrous old Kennedy hands to his camp, among them Arthur Schlesinger and Frank Mankiewicz, Bobby's former press aide. Craggy, Lincolnesque Muskie, glorying in the label "front runner," moved cautiously but move he did, from early morning until past midnight many days of the week, visiting cities, making speeches, holding news conferences, grinding out position papers. In September he stumbled in Los Angeles when, in a private talk with black leaders, he said in reply to a question that, if a black man were running as his vice president, "we would both lose." Supporters, heartened when no severe backlash developed, nonetheless wondered if the remark would rise afterward to haunt him.

Birch Bayh, handsome, dimpled, once a light heavyweight boxer, former Four-H Club tomato growing champion, went charging around the country in a minutely-planned campaign that recalled John Kennedy's: he blitzed across forty-six states in five months, touching every base he could; his staff telephoned brief spot announcements to radio stations everywhere he went on his latest pronouncements and activities; his money-raising divison was efficient and successful, "The only way I ever won anything," he said, "was by outworking my opponents."

Humphrey, ebullient and talkative as ever, was again in the fight, and highly rated in the polls. More important, he was popular with the professional politicians throughout the country, but the L.B.J. brand was upon him and some felt it was cut too deep ever to be erased. "Scoop" Jackson similarly was fighting the hawkish stand he took on Vietnam but he had strong appeal for the right wing and moderates of the party and older people.

Then, as that summer waned, along came tall, blond John V. Lindsay, the Mayor of New York, who switched to the Democratic Party and immediately began touring the nation, playing the game, acting like the candidate he said he was not. Unlike the others, he unleashed no high-powered blitz that would keep him out of City Hall for long periods of time and thus open him to charges of neglecting Fun City. Instead, Lindsay made quiet little getting-to-know-you trips to California, Florida, Indiana and other key states. He stepped up his network television appearances to give America a good view of his personality and his considerable charm. On the Dick Cavett show in October, where he was the sole guest for ninety minutes, he was by turns serious and jocular. He was not running for anything, he assured Mr. Cavett. "After the show, I'm going straight home to my wife, Mary Bird." (It was funny when Bobby Kennedy invented the remark but no matter — it was good once more.) And he said that he was elected president of his Sixth Form at St. Paul's School in Concord, New Hampshire, even though he wasn't running, and the audience could make what it wanted out of that.

As for Ted Kennedy, all through 1971 he was behaving as much like a candidate as any of these and, as a friend said, sitting in the cat-bird seat, "having himself one hell of a time not running — and staying very much in it at the same time." Since he "was not a candidate," he was not obliged, like the others, to tiptoe gingerly around the issues, fearful of offending some political boss or alienating any segment of the electorate. He could have his political cake and eat it too, speak out on any subject he pleased, go anywhere, do anything.

And he did a great deal. He traveled across the country with his health subcommittee, nipping at the flanks of the American Medical Association and getting growled at in return. He accused President Nixon and the AMA of forming a "marriage of convenience" opposed to meaningful reform of the nation's health care system. "Indeed," he said, "it is not too much to say that the AMA and Administration are one and the same — Tweedledum and Tweedledee." The AMA published four pages of rebuttal in its official newspaper, documenting its position and refuting the senator's charges of obstructionism.

When Vietnam war veterans gathered in Washington for their May Day demonstration, he went out at midnight to the Mall at the foot of the Capitol where they had set up camp. Combat-garbed, the veterans were trying to keep warm in the chill. Kennedy drank wine with the men and sang songs with them until 2 a.m. Emerging from a closed session with their leaders in a command tent, he said: "I'm an admirer of these people. They've fought and they've fought gallantly. They are the best of the country." Next day, the administration routed the veterans and their supporters with the tactic of mass arrests in one of the more shameful episodes of recent Washington history. After the protesters tried to halt traffic during the rush hours as part of their avowed intention to "stop the Government," police swept thousands of them off the streets in mass arrests. Dispensing with legally required arrest procedures, Washington police packed all who looked young and wore long hair and dungarees into vans and trundled them to the jails. When these were filled, they put the overflow into the Washington Coliseum and in a practice field used by the Washington Redskins, immediately labeled Woodstockade by the youthful prisoners.

A few days later, Kennedy spoke out in anger during an address at Iona College, a Catholic school in New York: "Most of the arrested demonstrators were your children, your nieces and nephews or your friends' children and nieces and nephews. They included perfectly straight secretaries and professional men and women and serious students, and, of course, Vietnam veterans. We on Capitol Hill know, not only because we see them in the streets and in the detention camps but also because their parents are calling us to find out where and how they are." Hearing this, more than a dozen in his audience stalked out. Later, his Washington and Boston offices received indignant calls and letters: Why wasn't Kennedy standing up for law and order? Why was he defending those hippie kids who tried to stop the Government? They got what they deserved. Kennedy remarked later that if the Government had made the streets safe for cars that day, it also made them unsafe for citizens.

Kennedy invaded hawkish-minded Charleston, South Carolina, for a rare speaking engagement in the South. Addressing the South Carolina Jaycees, he reaffirmed his continuing opposition to the war, to increased military spending, to building the supersonic transport, to racism. *The News and Courier* had to caution Charlestonians in an editorial called "Good Manners" to give Kennedy "the same courtesy they want shown Senator (Strom) Thurmond in other states." There were no untoward events, though Kennedy was closely guarded by Charleston police.

In May, he sent a cablegram to Chou En-lai asking for permission to visit China. In August he flew to India to see for himself the plight of the 7,500,000 refugees fleeing East Pakistan after the West Pakistani Army brutally undertook to crack the separatists' rebellion. Barred by the Pakistani Government from entering the country, presumably because of his criticisms of its administration and of American arms shipments there, he toured refugee camps in India and saw the damage inflicted on men, women and especially children. He was shocked to the core of his being by a tragedy that, he said, "was unequaled in modern times." He saw starvation, babies whose faces were black with gangrene, old men whose skin was stretched loosely over bones, whole families living in holes scooped from the ground. People died all around him as he walked. He saw genocide and he didn't hesitate to call it that.

All this activity was obviously intended to keep Kennedy's name and face before the public. Observers pointedly noted that the senator had not made any Shermanesque statement, had never said he wouldn't run if nominated nor serve if elected. Sargent Shriver, while accepting Kennedy's disclaimer at face value, commented: "What a man says can be changed by events."

2. The Deepest Concern

It isn't far by road from the heart of Boston to the small city of Haverhill, which sits on a bend of the Merrimack just below the New Hampshire border. Even with fairly heavy traffic, Edward M. Kennedy drove the thirty-five miles in less than an hour, arriving shortly before noon. Mayor James A. Waldron, heading the committee of local dignitaries that greeted him, was grateful he had come because this mid-June day in 1970 was special in Haverhill.

The thriving little community, once a colonial frontier town and the birthplace of the Quaker poet John Greenleaf Whittier, was celebrating the 100th anniversary of its elevation to the rank of city. There had been rallies and dinners all week long and now a fine parade, with floats in preparation for months, marching bands in full regalia and high-stepping drum majorettes, was to wind through the streets as a grand climax.

Senator Kennedy stood in the hot sun beside his car in a large square, talking with Paul Kirk and another staff aide as he waited for the parade to begin. Around them milled costumed bandsmen and other forward elements, ready to step out at the marshal's call. Without warning, an explosion — sharp and loud and very sudden — rocked the square. It startled everyone. Edward Kennedy staggered.

A few feet from the senator stood James Spada, a college student from Staten Island, New York, who is an ardent Kennedy supporter. Young Spada edits a small quarterly called EMK, devoted to the life and times of the senator, and he has accompanied Kennedy on campaign tours and other public appearances.

This is what Spada saw:

"Ted Kennedy gave a cry — 'Ho!' — and doubled up, both hands grabbing his stomach as though he had gotten a severe pain. He fell back inside the opened door of his car, on the seat.

"His face was white. It looked totally drained of expression. He was staring straight ahead.

"Then, in just a few seconds, he relaxed. His face took on color and he was smiling and jaunty as though nothing had happened."

A portable cannon, trundled into the square to signal the start of the march, had been practice-fired a few dozen feet away by men dressed as Revolutionary War soldiers. Paul Kirk called to Spada and Phillip Heller, a young campaign worker standing with him: Would they ask the men to refrain from firing again until Mr. Kennedy had gone out of the area? The men complied.

This was not an isolated happening. When sudden loud reports occur within his hearing, Ted Kennedy reacts. Only a few months earlier, another cannon had boomed near the senator during a St. Patrick's Day parade in Lawrence, north of Boston, and he had flinched severely. His wife, Joan, who was walking beside him, had quickly grasped his arm.

Always the recovery is prompt. At Haverhill, moments later, the lead band struck up and Ted Kennedy, his blue suit clinging damply in the heat but a broad smile on his face, strode the entire four-mile length of the march, waving at the crowds lining the sidewalks.

The thought that he is a child of tragedy is never far from Ted Kennedy and his family, and the people who work with him. It is almost never spoken aloud, but in his home and offices there is never any doubt of its chilling presence.

His Senate office, usually busier than a newspaper city room at press time, does wind down eventually and then the thought can surface. The staff can even make jokes about it. "We plan the best funerals," one top aide remarked after Robert Kennedy's assassination in June, 1968.

Dick Drayne says the feeling runs so deep that "only humor can get us through." Humor is an escape valve for the staff, and sometimes even Ted Kennedy will make grim jokes about himself. He knows — and lives with — the thought every day of his life.

The U.S. Secret Service reports that in the years between 1964 and 1971, 355 threats were made against Kennedy and members of his family, three times more than any other senator. Crank and hate mail comes regularly into his office. One close friend says: "His life is threatened weekly. Stories that he receives a hundred phone calls a week are exaggerated, but I can tell you they are damned numerous."

So numerous that Kennedy's wife and two older children have become anxious about his safety. When the senator is away from home, he will telephone frequently. During these conversations, he will ask the children about school work, discuss a forthcoming camping trip, tell little stories of what was happening, all to re-assure them — and Joan too — that he is well. Sometimes, the family will call him.

In the rare times she talks about it, Joan reveals that she is living with the tension all the time. Once a visitor to her McLean home pointed to the senator, who, in bathing trunks, was con-ferring with an aide on the terrace. "Look," the visitor said to Joan. "Couldn't someone just come down the road, into the house and . . ." He didn't finish because Joan's eyes were filling with tears.

The thought is with Rose Kennedy, too. Fred Sparks, in a syndicated series of articles published in July, 1970, wrote that Rose "determined to see her sole surviving son, Senator Edward M. Kennedy, in the White House," made him promise to make the attempt. "Rose really socked it to him," Sparks continued, "and buttoned up the ball game one day, I am told, when she said: 'I'm going to be 80 and I want to see another son in the White House. Ted, will you promise to try? Your promise will be my birthday gift.' What could a fellow do? Ted Kennedy gave Rose her birthday gift. Mother, as usual, had the last word."

The story received widespread circulation at the time, and added to Rose Kennedy's reputation as a power behind her sons' ambitions.

I asked Ted Kennedy if the story were true. His mother, he said, at *no* time asked him to run nor extracted any kind of pledge.

Actually, according to her friend Marie Greene who has known her from childhood, Rose does *not* want Teddy to seek the Presidency, though she has never asked him not to run. "She hopes he would continue to be a good public servant, but not in the highest office," Mrs. Greene told me. "The reasons are obvious, aren't they? As a mother who has had such trage-dies . . ."

His family's feelings have had a strong effect upon Kennedy's attitude toward the Presidency.

"I certainly have ambitions," he told me, "but my own career as a political figure is heavily conditioned by other factors and forces that are perhaps not as weighty with other people. How these forces will balance and mix in the future is something which is unresolved in my own mind."

He made it clear he was talking about the assassination factor. ("The forces I'm talking about are kind of self-evident," he said.) When his brother John was moving forward in politics, he told me, this did not exert the kind of restraint it does now.

"Obviously," Kennedy said, "these forces are not inhibiting me completely or I wouldn't stay in public office."

Here, then, is his most profound concern. He is aware of how Joan feels, of his mother's worries, the effect upon his children, his responsibilities to them all, and therefore he hesitates.

As for himself, he has resolved the problem of personal fear. Though he may react viscerally to sudden loud noises, he has done considerable soul-searching and decided that he will not allow fear to paralyze him, to dominate his life or to drive him from what he wants to do, even though he reportedly said: "I know that I'm going to get my ass shot off one day and I don't want to."

On his desk in his Senate office, between the two works of Thoreau, is a slender, blue-bound volume of Shakespeare that can be slipped into a coat pocket. The play is "The Tragedy of Julius Caesar," a drama about an assassinated head of state.

On page 36, this passage is underlined in red ink and marked it with an asterisk:

Cowards die many times before their deaths;
The valiant never taste of death but once.
Of all the wonders that I yet have heard,
It seems to me most strange that men should fear;
Seeing that death, a necessary end,
Will come when it will come.

Kennedy lives by this thought. He will not be terrified into hiding or retiring from public life, though some of his close friends and associates advise this. Gerry Doherty, for one, has anguish in his voice as he cries: "I hope to God he and Joan would just go somewhere and live long, happy lives, that he won't try to be President. Because if he does . . ." He pauses.

"When I tell him this, he just shrugs and says, 'What will be, will be. What God ordains will happen.' He tells me that if he must fulfill a challenge, he will."

"Tip" O'Neill, the veteran Cambridge congressman who has known Ted most of his life: "This man was bred to be President,"

Majority leader Mike Mansfield: "It's preordained with Ted. I'm afraid it's not a question of choice but a matter of destiny."

Edmund Muskie: "I would not count a Kennedy out of anything."

Sen. George S. McGovern: "I fully expect to see Senator Kennedy President of the United States some day."

James A. Farley: "Ted is going to wind up President."

Dick Clasby: "I know this man as well as anybody and I know he will never say I've gone this far and this is as far as I want to go. If he feels it is right, that he is suited to go on, then he will."

At Squaw Island, I put one final question to Ted Kennedy: "You have said that these forces, these concerns, are not inhibiting you completely or you would not remain in public office. But will they inhibit you from *ever* seeking higher public office?"

He replied: "I won't say that perhaps some time in the future I won't have a turn of interest or heart, or be a good deal more active, or pursue a higher ambition. It isn't something I'm bothered about or thinking about now — today. But I cannot say whether that will be so or won't be so sometime in the future."

He walked with me to the driveway, flame-haired Patrick at his side. As I drove back to the mainland, past the hamburger stands and seafood taverns along Route 28, I thought of what an old Boston politician had told me a few weeks before as he sat in his law office on Beacon Street. "As sure as those lawns on Boston Common turn green in the spring of the year," he had said in his richly embroidered prose, "that boy is going to run for the job one brother had and another brother wanted."

There was no doubt in my mind, that end-of-summer day in 1971, that Edward Kennedy had just told me precisely that.

B
K352
d

Ted Kennedy, triumphs and tragedies.